VIOLENCE
Basic and clinical science

THE MENTAL HEALTH FOUNDATION

The Mental Health Foundation is Britain's leading grant-making charity concerned with promoting and encouraging pioneering research and community care projects in the fields of mental illness and learning disabilities.

The Foundation aims to prevent mental disorders by funding and encouraging research into the causes and treatments of mental illness and learning disabilities, and to improve the quality of life for people with mental health problems and their families.

The Mental Health Foundation distributes its grants through five committees. Members are leading medical, academic, legal and healthcare professionals, who give their expertise at no charge to select the proposals most likely to yield innovative, effective or relevant results and findings.

The committees are increasingly setting the agendas for priorities and work in key areas, with internationally acclaimed results. The Foundation works in partnership with other organisations to maximise effectiveness and the dissemination of results.

VIOLENCE
Basic and clinical science

Edited by

CHRIS THOMPSON
BSc, MPhil, MD FRCPsych

*Honorary Secretary to the MHF Research Committee, Professor of Psychiatry,
University of Southampton, Royal South Hants Hospital, Southampton*

and

PHIL COWEN
MD, FRCPsych

*Deputy Honorary Secretary to the MHF Research Committee, Littlemore Hospital,
Oxford*

in association with

Butterworth-Heinemann Ltd
Linacre House, Jordan Hill, Oxford OX2 8DP

℞ A member of the Reed Elsevier group

OXFORD LONDON BOSTON
MUNICH NEW DELHI SINGAPORE SYDNEY
TOKYO TORONTO WELLINGTON

First published 1993

British Library Cataloguing in Publication Data
Violence: Basic and Clinical Science
  I. Thompson, Chris II. Cowen, Phil
  616.89

ISBN 0 7506 0926 5

Library of Congress Cataloguing in Publication Data
Violence: basic and clinical science/edited by Chris Thompson and Phil Cowen.
  p. cm.
  "This book is the result of a conference organized by the Mental Health Foundation at Balliol
  College, Oxford" – Pref.
  Includes bibliographical references and index.
  ISBN 0 7506 0926 5
  1. Violence – Psychological aspects – Congresses.   2. Violence – Physiological aspects –
  Congresses.   I. Thompson, Chris.   II. Cowen, Philip.   III. Mental Health Foundation
  (London, England)
  [DNLM: 1. Aggression – congresses.   2. Violence – congresses.   BF 575.A3 V7947]
  RC569.5.V55V564   1993
  616.85'82–dc20   92–48198 CIP

Typeset in Great Britain by Latimer Trend & Company Ltd, Plymouth
Printed and bound in Great Britain by Redwood Press Limited, Melksham, Wiltshire.

Contents

Contributors

Patricia Allderidge MA
Archives and Museum, Bethlem Royal Hospital, Beckenham, Kent

Per Bech MD
Frederiksborg General Hospital, Denmark

Dora Black MB
Department of Child and Adolescent Psychiatry, Royal Free Hospital, London

Ronald Blackburn MA, MSc, PhD, CPsychol, FBPsS
Directory Research Unit, Ashworth Hospital, Liverpool

Alyson J. Bond BA, MSc, PhD
Department of Psychiatry, Institute of Psychiatry, University of London

Man Cheung Chung PhD
Research Fellow, Department of Psychiatry, University of Birmingham, Queen Elizabeth's Psychiatric Hospital, Birmingham

Emil F. Coccaro MD
Associate Professor and Director, Clinical Neuroscience Research Unit, Department of Psychiatry, Medical College of Pennsylvania, USA

Phil Cowen MD, FRCPsych
MRC Unit of Clinical Pharmacology, Oxford

Kenneth A. Dodge PhD
Department of Psychology and Human Development, Vanderbilt University, Nashville, USA

Peter Fenwick MB BChir(Cantab), DPM, FRCPsych
The Maudsley Hospital, London

Jean Harris Hendriks MB, FRCPsych, DPM
Department of Child and Adolescent Psychiatry, Royal Free Hospital, London

Joe Herbert MA, BSc, MB ChB, PhD
Department of Anatomy, University of Cambridge, Cambridge

Tony Kaplan MB, MRCPsych
Department of Child and Adolescent Psychiatry, Royal Free Hospital, London

Richard J. Kavoussi MD
Assistant Professor and Medical Director, Clinical Neuroscience Research Unit, Department of Psychiatry, Medical College of Pennsylvania, USA

Gary M. Jackson MBBCh, MRCPsych
UCMSM, Academic Department of Psychiatry, Middlesex Hospital, London

Norman Kreitman MD, FRCP(Ed), FRCPsych
Medical Research Council Unit for Epidemiological Studies in Psychiatry, University of Edinburgh

Tony Maden MD, MRCPsych
Department of Psychiatry, Institute of Psychiatry, London

Gillian C. Mezey MB, BS, MRCPsych
Department of Forensic Psychiatry, St George's Hospital, London

Glynis Murphy BA, MSc, PhD
Psychology Department, Institute of Psychiatry, University of London

Rachel Rosser MBBS, MA, FRCP, FRCPsych, PhD
Department of Psychiatry, University College, London

Scott Stehle MD
Instructor and Research Psychiatrist, Clinical Neuroscience Research Unit, Department of Psychiatry, Medical College of Pennsylvania, USA

Digby Tantam MA, MPH, PhD, FRCPsych
School of Postgraduate Medical Education and Department of Psychology, University of Warwick, Coventry

Chris Thompson BSc, MPhil, MD, FRCPsych
Department of Psychiatry, University of Southampton

James Thompson BA, PhD, Dip Clin Psychol, FBPF, CPsychol
Department of Psychiatry, Middlesex Hospital, London

Simon Wessely MA, BM, BCh, MSc, MRCP, MRCPsych
King's College School of Medicine and Dentistry; Institute of Psychiatry, London

Preface

This book is the result of a conference organized by the Mental Health Foundation at Balliol College Oxford in the autumn of 1991. The impetus for holding a conference on this subject was the growing consensus that research on and services for the mentally abnormal offender were inadequate. Indeed the Foundation had recently responded to this by setting up a special committee in the Foundation to create initiatives in collaboration with the Department of Health and the Home Office.

There is a common misconception about the mentally ill that they are all in some way potentially violent – the mad axeman at the top of the stairs is a powerful televisual image. And yet this notion could not be further from the truth for the vast majority of the mentally ill who, if anything, are insufficiently assertive about their rights to good treatment and sometimes passive in the extreme.

However, there is a group of patients for whom violent and aggressive behaviour is a serious problem; such patients are often seen in forensic psychiatry services and diagnosed as having psychopathic personality disorder. In addition some psychotic patients have delusions or hallucinations which cause them to behave violently towards imagined persecutors. So the violence dimension in psychiatry is a real one. It is a subject which, perhaps for fear of adding to the 'mad axeman' stigma, has been little debated or researched until recently, although there are now signs that this is changing.

But we should also not forget that violence of a different kind runs throughout psychiatry. That is violence towards the self, which is common in psychiatric patients not only with the intention of committing suicide but also with the sole intention of causing physical damage short of death. This extremely distressing and challenging behaviour is barely understood, although some insights affecting the cause and the possible treatment are discussed in this book.

The psychiatric patient has more often been a victim than a perpetrator of violence and so it is right that some of the space in this book should be devoted to that topic. Children subjected to violence in their early years may be more likely to be mentally ill adults. Adults subjected to violence develop acute psychiatric syndromes.

All of these aspects of violence can perhaps be woven into a common thread, based on scientific research on all fronts, from the neuroscientist to the psychiatrist, from the child development specialist to the lawyer. The results are likely to have implications not only for the classification of psychiatric disorders and the treatment of psychiatric patients but also for society at large, since violence is a feature not only of individuals but also of societies.

Chris Thompson
Southampton

Phil Cowen
Oxford

Part 1 *Behavioural science*

1 The nature of aggression in humans

DIGBY TANTAM

Although my title quite specifically excludes non-human animals, it is impossible to begin without some mention of them. Particularly offensive violence is, after all, termed 'bestial', and it is said of its perpetrators that they behave 'like animals'. 'Every man has a wild beast inside him', wrote Frederick the Great to his mentor, Voltaire, and, although this beast can be tamed by civilization and curbed by society it has a tendency to break out, sometimes lamentably.

This sort of conception of humanity seems to have influenced Freud. In *Civilization and its Discontents*, Freud (1930) writes that (in J. Rivire's translation) 'the tendency to aggression is an innate, independent, instinctual disposition in man' and 'Culture has to call up every possible reinforcement in order to erect barriers against the aggressive instinct. . .' (p. 62). Freud originally 'took as my starting-point. . . Schiller's aphorism, that hunger and love make the world go round' and concluded that the aggressive instinct was one of self-preservation, but later concluded that it was a death instinct which was in direct opposition to the life-giving, prosocial erotic instinct and to the society that that instinct creates. Nietzsche's view of the matter was more cynical, but surprisingly similar: 'The purpose of all civilization is to convert man, a beast of prey, into a tame and civilized animal, a domestic animal' (Nietszche, 1967).

This Hobbesian conception of the social contract bridling the animal violence of human beings coexists with a very different one: that it is civilization which is the wellspring of violence because, as Rousseau wrote, 'Civilized man is born, lives, and dies in slavery. . .So long as he retains human form he is fettered by our institutions' (Jimack, 1911). Pliny the Elder cannot have been the first, and certainly has not been the last, to make the erroneous but persuasive observation, in his *Natural History*, that 'lions do not fight with one another; serpents do not attack serpents, nor do the wild monsters of the deep rage against their like. But most of the calamities of man are caused by his fellow-man'.

For a modern Plinean view we need go no further than the Pelican edition of Anthony Storr's admirable book *Human Aggression* which has this on the cover: 'that man is an aggressive creature will hardly be disputed. With the exception of certain rodents, no other vertebrate habitually destroys members of its own species . . . The sombre fact is that we are the cruellest and most ruthless species that has walked the earth' (Storr, 1970). This perception, it is easy to see now, is strongly biased. Accounts of human aggression are collected from large populations observed continuously for prolonged periods. No non-domestic animals have been studied with anything like this degree of intensity until recent long-term studies of primate colonies, and this research, much of it conducted in feral populations, has uncovered castration, murder and even war (De Waal, 1989) at a frequency that is probably higher than in human populations.

The quotations from Freud and Pliny referred to 'man', but it has been argued that what is true of aggression in men may not be true of aggression in women. Women are less frequently convicted of violent crime than men; they are less likely to describe themselves as being aggressive, and they are more likely to react non-aggressively to others' aggression. Many of these differences can be attributed to the different social training that girls and boys receive, but not all (Geen, 1990). Social learning is an important influence on aggressiveness as well as on the inhibition of aggression, but is probably not sufficient to account for all the differences between individuals and between the sexes. Some degree of innate, biological determination must also be invoked. Possible factors in this will be considered later in this volume.

There is a tendency for the differences between the sexes to become less with age. Geen (1990) considers that there is 'considerable evidence' that women are more likely than men to react to their own aggression with anxiety. The smaller size of women than men, with its corollary of their overall disadvantage in physical conflicts between sexes, may be a contributory factor to this. Perhaps it is in response to the frequency with which men attack women that some feminist writers have held that all aggression originates with men, and proposed that a society ordered by women would have a considerably lower, perhaps negligible, level of violence. The differences between men and women are greatest when violence leading to physical pain or suffering is considered. However, this may be because men are more likely to strive for dominance than women and therefore to engage more in competitive aggression.

The Plinean, Freudian, and feminist views all seem flawed, and yet continue to command attention; why? One possible reason is that whenever aggression strains social cohesion, it is usually condemned as bad or evil. Indeed etymologists suggest that these words derive from words meaning against the group. When violence produces new social arrangements that turn out to be preferable, it ceases to be violence by virtue of being relabelled as freedom-fighting, self-assertion, or even peace-keeping. The 'nature red in tooth and claw', the 'slave of culture', and the male bully theories all imply that a life without violence is possible – by reversion to a state of nature, by the perfection of civilization, or by adoption of the feminine principle – and assume that this would be desirable, whilst accepting that it is utopian.

A quite different point of view, which is the one that I think fits best with psychiatric insight into human nature, is that aggression is normally socially valuable. This is trivially true of aggression which is mandated by society as a means of preventing greater aggression: in self-defence or as a member of a police force or an army, for example. This type of aggression is sometimes termed instrumental, in contrast to affective aggression, because it is assumed that there is an opposition between violence directed towards an end, and violence associated with strong feeling. This is not a useful distinction for the clinical psychiatrist. He or she may be concerned with people who are suffering long-term emotional disorders as a result of committing an act of justified and legitimate aggression, as well as those whose aggression is illegitimate but not apparently associated with a display of feeling either at the time or afterwards.

Even affective aggression makes a positive contribution to human adaptation, including social adaptation. Ethological observations of animals suggest that 'a personal bond, an individual friendship, is found only in animals with highly developed intra-specific aggression, in fact this bond is the firmer, the more aggressive the particular animal and species is' (Lorenz, 1967; p. 186). One possible explanation for this is that a personal bond requires some compromise between the interests of the individual and those of the dyad. Aggression is one means of shifting the balance between these two and, if successful, is likely to give greater strength to the relationship. Courting couples often find that a violent disagreement is the immediate precursor of a decision to split up, or to enter into a more permanent relationship.

The inevitability of hostility in close relationships has been repeatedly emphasized by psychoanalysts, particular those with an object relations orientation. The relationship must 'contain', in Winnicott's useful term, some degree of hate. Klein, whose work on the vicissitudes of aggressive impulses has been particularly influential, attributed them, in a lecture given in 1956 (Klein 1986), to envy. Envy, in the sense that Klein uses it, implies the persecutory belief that something valuable is being withheld which could be given. Ill-feeling of this kind cannot easily be contained in a close relationship. Experimental studies suggest that aggression is greater and more resistant to being switched off when the victim is seen as malicious and this type of bad feeling leads to a deterioration in the capacity for intimacy. As Blake put it:

'I was angry with my friend:
I told my wrath, my wrath did end.
I was angry with my foe:
I told it not, my wrath did grow'   (*A Poison Tree*)

Once 'the patient realizes his own destructive impulses and projections, [he] revises therefore his first object relations and establishes, in retrospect, his good object more securely' (Klein, 1986; p. 228). Consequently 'his capacity for enjoyment, and the appreciation of the gifts received from the good object, increases step by step and envy is diminished and gratitude becomes possible' (Klein, 1986; p. 229). With gratitude comes a deepened capacity for love and affection.

Averill (1982) conducted a questionnaire study of angry incidents, and found that the most common targets of anger were friends, acquaintances or close family and that 'loss of personal pride, self-esteem, or sense of personal worth' following the harmful action of the other person was a commonly reported cause of anger. The motive for anger was most often 'to reassert. . .authority or independence, or to improve [one's] image'. Anger therefore seems, as Erikson (1963) suggested, to contribute to the development and maintenance of autonomy by promoting mastery. However where aggression cannot lead to an effective response, anger is either suppressed or builds up into futile, but poorly controlled aggression. This is a more specific hypothesis than, but clearly linked to, one of the most researched psychological theories about aggression: the frustration hypothesis, first put forward by Dollard *et al.* (1939). Berkowitz (1989) summarizes the main points of a modern version of this theory as follows:

1. frustration leads to an increase in negative affect;
2. there are associations between negative affects and aggression, angry thoughts, and feeling angry;
3. negative affects may or may not lead to aggression; and
4. anger does not cause aggression, although it may accompany it.

Frustration–aggression theory potentially explains why distractors like noise or discomfort increase the risk of violence, by disrupting intentional activity. It does not explain why other environmental stimuli such as ambient temperature, pain, or an increase in atmospheric negative ion concentrations also increase aggression. Nor does it explain why, when the frustration is due to another person's behaviour, their motives influence the degree of aggression shown.

The cathartic effect of aggression was one of the original presumptions of frustration–aggression theory. Recent evidence (reviewed by Geen, 1990) suggests that catharsis is not, however, the result of the expression of an aliquot of destructive energy, but requires the achievement of a goal such as a greater degree of dominance or affiliation. Aristotle wrote: 'anger, even violent anger, against another person will cease if vengeance is taken on another' and Breuer and

Freud's formulation of catharsis echoes this: it was not, as is commonly assumed, drive-reductive but goal-directed. They wrote: 'The reaction of an injured person to a trauma has really only...a "cathartic" effect if it is expressed in an adequate reaction like revenge' (quoted in Breuer and Freud, 1961; p. 5).

Men are more aggressive than women, and show more rapid autonomic recovery after aggression (falling blood pressure and pulse rate) if they respond with aggression than if they do not. Women show more rapid recovery if they reward the aggressor (Hokanson *et al.*, 1968). Men are more likely to respond to aggression with aggression. Male chimpanzees are also more aggressive than female chimpanzees, but also spend considerably more time in male-to-male conciliation (De Waal, 1989). One function of this in chimpanzees is to ensure the stability of the male dominance hierarchy and it is interesting to speculate whether this may be a particular function of the aggression of men. Aggression towards higher-status people is inhibited, and if forced is less likely to lead to autonomic recovery (Hokanson, 1961; Hokanson and Shetler, 1961). It seems that, as in chimpanzees, it is best to conciliate your boss unless you are sure that you can take over his or her chair.

I have assumed, in considering the virtues of aggression, that it is both ubiquitous and inevitable. This does not imply either the Kleinian hypothesis that children are born with envious feelings about their mothers, or Freud's idea that they are born with a quota of destructive instinct, neither of which seem to me to be tenable. It does suggest that inborn dispositions in relation to other people, for example dispositions to affiliate and to get mastery over, are in conflict; and that some aggressive displays are also innate. This relatively weak hereditary component to aggression does not preclude – indeed it requires – that a good deal of learning, for example by social imitation, about aggressive responses and the social conventions governing them takes place after birth. Imitation remains an influence on whether or not anger is expressed, particularly in marginal situations, throughout life: hence the concern about the effect of exposure to broadcast violence and the notorious disinhibiting effect of crowds.

'We praise a man who is angry on the right grounds, against the right persons, in the right manner, at the right moment, and for the right length of time' wrote Aristotle in the *Nicomachean Ethics*, and modern research has borne out the importance of evaluative processes in aggression, particularly in its inhibition.

Anger may be inhibited by the higher status of the potential target, by the fear of retaliation, by the suffering of the victim, and when it is a response to inadvertent harm by another person rather than deliberate harm.

The 'rightness' of which Aristotle wrote is no longer the objective truth which he would have considered it, but more a matter of social practice. In the case of legitimate violence, these practices are codified as rules or conventions (the Queensberry rules, the Geneva convention) or are institutionalized in command structures in which precise limits to action are determined by rank. The rightness of other types of aggression is much more open, and is likely to be differently judged by groups with different relationships to the aggressor and the victims. The mindless violence of the terrorist may strike other members of the community as the justified retaliation of the freedom-fighter.

Ascribing pathology to aggression is therefore potentially difficult. However, I think that we are on fairly safe ground if we assume that aggression is pathological if no one considers it right, other than the aggressor and any accomplices. Conversely we might be safe to assume it is non-pathological if the victim considers it justified. The subjugation of passion to the yoke of convention is also true of sexuality, and the most commonly used criterion of sexual pathology, the consenting partner criterion, is similar to what I am proposing for aggression.

The analogy between the two is such that disorders of aggression might usefully be usefully be classified in the same way as sexual disorders into abnormalities of:

1.   disposition to be aggressive;
2.   choice of victim;
3.   type of aggression displayed; or
4.   consummation.

Biological approaches to aggression have tended to focus on the concept of drive strength, and particularly on abnormally high drive strength. However, in clinical practice, overly aggressive behaviour may more often be due to other emotions, notably anxiety being expressed aggressively, than to any biological abnormality in aggression itself. A heightened tendency to aggression strength may also be the consequence of learning or of cultural factors, and twin studies suggest that these determinants are at least as important as hereditary ones. Moreover the drive strength concept has received little support from recent studies: the outflow of aggression is more likely to increase the frequency of subsequent aggression than to reduce it. What distinguishes abnormally aggressive individuals is rather an emotional set of suspiciousness or rancour, and a cognitive set towards presuming hostility or threat by others in marginal situations where less aggressive people would make other attributions.

De Waal (1989) has suggested that more emphasis should be placed on the factors that lead to the offset of aggression. These include social responses from others – the 'peace-making' of De Waal's title – but also the inhibitory factors which limit aggression. Empathy is the one that is probably of most immediate clinical relevance. Aggression is inhibited by signs of suffering in the victim, but only if the aggressor can identify with him or her. The manifest suffering of victims who are racially different from their attackers, for example, does not inhibit. Empathy would thus appear to have two components: identification and an emotional response to the suffering of others.

The psychotherapeutic treatment of violent offenders has long fostered greater identification between the offender and his or her potential victims. Recently this has formed an explicit part of some programmes in which victims confront the offender with the consequences of his or her act. Some of the obstacles to identification have already been considered. They include emotions such as envy or hatred of the victim, or actions by the victim which are perceived as rejections or betrayals.

The factors determining a sympathetic response to the suffering of others have received less attention, despite the widely held commonsense views that repeated exposure to violence without the exercise of compassion inures one to further violence, and that the aggression of callous individuals is dangerous. Clinical research into the characteristics of violent individuals may benefit from a consideration of their sensitivity to the emotional responses to others, and the extent to which they identify with other people.

REFERENCES

Aristotle, *Nichomachean Ethics*, **IV**
Aristotle, *Rhetoric*, **II**
Averill J. (1982). *Anger and Aggression: An Essay on Emotion*. New York: Springer-Verlag.
Berkowitz L. (1989). The frustration-aggression hypothesis: an examination and reformulation. *Psychological Bulletin*; **106**: 59–73.
Breuer J., Freud S. (1961). *Studies in Hysteria*. Boston: Beacon Press (originally published 1894).
De Waal F. (1989). *Peacemaking Among Primates*. Cambridge, MA: Harvard University Press.
Dollard J., Doob L., Miller N., Mowrer O., Sears R. (1939) *Frustration and Aggression*. New Haven, CT: Yale University Press.
Erikson E. (1963) *Childhood and Society*, 2nd ed. New York: W.W. Norton.
Freud S. (1930). *Civilization and its Discontents*. Translated by J. Riviere, 1958. Garden City, NY: Doubleday.
Geen R. (1990) *Human Aggression*. Milton Keynes: Open University Press.
Hokanson J. (1961). The effect of frustration and anxiety on overt-aggression. *Journal of Abnormal and Social Psychology*; **62**: 346–51.
Hokanson J., Edelman R. (1961). Effects of three social responses on vascular processes. *Journal of Personality and Social Psychology*: **3**: 442–7.
Hokanson J., Willers K., Koropsak E. (1968). The modification of autonomic responses during aggressive exchanges. *Journal of Personality*: **36**: 386–404.

Jimack P. (1911). *Introduction to Rousseau's Emile*. London: Dent

Klein M. (1986). A study of envy and gratitude. In: *The Selected Melanie Klein* (Mitchell J., ed.) Harmondsworth, Middx.: Penguin.

Lorenz L. (1967). *On Aggression*. London: Methuen (originally published as *Das Sogenannte Bose*, 1963).

Nietszche F. (1967). *On the Genealogy of Morals*, translated by W. Kaufmann. New York: Random House.

Pliny, *Natural History*, **VII**, 77

Storr A. (1970). *Human Aggression*. Harmondsworth, Middx.: Pelican.

2 Aggression in suicide and parasuicide

NORMAN KREITMAN

It would be possible to discuss from many viewpoints the relationship between aggression and suicidal behaviour, and the light each may throw on our understanding of the other. My own approach will be highly selective; contrary to what the given title may suggest, I propose to worry about the definition of aggression in humans, not in order to advance a particular formulation so much as to review in outline what kinds of definition are available and their apparent strengths and weaknesses. The relation of aggression to suicidal behaviours is an allied theme which can usefully be considered at the same time. These behaviours are sometimes described as aggression towards the self – a view I find very questionable – and sometimes as a manifestation of hostility towards others. It is this latter aspect which may be particularly relevant to the definition of human aggression. However, it would be logical to start by considering the problem of aggression more generally.

DEFINITIONS OF AGGRESSION

It appears on initial consideration that only two kinds of definition of aggression are available – the behavioural and the intentional. Each merits attention.

At first sight the behavioural approach seems attractive. It is of course the only one applicable to laboratory or field studies of, for example, animal behaviour, when the investigator needs do no more than declare that he or she intends to regard a certain group of behaviours as falling within the rubric of aggression. The same applies in the psychological laboratory when the investigator takes certain patterns of behaviour or questionnaire responses as being what he or she means by such terms as hostility or aggression (though the experimental psychologist, unlike the animal behaviourist, will usually try to validate the methods used by testing criterion groups). The immediate problem that arises is precisely what does link these various instances of aggressive behaviour, that is to say, what is the definition of the set of behaviours so designated? (In formal terms, the problem is how to move from a definition which is ostensive and extensive to one which is intensive.)

This problem becomes much more acute outside the laboratory context, and any attempt to apply a purely behavioural definition of aggression to spontaneous human activity seems doomed to immediate failure. We might, for example, consider that the act of putting a knife into someone is a *prima facie* instance of aggression. Our views would, of course, immediately change if the actor was a surgeon and the recipient his patient. In everyday life, and even more for legal purposes, we attach great importance to distinguishing non-intentional, incidental and accidental behaviours from those that are deliberate, not simply for moral evaluation but as the very basis of our definitions and classifications of action.

Yet within a scientific as distinct from a humanistic psychology, the notion of intention poses two formidable difficulties. The first is that of reliable identification and specification, that is, the problem of determining unequivocally whether a particular intention is present or absent, and further, of distinguishing it from other intentions; clearly without such a foundation no progress can be made. The methodological problem is complex. Often the accounts of the actor will be the primary basis for ascertainment, but such accounts always need to be evaluated critically since they may be at variance with what the agent has done or with his or her overall emotional orientation. Sometimes the agent can give no account of intent – as is often the case with abnormal behaviours. In all such situations motivation will have to be inferred using methods analogous to the motivational analysis of animal ethologists. It cannot be claimed, however, that with humans such techniques are rigorous.

The second problem is more conveniently considered later. At present we need simply note that a definition of aggression based on intent, or the allied concept of motivation, rather than on behaviour alone shifts the issue into an area which is itself problematic.

A sophisticated view which appears to avoid some of the difficulties can be derived from writers such as Bowlby and Waddington. The former was renowned for having brought into psychiatry some of the concepts of ethology, and proposed that sets of actions were functionally organized to specific biological ends, such as reproduction, or attachment to salient others, such as the mother. Intentions and emotional states arise as epiphenomena; what the individual envisaged or experienced in the course of action directed to these functional ends was to be understood as no more than the psychological correlates of basic biological patterns.

Waddington proposed the interesting concept of homeorrheosis. This he regarded as a pattern of action (i.e. a response to a changing environment) such as to maintain the individual's continuation of a particular development such as growth or reproduction, in contrast to homeostasis in which the pattern of responses was directed towards maintaining stability. However, from both these viewpoints, particularly perhaps from that of Bowlby's, the difficulty again emerges of specifying how many primary functional drives or lines of development there may be, and how they are to be characterized and distinguished. (Many have attempted the task of classifying basic drives, but there seems to be little agreement.) Neither Bowlby nor Waddington, however, have suggested that aggression should be seen as a primary drive – though admittedly others writers, notably Lorenz, take a different view. Bowlby and Waddington imply rather that aggressive behaviour arises incidentally in the course of the pursuit of some end-state as defined in their respective theories. Aggression, in this view, is a style of action, not a class of actions *per se*. This is an important point, but it still leaves the problem largely untouched; it is simply reformulated, not resolved.

So the dilemma remains; it is impossible to understand human action without incorporating intention in some sense, yet we have no cogent definition of intent suitable for scientific purposes. However, rather than continue pursuing the matter purely theoretically I will now turn to illustrating some of the points already adumbrated by considering aspects of suicidal behaviour. Pending a more satisfactory definition I shall use the word 'intent' as a disposition to act so as to achieve some envisioned end-state; thus if someone is standing on my foot and I can envisage a situation in which this no longer pertains, then I will ask them to move with the intention of bringing about a more desirable state of affairs.

PARASUICIDE

This term refers to any deliberately initiated but non-fatal act of self-harm. It was introduced at a time when it was already established that most acts of self-poisoning or self-inflicted injury could not appropriately be considered as failed suicides since such patients differed in numerous epidemiological and clinical respects from the group of completed suicides. It is a form of behaviour which, as the anthropologists say, has attracted 'thick description'. Many of these accounts are of limited relevance for present purposes; it does not clarify matters very much to note that most parasuicides are impulsive, and that some may be patterned on examples already familiar to the patient or latent within the culture. Of greater concern in view of the preceding discussion is the pattern of underlying motivations and intentions.

Apart from innumerable clinical reports, a handful of research studies have tried to describe the intentions underlying parasuicide.

They have been concerned with both intentions as volunteered on systematic enquiry and with those which may be reasonably attributed to the patient on various grounds, even if he or she finds it difficult to articulate them. The methods used range from structured interviews to formal procedures such as the Osgood semantic differential test and the repertory grid test. A number of intentions have been described, none of which are considered to exclude others, since parasuicide is a splendid example in which multiple or even contradictory intentions may coexist. Though investigators have presented their findings in different ways it seems that the intentions reported can be ordered into two main groups, or perhaps better, along two axes. The first relates to tension discharge; the second concerns the interpersonal or signal function of the act – the original 'cry for help'. The importance of the first set or axis is often overlooked; it seems easier for observers to latch on to what Freud termed the secondary gain and to overlook the primary gain altogether, ignoring the discharge of non-specific tension and the patient's need for respite. By contrast, the second aspect is widely recognized, perhaps because the interpersonal function of parasuicide is usually so dramatically evident. Descriptions of the signal function commonly include reference to a desire to influence significant others by eliciting sympathy or inducing guilt and anxiety. Ill-trained professionals and lay observers alike tend sooner or later to use the blanket term 'manipulative' to this aspect of parasuicide. To do so seems to me profoundly unhelpful, not because it is wrong but because it is too vague. Virtually all our behaviours form part of a social system and have the effect of modifying or manipulating that system, however marginally; saying 'Please pass the marmalade' or even a simple 'Good morning' to one's colleagues can be considered manipulative in this sense.

However, the response by others to a patient's parasuicide is quite often not one of solicitude or remorse but of irritation or anger, especially if the act is repeated, and it is here that we may perhaps obtain a glimpse of its aggressive component. What appears to engender the resentment in such instances is not the content of the 'message' but a sense that the patient has resorted to a primitive method of social interaction of a kind which arouses high levels of anxiety, and that the forcefulness of the communication has exceeded socially accepted boundaries. If so it would suggest that a definition of human aggression might be found in the area of social norms, in contrast to the behavioural and intentional types of definition already noted.

SUICIDE

Completed suicide, a deliberately caused act of self-harm with a fatal outcome, has also received close attention from the perspective of social psychology, and various subtypes of suicide have been described. The classification proposed by Durkheim (trans. 1951) was based upon the level of social bonding of the subgroup to which the individual belonged. His analysis is still widely used a century after its original publication, though it is obviously incorrect in some aspects such as the postulate of a universal motivation towards suicide which is only held in check by various kinds of social regulation; there is of course no evidence of any such drive. His account is also incomplete in that he had no interest in the subjective significance of the act of suicide or of what has been referred to as the primary gain in the parallel instance of parasuicide (albeit in suicide it is the desire to terminate rather than intermit a condition which the person perceives as a painful and irremediable state). Nevertheless, Durkheim's account of the social face of suicide, so to speak, remains cogent and for present purposes we should note that at no point does he find it necessary to invoke the notion of aggression or coercion in any sense.

A quite different view has been taken by some psychoanalytic writers, especially at the begining of this century. Much of suicidal behaviour is related to depression, and in formulations such as those of Abrahams severe depression is viewed as a state of introverted hostility. It is difficult to strip these accounts of their dramaturgic trappings but the central notion appears to be rather similar to that later developed by the 'reservoir' theorists, who also considered that aggression could be thought of as a drive which could be variably directed to different ends. In psychoanalytic theory melancholia is a state of increased hostility which is primarily directed against the ego but which can be externalized, however briefly, and directed against the external world. Hence the irritability of many patients with depression, and hence too the often-noted association between depressive states and acts of murder.

The notion that hostility might variably be channelled internally or externally has received considerable attention. Epidemiologists have enquired whether the murder rate and suicide rates across different communities are inversely correlated, as the theory would predict; the better studies find no correlation whatsoever. Similarly, clinical psychologists such as Foulds (1965, 1976) have devised methods of measuring hostility directed to others and, separately, punitive attitudes towards the self. These two measures when applied over time to the same group of individuals have also been found to vary independently. There is no clinical evidence of which I am aware which would support the 'hydraulic' theory of aggression. The undoubted irritability of depressed patients can I think be more parsimoniously explained in terms of arousal, while murder by depressives appears to have more to do with delusional thinking than a simple increase in hostility.

Other accounts of suicide have been formulated in other cultures, most notably those of the Far East. These long preceded the Durkheimian formulation, to which they nevertheless have certain similarities in their emphasis on the social dimension. The most developed account is to be found in Japanese culture, in the concept of *seppuku*. This refers to suicide in socially prescribed situations; other types of suicide are recognized but considered unworthy of close attention. Various subgroupings of *seppuku* have been proposed and a recent account lists no less than 16. They are based entirely on the varieties of moral and social conflict in which an individual might find him- or herself. The suicidal act is carried out according to a detailed ritual, which subtly varies according to the social prescription in question. While each type is considered to achieve quite precisely specified ends, all of them also serve to reintegrate the individual into society; he or she is no longer viewed as a deviant on account of preceding voluntary or involuntary actions and, if the context is appropriate, is considered to have resolved any conflict of obligations. Thus honour – one's place in society – is restored; indeed by his or her act the suicide has reinforced the social order for the sake of which he or she has given his or her life. Once again there is little reference in these accounts of any aggressive component, although it is said that that the other actors in the drama are sometimes expected to feel remorse.

The theme of aggression is more fully developed in the earlier Chinese accounts of suicide, on which the Japanese versions were based. One important variant in the Chinese description was the form of suicide (reserved for the use of the upper classes) which is explicitly a form of revenge. In this the man who has been intolerably wronged but has no other redress kills himself on the doorstep of his enemy in order that his ghost may haunt that person for the rest of his life. Here then is another example of hostility – the imposition of one person's desires on the feeling and behaviour of another beyond what is customary within the everyday rules of society. The society in question may seem exotic, but we commonly find hints of the same theme in our own culture – the motif of 'I'll die and then you'll be sorry'. But, as in the instance of parasuicide, it seems that so far as aggression is concerned, we are here dealing with a kind of behaviour of which the chief characteristic is that the standard boundaries of what is permissible by way of influencing other people have been transgressed.

Finally, it might of course be argued that the act of self-murder should be regarded as an aggressive act according to our everyday vocabulary, since it involves the wilful destruction of a human being. But if common usage is to be the court of appeal then it must be noted that we usually speak of aggression as referring to an action by a person on another person or thing. To declare by fiat and without collateral evidence that the meaning should be extended to the self does not advance matters materially.

SUICIDAL BEHAVIOUR AND INTENTIONS

What emerges from this discursive consideration of both parasuicde and suicide is that a definition of human aggression might be attempted along the lines of saying that an act is aggressive in so far as it attempts to manipulate against their will the behaviour or attitudes of other persons by techniques which are socially proscribed. Some modification of this formulation would be necessary for phenomena such as harm to others arising from a rage reaction, but I think these could be accommodated. Moreover, this definition is capable of being operationalized and hence used for scientific purposes. But I am still worried about the omission of the component of subjective intent which, as already discussed, is inseparable from any discussion of human activity, and I would like now to return to the theme of intention as illustrated in suicidal behaviour.

Something has already been indicated of the diversity of intentions that might underlay suicidal acts. Those associated with parasuicide have already been touched on. Those which appear to be linked to completed suicide may be brutally summarized into four main types or classes. First, there is the desire to terminate a painful state. Secondly, there is the wish to convey some kind of message to significant others; this may be affectionate, e.g. to relieve others of the burden of care, or hostile, as in the example of exotic Chinese revenge suicides, or both. Thirdly, there is the aspect of reinforcing social bonds and the social order even at the cost of life itself. Lastly, there is the interesting type or component of completed suicide in which death is seen as a stepping stone towards reunion with predeceased loved ones. This last raises a new question. It is now commonly accepted by psychologists that plans and intentions are serially, or sometimes hierarchically, organized. Thus with reunion suicide, an individual embarks on a course of action which will result in death, and we can say that death is the end-point of the first phase of the plan. But being dead is in turn a stepping stone towards the second aim, which is that of being reunited with someone. There is no reason to stop at that point; one could, for example, ask why the individual wishes to rejoin those who have preceded him or her out of this world. This problem of the ever-receding end-point of action has of course been noted by many writers on the general topic of intention. I wish to do no more than to indicate its relevance in the present context, with the implication that any intentional definition would have to specify that the intention in question related only to the proximal objective. Ultimate goals appear to be beyond analysis.

CONCLUSIONS

After this rather discursive review it might be helpful to try to summarize the points that have emerged. These are as follows:

1. There is no generally agreed definition of aggression, but two main approaches have been widely used – the behavioural and the intentional.
2. A purely behavioural definition is of limited theoretical power and of no practical value for the study of human aggression.
3. Intent appears to be an irreducible element of any definition of aggression. Intent, however, is difficult to identify and classify. There is also the important problem that human intentions are sequentially organized with the attendant difficulties of specifying their stage or level.
4. There is no evidence that suicide *per se* is basically a form of aggression, but there are aspects of both parasuicide and completed suicide that are experienced by others as cooercive. These may therefore be called aggressive in the everyday use of the word. It transpires that the boundary between aggressive and other kinds of interpersonal behaviour is defined by social norms. This offers a possible third approach to the question of definition.
5. Overall it seems that since a single, comprehensive definition of aggression is not currently available, different criteria will have to be employed by the behaviourist, the psychologist and the the sociologist according to their own needs, but a more comprehensive perspective is obviously an important goal for the future.

REFERENCES

Durkheim E. (1951). *Suicide: A Sociological and Statistical Study*. English edition. Translated by Spaulding J. and Simpson G. New York: Free Press.

Foulds G. (1965). *Personality and Personal Illness*. London: Tavistock Publications.

Foulds G. (1976). *The Hierarchical Nature of Personal Illness*. London: Academic Press.

3 *Studying mechanisms in the cycle of violence*

KENNETH A. DODGE

The goal of our research programme has been to understand how it is that some children come to be chronically aggressive toward others in the first 6 years of life.

From research reviewed by Parker and Asher (1987), Loeber and Dishion (1983), and Olweus (1979), we know that by the time that a child reaches the age of 8, individual differences in aggressive behaviour patterns are fairly stable and are predictive of maladaptive outcomes in adolescence. Change is still possible, but many forces from this point onward act to perpetuate patterns rather than to instigate change. Numerous studies have shown that the initial onset of chronic antisocial behavior in adolescence or adulthood is rare (Robins, 1966). Certainly we know about transient delinquency that arises in adolescence, but the work of Lee Robins and others has taught us that chronic aggressive behaviour almost always has its beginnings in early childhood. So the focus of this work will be on factors that lead to aggressive behaviour patterns up to the age of 8 years.

The study of aggressive behaviour problems and conduct disorder is complicated by the fact that this is not a unitary phenomenon having a single form, a single etiology, and a single life-course (Kazdin, 1985). In medical research, we seek to identify a disease by its single cause, such as human immunodeficiency virus (HIV) being the necessary cause and defining characteristic of acquired immune deficiency syndrome (AIDS)-related disease. The goal of medical research is to move from a vague hypothetical construct, such as AIDS, to an operationally definable phenomenon, such as the presence of HIV. Conduct disorder, on the other hand, is a hypothetical construct and will never be anything more. Conduct disorder and aggressive behaviour problems are more like cancers, with multiple forms and multiple causes. We will never identify a single cause of chronic aggression, just as we will never identify a single cause of cancer. We speak of cancers, and perhaps we should speak of aggressions, with different structures and etiologies.

A related problem is that our inquiry requires analysis at multiple levels, from the very proximal level of the dynamics of a single act of aggression to the distal epidemiological level of factors in socialization that contribute to risk for aggression. Borrowing again from cancer research, we study both distal risk factors such as cigarette smoking, and proximal mechanisms such as cellular changes that mediate the relation between smoking and cancer. A comprehensive understanding of aggression requires analysis at multiple levels, including neurochemical action during an aggressive episode, genetic predispositions, and ecological influences such as the rate of crime in a neighbourhood or a culture in which a child lives. This chapter will focus on just two levels, that of the cognitive dynamics in a single act of aggression and that of socialization influences, specifically physical abuse of a child in the first few years of life. This chapter will emphasize the relation between these two levels, that is, how a distal factor such as past physical abuse might affect the proximal dynamics of a specific act of aggression. In so doing, the two psychologies of individual differences research and research on normal developmental processes will be bridged.

MENTAL PROCESSES IN AGGRESSIVE BEHAVIOUR

Observations of children's play (Dodge, 1991; Dodge and Coie, 1987; Dodge, *et al.* 1990a) have identified at least two kinds of aggressive acts, called reactive and proactive aggression.

In a prototype of reactive aggression, a peer pushes or teases a child, who then retaliates with overt anger and hostile aggression, leading to a fight. If the child actually had been provoked, we would speak of *defensive* aggression, which some would not want to call aggression at all. If the child had not been objectively provoked into aggression, a characteristic of reactive aggression is that it still seems so, at least to the aggressing child. That is, even though we as objective observers see no provocation, it seems that the child believes that there was a provocation.

A key to understanding this event is an analysis of the perceptions and mental processes of the child during this encounter. I use the term 'mental processes' (suggested to me by Jack Block) rather than cognitive processes because it is obvious that these processes are highly emotional as well as cognitive. These processes are both conscious and unconscious, and they occur in microseconds. Even if the child lacks awareness of what has happened, it appears as if the child has attended to the peer provocation, interpreted this provocation as intentional and malicious, and decided indignantly and frenetically that retaliatory aggression is justified and necessary.

The second kind of act is proactive or instrumental aggression, in which a child apparently desires some object, such as a toy, or an outcome, such as enhanced status among peers. This child is not angry, but rather employs aggressive behaviours instrumentally and somewhat methodically. A key to understanding this event is an analysis of the aggressing child's decision-making process, a process that includes the recognition of a desired end-state (such as the ball that is in the hands of another), the accessing from long-term memory a strategy of coercion to reach that end-state and, possibly, the anticipation that coercion will achieve this end-state successfully.

These two kinds of aggressive acts represent extremes on a continuum, in that most acts include elements of each type (Dodge, 1991). Consider, for example, the coercion episode classically described by Patterson (1982), in which the child attends to an aversive stimulus, such as a mother trying to get him or her to go to bed, and then employs a temper tantrum to achieve a desired end-state of staying up. The child is reacting angrily to the mother's aversive stimulus, but is also instrumentally employing aggression to achieve goals.

In all of these cases, consideration of the child's processing of social information enhances our understanding of the dynamics of the aggressive act. A general model of this processing can guide our thinking about aggression (Dodge, 1986). According to this model, a child comes to the social event with a set of biological characteristics, uch as attentional capacity and homeostatic inclinations, and a social history stored in memory. This history serves as a database for the processing of current cues. The child's behaviour occurs as a function of processing steps, steps that include attention to and encoding of the social stimuli, interpretation and mental representation of those stimuli, experience of emotion, accessing of one or more behavioural strategies or responses, possible evaluation and decision about a strategy, and enactment of a selected behavioural response. This model is not sacred, and it is similar to those used to describe non-social processes such as solving maths problems. Biases or deficits at each step of processing could lead to reactive or proactive aggression.

The reactively aggressing child who was seemingly provoked is hypervigilant to the aversive stimulus, has encoded that cue, and has interpreted that cue as threatening, hostile or malicious. These steps of the process seem crucial to understanding this event. The proactively aggressing bully has a goal of achieving a desired end-state; he or she readily accesses coercive, and only coercive, means to achieve that state, and anticipates that these coercive means will be successful. The steps of response access and evaluation seem crucial to understanding the dynamics of this event.

Researchers have devoted considerable attention to empirical examination of these processes as correlates of aggressive acts. Peer behaviour in play groups as well as case records of extremely violent adolescents in treatment have been analysed. The empirical findings are very strong at the level of the individual act. For example, it is overwhelmingly clear that when a child interprets a peer's provocative behaviour as hostile, that child is more likely to display retaliatory aggression than when he or she interprets the same stimulus as accidental or benign (Dodge, 1980). This pattern holds for hypothetical events as well as experimentally manipulated real events (Steinberg and Dodge, 1983). In one study, when the provocation was perceived as hostile, the probability of an aggressive behavioural response was 0.75, in contrast with just 0.25 when it was perceived as benign (Dodge, 1980). These findings hold for both highly aggressive as well as non-aggressive children. Hartup and colleagues (Sancilio *et al.*, 1989) have demonstrated the same effect, and have noted that this factor does not account for *all* of aggressive acts.

Just as strong are findings that instrumental aggression is accompanied by the prior judgement that aggression will be successful in achieving a desired end-state, and that restraint from instrumental aggression is accompanied by the judgement that its enactment would lead to negative interpersonal, intrapersonal, instrumental or moral outcomes. Bandura's analysis of fights, conflicts and international aggression are the best evidence here (Bandura, 1988, 1989).

Also robust, but not as strong, are correlational findings at the level of individual differences. That is, children who characteristically, or habitually, process information in deviant ways are likely to display characteristically high rates of aggression toward others, as evidenced in teacher ratings, peer nominations and direct observations (Dodge, 1986).

Gouze (1987) has found that aggressive children attend more closely to hostile cues in the social environment than do non-aggressive children, and they have a harder time shifting attention away from these cues. We have found that chronically aggressive 8-year-olds attend more to irrelevant cues than do non-aggressive children (Dodge *et al.*, 1986). For example, when a situation calls for attention to another's facial expression to recognize an accidental provocation, aggressive children are more likely to attend to irrelevant details such as the other's shoe colour, or details of outcome, such as how severely they had been injured.

At least 26 studies have shown that aggressive children are relatively biased in their attributions of ambiguous peer provocations as being hostile (Crick and Dodge, 1991). Another way of stating this finding is that non-aggressive children are biaseds toward interpreting such stimuli as benign, relative to aggressive children. In the typical study (e.g. Dodge, 1980), the aggressive group of boys is 50% more likely to make an interpretation that a hypothetical peer was being hostile than was the non-aggressive group of boys.

Aggressive children are not only likely to interpret ambiguous provocations as hostile; they are also more likely to demonstrate actual errors in interpretation when the cues are clear (Dodge *et al.*, 1984). Consistent with the hostile attributional findings, most of their errors are ones of presumed hostility when the objective cues indicate otherwise.

Numerous studies show that aggressive children more readily access from memory aggressive responses to social stimuli (Crick and Dodge, 1991). They access larger numbers of aggressive responses, and they do so more quickly than others do. They access aggressive responses in both hypothetical and real situations, and both after goal-blocking as well as without goal-blocking. It is clear that this response category is more available and more accessible in the memory stores of chronically aggressive children than of other children.

Several researchers, most notably Perry *et al.* (1985) and Crick and Ladd (1991), have found that aggressive children evaluate the potential outcomes of aggressing more favourably than do other children. These outcomes include the interpersonal, instrumental, intrapersonal and moral consequences of aggressive behaviours. In addition, these evaluations are related to proactive aggressive behaviour rates but not to reactive aggression (Crick and Dodge, 1991).

Finally, when asked to enact competent responses, such as asking to gain entry to a peer group, chronically aggressive children perform less skilfully than do non-aggressive children (Dodge *et al.*, 1986).

There are many caveats to these findings, and I do not wish to represent them as particularly strong in magnitude or pervasive across all aggressive children. They hold in some social situations but not others. The findings hold more strongly when the contexts of assessment simulate real-life conditions than in artificial hypothetical situations. They hold more strongly when children are aroused emotionally than when they are cold observers of meaningless irrelevant events (Dodge and Somberg, 1986). Still, these findings are robust. They have been replicated numerous times, in study after study by independent laboratories.

Even though any single finding might be of small to moderate magnitude, it has been found in at least four studies that aggregation of findings across the processing steps, in the form of multiple regression, yields powerful correlations with aggressive behaviour rates, accounting for 50–90% of the common variance (Dodge *et al.*, 1986). Also, these processing patterns tend to accumulate, so that a comprehensive assessment of multiple processing patterns in multiple social domains reveals that 70% of chronically aggressive children display at least three processing biases or deficits, in contrast with fewer than 10% of non-aggressive children.

SOCIAL INFORMATION PROCESSING AND
CHILD DEVELOPMENT

To summarize thus far, social information processing responses have been shown to correlate with aggressive behaviour responses at the level of specific aggressive acts. Also, patterns of processing social information, such as hostile attributional biases and the belief that aggression leads to favourable outcomes, correlate with individual differences in rates of aggressive behaviour. It appears, then, that these processing patterns are a reasonable description of the proximal brain mechanisms for aggressive responding. It might be more conservative to state that these processing patterns *describe* the phenomenology of aggressive behaviour, rather than causally explain aggression. The patterns are a description of what happens when a child aggresses. As a scientific theory, these findings are suspect, because they are only correlational; they are often collected outside of actual aggressive occurrences, and they are subject to alternative explanations. Still, they can be extraordinarily useful in understanding how the socialization of aggression might operate.

It is hypothesized that chronic patterns of processing social information are acquired through social experiences, particularly those in the first 5 years of life. An assertion is made about the primacy of early life because these patterns tend to self-perpetuate once they have been learned. It is hypothesized further that socializing influences on the development of chronic aggression are those that will affect processing styles. That is, experiences that will predispose a child towards aggressive behaviour are those that are likely to engender processing styles that characterize aggressive acts.

Consider first the development of angry reactive aggression, which occurs as a function of hypervigilance to hostile cues and hostile attibutional biases. Any experience that will lead a child to see the world as hostile should place a child at risk for reactive aggression. So, we posit that actual experiences in early life of chronic danger, trauma, being the object of violence as in abuse, or privation of relationships (Rutter's term, 1972) will lead to increased rates of aggressive behaviour, especially reactive aggression.

Likewise, it is hypothesized that proactive aggression will be socialized by experiences that place aggressive strategies at the top of a child's memory bin and that lead a child to believe that aggression results in favourable outcomes. These experiences might be exposure to aggressive models; environmental endorsement of aggression; the lack of competent, non-aggressive models; and direct or vicarious reinforcement of aggressive behaviour.

One major socializing influence is on the experience of physical harm by an adult. Harsh discipline is a common event in the USA. It has been estimated that 10–15% of all children in the USA have been physically abused in the first 5 years of life (Straus and Gelles, 1990). Hypothesizing that abuse increases the risk of child aggression is not a novel idea. Indeed, it is consistent with most theories of aggressive development. I will argue though that these theories actually posit some form of processing pattern as a mediating link in this chain.

Social learning theory (Bandura, 1977) posits the central role of modelling and imitation of others' behaviour, particularly successful behaviour, in behavioural development. Exposure to aggressive models places the response of aggression in a child's memorial repertoire. Repeated or dramatic models are placed more deeply in memory and are likely to be highly accessible and available in memory.

Patterson's coercion theory (1982) frames the problem in terms of discipline. The harsher the discipline (especially when it is inconsistently applied or followed by capitulation to a child's demand), the more likely it is that the child will become aggressive. The child learns that coercive tactics are likely to lead to favourable outcomes.

The frustration–aggression model, as described by Berkowitz (1989), posits the necessity of goal-blocking and highly frustrating events such as the experience of physical harm in the socialization of aggression. These goal-blocking events are particularly frustrating if they are intentional and malicious and likely to continue.

Finally, attachment theory has highlighted the role of early interpersonal relationships, particularly those that are characterized by insecurity and physical violence, as causal links in aggressive development. Crittenden and Ainsworth (1989) have speculated on the mechanisms in this relation. They postulate that children who have been physically abused become hypervigilant to hostile cues, and that 'such vigilance resulting from internal models of conflict and dominance could easily lead the abused child to misinterpret the behavior of others and to respond with aggression himself' (p. 453).

RELATION BETWEEN PHYSICAL ABUSE AND AGGRESSIVE DEVELOPMENT

In spite of these numerous theories, there exist relatively few good studies on the effect of physical abuse on aggressive development, and virtually none on the mechanisms of action. There are, of course, hundreds of case accounts of formerly abused individuals who grow up to become abusive parents or violent criminals. Most of the studies, however, are retrospective accounts in which the occurrence of abuse has not been independently verified and is subject to the victim's biased recall.

Almost all of the prospective studies have relied on a sample of abused children selected from the juvenile courts. Juvenile court samples are problematic because they are undoubtedly a biased group of abused children, likely to be more aggressive and noticeable to authorities than most abused children. Also, these studies confound the occurrence of abuse with subsequent intervention by the court, which usually includes separation from the home, labelling and professional treatment, all of which might be iatrogenic. What is needed is a prospective study of children who have been severely harmed in early life but who have not necessarily been identified by public agencies.

Another problem with longitudinal studies in this area is that the occurrence of abuse and harsh discipline is likely to be correlated with other factors that may account for any increased risk in the victims. It is known that abuse is likely to occur in an ecological context of other risk factors (Widom, 1989). Abuse is more common among highly stressed groups, including single-parent families, families with marital conflict and violence, and lower socioeconomic classes.

Also, it has been speculated that certain biologically based characteristics of the child lead adults to engage in physical harm towards that child, and perhaps it is those child characteristics that are also responsible for the high risk. According to an extreme child effects model, which smacks of blaming the victim, physical abuse is a marker of risk without contributing to the risk. Clinical evidence suggests that infants with a difficult temperament are at risk for abuse, as are infants with health problems, such as low birth weight. To date, no study has controlled these ecological and child biological factors while examining the possible aggressogenic effects of abuse on children.

THE CHILD DEVELOPMENT PROJECT

This background led Jack Bates, Greg Pettit and me, with the participation of numerous others, to initiate the Child Development Project, a prospective study of two cohorts of about 300 children each. The children come from three geographical sites: Nashville, Tennessee, with several urban, high-crime neighbourhoods; Knoxville, Tennessee, with a low-income rural population; and Bloomington, Indiana, with a working-class population. The sample is multiracial, socioeconomically mixed and of varied family backgrounds. The sample is representative of the populations in these respective areas.

The children were recruited 5 months prior to the beginning of kindergarten, at age 5, and have been followed since that time. Three kinds of measures have been collected.

The first kind has to do with early social and family experiences that might place the child at risk. These data were collected through private interviews with parents, written responses, and direct observations of parent–child interaction in the home. After soliciting information about early health problems and developmental history, the interviewer conducted a clinical interview about the child's disciplinary history and physical harm. The interviewer asked whether the child had ever been physically harmed by an adult to the point that the child required medical attention or showed visible bruising. These questions were asked separately for the period from the child's birth up to 12 months ago, and again for the past year.

Children were classified into groups of ever having been severely harmed versus not harmed, with 12% of the sample fitting the harmed group (Dodge *et al.*, 1990b). As noted earlier, this rate is consistent with national estimates by Straus and Gelles (1990). But abuse is often not only a single isolated incident. One could define the experience of abuse dimensionally, based on the frequency and severity of harm. Such ratings were made on 5-point scales for each of the eras of early life. Both the categorical and dimensional scores correlated significantly with parents' reports on the conflict tactics scale. It is assumed that these scores are subject to some error because of the parent-report nature of the data. However, it is also assumed that most of the error is under-reporting of abuse. The prototypical case was of a mother reporting that the child had been severely beaten by a current or former husband or boyfriend who was not currently exhibiting this behaviour.

In a separate interview with a different adult, the child's patterns of processing social information were assessed. Video-recorded stimuli were used to solicit the child's responses to questions about the child's attention to relevant cues; interpretations of peers' intentions; accessing of aggressive strategies; and evaluation of the probable outcomes of aggressing. These assessments are the same as those described in the earlier studies.

Finally, individual differences in children's interpersonally aggressive behaviour were assessed 6–9 months later in school, through direct observations on the playground, peer nominations, teacher ratings, and parent ratings. Because the parent ratings are the only scores subject to rater bias problems with other measures, these measures have been dropped from the analyses of aggressive outcomes in school.

The data have been analysed separately for each cohort, as a built-in replication of the findings (Dodge *et al.*, 1990; Weiss *et al.*, 1991). First, the hypothesis was tested that physical harm and abuse in the first 5 years of life are predictive of later aggressive behaviour. Categorical analyses revealed that the harmed group, relative to the unharmed group, received 93% higher scores on the aggression scale of the teacher report form. This finding means also that over 36% of the harmed group received scores in the clinically significant range,

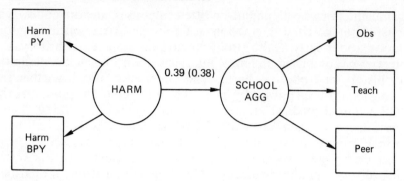

Fig. 3.1 *Structural equation model predicting school aggression (observed, teacher-rated and peer-rated) from being the object of physical harm at home before the past year (BPY) and in the past year (PY).*

contrasted with just 13% of the unharmed group. In peer nominations, the harmed group averaged twice as many nominations for aggressive behaviour as did the unharmed group. Direct observations yielded rates of aggressive acts that were 30% higher for harmed children over unharmed children, with a more dramatic effect for angry reactive aggression than proactive bullying.

Dimensional analyses were conducted with structural equation modelling, in order to aggregate across multiple measures of a construct, disattenuate for error and test hypotheses. Harm, as assessed by the combination of the two eras of the past year and before the past year, was found to predict later aggression, assessed by the observations, teacher ratings and peer nominations (Fig. 3.1). This simple model fitted the data well, as indicated by standard goodness-of-fit indices. The magnitude of the path coefficient was 0.39 in the first cohort and 0.38 in the independent replication cohort (indicated by the figure in parentheses). These effects are highly significant, but we were not yet convinced because of the numerous correlated factors that might account for these findings.

Next, we tested the possible confounding effect of marital violence. Because over a third of the sample involved single-parent families, this test was necessarily conducted with a subset of subjects. We assessed marital or partner violence in two eras – the past year and before the past year. As expected, this construct was related to physical harm of the child in both cohorts. However, this construct did not account fully for the relation between harm and later child aggression, which remained significant after this construct was partialled out.

The next tests concerned the effects of socioeconomic status and child temperament as possible confounding factors. Socioeconomic status was assessed by the Hollingshead 4-factor index, including mother and father education and occupation. This measure correlated significantly with harm to the child in both cohorts. Child temperament was assessed by the mother's retrospective rating of her child at 6 months of age with the Bates infant characteristics questionnaire, which yields scales of fussiness, unadaptability and resistance to control. This construct related significantly to child harm in the second cohort only.

Even though these constructs were related to harm, they did not account for the predictability of child aggression from physical harm. This relation again remained significant in both cohorts. So, as far as we can presently determine, the relation between physical harm to the child and later child aggressive behaviour is not due to socioeconomic status or child effects.

We went to some trouble to account for this relation by partialling out not only these factors, but also child gender, child health problems at birth, marital disruption and divorce and family stress in the first years of the child's life. Even when all of these factors were considered simultaneously, physical harm to the child continued to predict school aggressive behaviour in both cohorts. Thus, these data are consistent with the hypothesis of a causal effect, even though we know that data of this sort cannot satisfactorily answer a causal question.

We next turned to the possible mediating influence of social information processing mechanisms. It was hypothesized that:

1. processing styles would predict later child aggressive behaviour;
2. physical harm would predict these processing styles; and
3. processing styles would reduce the magnitude of the relation between physical harm and school aggression.

The predictability of school aggression in kindergarten from processing styles assessed prior to the beginning of kindergarten was tested next. The processing construct was indicated by four variables: irrelevance of encoding, hostile attributional biases, aggressive response generation and a favourable aggressive response evaluation. The path was significant in each cohort, with the coefficient being 0.48 in the first cohort and 0.28 in the second cohort (Fig. 3.2). All four of the indicators were significantly correlated with at least one of the aggressive behaviour outcomes, and they provided unique increments. These findings are consistent with past studies (see above) but are among the first in which the relation is tested prospectively, thus reducing the likelihood that they are accounted for by an opposite causal path.

Next, the path from physical harm to child processing patterns was tested. This path was significant in each cohort, with coefficients of 0.42 and 0.28. Physical harm to the child in the first 5 years of life significantly predicted at age 5 the child's tendencies to attend to irrelevant cues, attribute hostile intent to peers, and access aggressive strategies in response to interpersonal problems. Harm was not

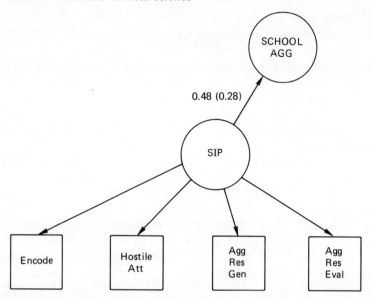

Fig. 3.2 *Structural equation model predicting school aggression from social information processing (SIP) patterns (encoding skill, hostile attributional biases, aggressive response generation, and aggressive response evaluation).*

related to evaluations of the outcomes of aggressing. These findings are the first indication that these processing patterns are related to a specific social history.

The final test was of the mediation hypothesis. Analysis by a structural equations model yielded an acceptable fit to the data in each cohort, and significant paths were found from physical harm to processing styles and from processing styles to school aggression, exactly as predicted by the mediation model (Fig. 3.3). Thus, the processing styles accounted for, or mediated, at least some of the effect of physical harm on child aggressive behaviour in school. In cohort 1, this mediation was large enough to account for all of the variance in the relation between harm and aggression. In cohort 2, it accounted for some but not all of the variance. A test was conducted with the two cohorts combined, and it was found that the paths from harm to processing and from processing to school aggression were significant, and the direct path from harm to school aggression was not significant. Thus, physical harm has an effect on aggressive development, but this effect is an indirect one that is mediated by the child's acquisition of social information processing styles.

These data are consistent with a model of aggressive behavioural development that includes distal factors such as physical harm to the child in the first 5 years of life and proximal mechanisms such as poor attention to relevant cues, hostile attributional biases, and accessing

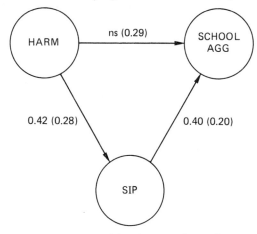

Fig. 3.3 *Structural equation model indicating the mediating effect of social information processing (SIP) patterns on the prediction of school aggression from being the object of physical harm.*

of aggressive strategies from memory. These findings must be accompanied by many caveats and alternative explanations, including the possibility of the effects of other common variables such as genes and as yet untested child effects on harm, processing styles, and aggressive behaviour.

It must be noted, however, that physical harm to the child is not the only socializing influence on child aggression. It is obvious that aggression is multidetermined, and that a comprehensive account will include numerous other factors, such as exposure to violence and lack of parental monitoring, and will be culturally specific.

Likewise, aggression is not the only likely outcome of physical harm to the child. Physical abuse could well have numerous other effects, although we did test the effect of harm on internalizing problems, which at the age of 5 and 6 are defined by Achenbach and Edelbrock (1981) as sadness, listlessness, withdrawal and social isolation. Harm did not predict such problems in either cohort. These findings might be attributed to age-specificity, that is, it might well be that early physical abuse will have a long-term effect on psycho-pathological outcomes such as anxiety disorder and depression in adolescence.

Perhaps we have proposed a weak developmental model of the relation between physical abuse and child aggression if it is one in which early physical harm leads to multiple outcomes and aggressive behaviour has multiple sources. What is exciting about these data, however, is the possibility that the temporal relation between early harm and later aggression might be mediated by the child's development of specific aggressogenic styles of processing social cues. This is indeed a developmental model and one that specifies mechanisms of action.

I do not wish to imply that social information processing patterns are the only proximal mechanism for aggressive behaviour. I have not addressed other simultaneous mechanisms, such as neurochemical pathways and psychophysiological mediators. I assume that such pathways will eventually be found, and I hypothesize that early physical abuse will be found to influence aggressive development by its influence on these neurochemical factors. Inquiry into these mechanisms is not at odds with the theorizing that I have articulated here, and I hope that the competitive battle across disciplinary, or perhaps theoretical, boundaries will be dropped. The advances in our understanding will come through an integration across domains, in somewhat the way that I have articulated an integration across the domains of distal socialization factors and proximal processing factors.

Unfortunately, these data have not yet distinguished among the socialization theories described earlier. Both attachment theory and social learning theory remain viable accounts of the development of aggressive behaviour in abused children. In fact, if anything, these data support the hypothesis that different theories best explain aggressive development in different children. Because we found evidence of multiple unique processing factors, and because these processing factors appear to mediate aggressive development, it might well be that different mechanisms apply for different children. One abused child might become aggressive as a function of an internal working model of the world as a hostile place, as predicted by Crittenden and Ainsworth (1989), whereas another abused child might become aggressive as a function of imitating violent models, as predicted by Bandura (1977). Still another might become aggressive by learning coercive tactics, as Patterson (1982) has shown. This is not to imply that these are poor or understated theories; rather, I mean to imply that studying aggressive behavioural development is a bit like studying cancer.

ACKNOWLEDGEMENTS

The author wishes to thank Greg Pettit and Jack Bates for stimulating ideas. He acknowledges the support of the following research grants: National Institute of Mental Health R01 MH42498 and National Institute of Child Health and Human Development K04 HD00806.

REFERENCES

Achenbach T. M., Edelbrock C. S. (1981). Behavioral problems and competencies reported by parents of normal and disturbed children aged four through sixteen. *Monographs of the Society for Research in Child Development*; (serial no. 188).

Bandura A. (1977). *Social Learning Theory*. New York: General Learning Press.

Bandura A. (1988). Self regulation of motivation and action through goal systems. In: *Cognitive Perspectives on Emotion and Motivation* Hamilton V., Bower G. H., Frijda N. H., eds, pp. 37–61. Dordrecht, Netherlands: Kluwer Academic.

Bandura A. (1989). Reflections on nonability determinants of competence. In: *Competence Considered: Perceptions of Competence and Incompetence across the Lifespan*. Kolligian J. Jr, Sternberg, R. J. eds. New Haven, CT: Yale University Press.

Berkowitz L. (1989). Frustration-aggression hypothesis: examination and reformulation. *Psychological Bulletin*: **106**: 59–73.

Crick N. R. Dodge K. A. (1991). *A review and reformulation of the relation between children's social cognition and social adjustment*. Unpublished paper, Vanderbilt University, Nashville, TN.

Crick N. R., Ladd G. (1991). Children's perceptions of the consequences of aggressive behavior: do the ends justify being mean? *Developmental Psychology*; **26**: 612–20.

Crittenden P. M., Ainsworth M. D. S. (1989). Child maltreatment and attachment theory. In: *Child Maltreatment: Theory and Research on the Cause and Consequences of Child Abuse and Neglect* Cicchetti D., Carlson V. eds, pp. 254–77. New York: Cambridge Press.

Dodge K. A. (1980). Social cognition and children's aggressive behavior. *Child Development*: **51**: 162–70.

Dodge K. A. (1986). Social information processing variables in the development of aggression and altruism in children. In: *The Development of Altruism and Aggression: Social and Biological Origins* Zahn-Waxler C., Cummings M., Radke-Yarrow M., eds, pp. 280–302. New York: Cambridge University Press.

Dodge K. A. (1991). The structure and function of reactive and proactive aggression. In: *The Development and Treatment of Childhood Aggression* Pepler D. J., Rubin K. H., eds, pp. 201–18. Hillsdale, NJ: Lawrence Erlbaum.

Dodge K. A., Coie J. D. (1987). Social information processing factors in reactive and proactive aggression in children's peer groups. *Journal of Personality and Social Psychology*: **53**: 1146–58.

Dodge K. A., Somberg D. (1986). Hostile attributional biases among aggressive boys are exacerbated under conditions of threats to the self. *Child Development*: **58**: 213–24.

Dodge K. A., Murphy R. R., Buchsbaum K. (1984). The assessment of intention-cue detection skills in children: implications for developmental psychopathology. *Child Development*: **55**: 163–73.

Dodge K. A., Pettit G. S., McClaskey C. L., Brown M. (1986). Social competence in children. *Monographs of the Society for Research in Child Development*; (serial no. 213, vol. 51, no. 2).

Dodge K. A., Coie J. D., Pettit G. S., Price J. M. (1990a). Peer status and aggression in boys' groups: developmental and contextual analyses. *Child Development*: **61**: 1289–1309.

Dodge K. A., Bates J. E., Pettit G. S. (1990b). Mechanisms in the cycle of violence. *Science*: **250**: 1678–83.

Gouze K. R. (1987). Attentional and social problem solving as correlates of aggression in preschool males. *Journal of Abnormal Child Psychology*: **15**: 181–97.

Kazdin A. E. (ed.) (1985). *Treatment of Antisocial Behavior in Children and Adolescents*. Homewood, IL: Dorsey Press.

Loeber R., Dishion T. (1983). Early predictors of male delinquency: a review. *Psychological Bulletin*: **94**: 68–99.

Olweus D. (1979). Stability of aggressive reaction patterns in males: a review. *Psychological Bulletin*: **86**: 852–75.

Parker J., Asher S. R. (1987). Peer acceptance and later personal adjustment: are low-accepted children at risk? *Psychological Bulletin*: **102**: 357–89.

Patterson G. R. (1982). *Coercive Family Process*. Eugene, OR: Castalia.

Perry D. G., Perry L. C., & Rasmussen P. (1985). Cognitive social learning mediators of aggression. *Child Development*; **57**: 700–11.

Robins L. N. (1966). *Deviant Children Grown up*. Baltimore: Williams & Wilkins.

Rutter M. (1972). *Maternal Deprivation Reassessed*. Harmondsworth, Midd: Penguin Books.

Sancilio M., Plumert J. M., Hartup W. W. (1989). Friendship and aggressiveness as determinants of conflict outcomes in middle childhood. *Developmental Psychology*: **25**: 812–19.

Steinberg M. D., Dodge K. A. (1983). Attributional bias in aggressive adolescent boys and girls. *Journal of Social and Clinical Psychology*: **1**: 312–21.

Straus M. G., Gelles R. J. (eds.) (1990). *Physical Violence in American Families: Risk Factors and Adaptations to Violence in 8145 Families*. New Brunswick, NJ: Transaction Publishers.

Weiss B., Dodge K. A., Bates J. E., Pettit G. S. (1991). *Some consequences of early harsh discipline: child aggression and a maladaptive social information processing style*. Unpublished paper, Vanderbilt University, Nashville, TN.

Widom C. S. (1989). Does violence beget violence? A critical examination of the literature. *Psychological Bulletin*: **106**: 3–28.

Part 2 *Neuroscience*

4 The neuroendocrinology of aggression: roles of steroids, monoamines and peptides

JOE HERBERT

AGGRESSION AS BEHAVIOUR: LIMITATIONS OF AN EXPERIMENTAL STRATEGY

Reductionism has ruled the experimental study of behaviour, as it has most other areas of neuroscience, and for much the same reasons. The whole life of any animal, including a human being, is a behavioural stream. Faced with the impenetrable complexities of behaviour, the experimental strategy has been to categorize behaviour into components, and then to study each component by itself, hoping to define the control processes and neural mechanisms associated with each behavioural subset. This strategy has had its successes. Sexual behaviour, commonly studied in the rat and similar species by observing pairs of animals, or even a single animal working for a sexual goal, has given huge amounts of information. We know a great deal about the hormonal control of this behaviour, and increasing amounts about the way that neural systems both respond to hormones or themselves operate to limit or define endocrine action. Eating and drinking, often studied separately, have also yielded to this approach. A good deal is known about variations in, say, incentive properties of food, the way this interacts with central states supposed to represent food lack (i.e. hunger), and how disturbing (usually lesioning) parts of the brain – say the hypothalamus – alters food intake. Drinking behaviour is less often studied in its own right (i.e. as a pattern of behaviour) but rather as part of the effort to disentangle the control of fluid balance. Nevertheless, we are beginning to understand something about its neural control, and about the chemical systems that operate to regulate this behaviour.

These strategies have been successful for two reasons. Though there are always blurred areas between behavioural categories such as these, nevertheless there is little doubt in an observer's mind (in most cases) as to the type of behaviour being displayed. Eating is obvious, simply from the point of view of the relatively stereotyped motor pattern the animal displays. So, too is drinking, or sexual interaction, or maternal behaviour. In parallel with this observable classification (we might refer to it as the proximate basis for categorization) is a second one: the different behaviours have equally distinct functions – the ultimate basis for their separate identities. There are, of course, numerous examples where several behavioural categories overlap; this is inevitable because behaviour is, as has been said, a continuous stream. Nevertheless, the function of sexual behaviour, say, is reasonably distinct from that of eating. Even eating and drinking, though they clearly share many affinities, have separable functions. The same is true for maternal behaviour, even though it shares with sexual activity the function of perpetuation of the species, rather than of the individual. The form of each behaviour, then, reflects its function: these functions are, to a degree at least, distinct, and hence the justification for, and success of, the reductionist approach to the experimental study of behaviour. Though when we separate and isolate each behaviour from the rest of the animal's repertoire we may lose some features of considerable importance (e.g. the way they interact with each other, or how they are controlled by common factors such as the animal's social system), nevertheless the rationale for this approach – so long as it is seen for what it is – is defensible; furthermore, as this brief overview tries to show, it has been quite successful, at least within the terms it has set itself.

It is natural, therefore, that this well-tried and profitable method should be applied to a behaviour so imperative as aggression. After all, it is also quite easy to recognize aggressive behaviour, even though this may become difficult as levels of interaction between members of a species become more complex, for example, in humans. Nevertheless, there are clear-cut types of behaviour which, it can be fairly said, no reasonable observer would categorize as anything other than aggressive. Ethologists have given us the means to recognize a behavioural repertoire which we can label as aggression. What is more, manoeuvres such as isolating animals and then confronting them with unfamiliar conspecifics, or pairing animals together and giving one an electric shock, reproduce in a consistent and quantifiable way aggressive behaviour. The stage is set, it seems, for a successful repeat of the experimental study of another category of behaviour – aggression. And yet, despite this justifiable expectation, despite the evident critical importance of aggressive behaviour to the understanding of social behaviour and the means whereby animals optimize their survival, despite the urgent need for a clearer understanding of both the psychological and physiological bases of aggressive behaviour to underpin clinical and social needs of our own species, despite a ready-made armamentarium of techniques, the reality is almost total disappointment. By comparison with any of the other behaviours listed in the paragraphs above, we understand very little about the neural and endocrine control of aggressive behaviour. An informal way to demonstrate this is to look in any standard textbook on the physiology of behaviour. The chapter on aggressive behaviour – if there is one – is truncated, confused and uninformative if set alongside those on the other behaviours. Whilst there is some general understanding of the principles by which sexual, eating and the other behaviours are regulated, all the information on aggression seems empirical and without any clear structure. Yet without experimental advances in the understanding of aggressive behaviour we are unlikely to get an adequate view of the pathophysiology of aggression, let alone a rational basis for any sort of treatment of aggressive disorders. What accounts for this state of affairs?

The explanation is simple to describe, though much harder to remedy. Because aggressive behaviour is so stereotyped and species-specific, the temptation has been to regard it as a unitary category of behaviour, comparable to sexual, material and eating behaviour, and so on. The fatal flaw has been to confuse the form of a behaviour with its function. Even in the better-categorized behaviours this can be a problem – there are plenty of examples of eating, say, being used in contexts other than the strictly nutritive. Nevertheless, as we have seen, the correspondence between form and function is maintained for these behaviours – to a degree at least. For aggression it is totally absent, as aggression is a means, not an end, a behavioural tactic in the competitive strategy. Aggression may appear to occur by itself, but it never does; it is always part of another behaviour (Attili and Hinde, 1986). For example, the aggressive behaviour of male monkeys or stags towards each other during the mating season is part of sexual behaviour, and is thus driven by the controls that regulate sexual activity (testosterone levels, position in the dominance hierarchy etc.; Wilson and Boelkins, 1970). Defence of the young by attacking potential threats to them is part of maternal behaviour (Hansen and Ferreira, 1986). It is not surprising, therefore, that the effects of hormones on the two types of aggression are different (Herbert, 1989b) since the endocrine regulation of the underlying behavioural state is also different. Classifications of aggression have reflected this confused view; for example, that proposed by Moyer (1968) – and perhaps, at last, being abandoned – confounds stimuli, contexts and functions in its attempts to clarify different sorts of aggression. So when we separate aggression from other behaviours, in order to study it 'alone' in a simplified condition, we are in grave danger of making it irrelevant and of removing or obscuring the essential context in which aggression occurs. This does not necessarily mean that studying isolated aggression is always a waste of time; but the underlying function (context) of the aggression must always be considered, even though experimental conditions may make it difficult to perceive. Ignoring this has led to aggressive displays of similar appearance but different function being lumped together; thus it becomes almost impossible to design experiments that can reveal physiological control systems of the behaviour. Hinde (1974, quoting Karczmar and Scudder, 1969) gives the example of different strains of mice, whose relative scores of aggressive behaviour varied according to the situations (defence of pups, after isolation etc.) in which they were tested. There are two questions that are important: why do (some) animals use aggression as a tactic some of the time, and what is the consequence both for the animal concerned and for its conspecifics of adopting aggression as a tactic? It will not have escaped notice that these questions are also profoundly relevant to the study of human aggressive behaviour.

AGGRESSION IN SOCIETY: THE DOMINANCE HIERARCHY

Whilst the study of any behaviour is liable to be impoverished by removing it from its social context, that of aggression loses much of its point. For aggression is the means whereby members of the same species regulate each other's behaviour and, in so doing, gain or lose access to prized resources that are in short supply (e.g. food, shelter, mates). The mammalian brain, and particularly the primate brain, is well-equipped to learn significant facts about both the physical and the social environment, and make use of this information to plan behaviour or adapt responses. So animals living in long-standing groups (such as most primates) can not only regulate each other's behaviour by aggressive actions or threats of such action, but can also learn from their outcome. This learning process gives rise to the dominance hierarchy that characterizes such societies. This hierarchy is defined, not by who gives (or receives) the most aggression, but the direction of aggressive interactions. Commonly, they are linear and one-way, though more complex arrangements often exist. The main function of such a hierarchy, often stated, is to reduce the amount of direct aggression between its members, since each comes to know the likely outcome of attempting to compete with others, or of indulging in behaviour that may elicit aggressive responses. Monkeys, for example, seem to learn which individuals control the group's behaviour (and spend much time monitoring them – Keverne *et al.*, 1978; see Fig. 4.1) and also the rules by which they are regulated (i.e. the circumstances that are particularly liable to elicit aggression towards them). Humans may do likewise. However, the dominance hierarchy, though it often appears very stable over a prolonged period of time (an observer will be able to predict accurately which individual takes precedence in competitive situations), is nevertheless in a state of constant tension. This is because the more subordinate animals must

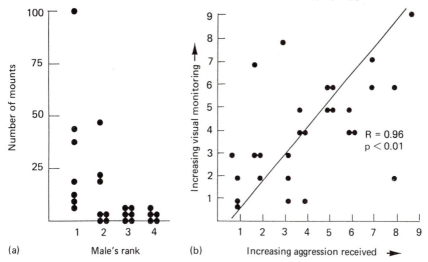

Fig. 4.1 *The effect of social subordination (associated with persistent threat of aggression) on behaviour in captive groups of talapion monkeys. (a) the relation between the male's rank and the expression of sexual behaviour. Behaviour is suppressed in subordinate animals (ranks 3 and 4). (b) The relation between visual monitoring, a form of vigilance behaviour, and the amount of aggression received by individual animals. Each animal has been ranked according to its level of visual monitoring and the amount of threatening behaviour or overt aggression received from other group members. The two parameters are positively correlated.*

persistently monitor the more dominant (Fig. 4.1), so as to react to (or forestall) aggression from others who are likely to outclass them and also because there must be some mechanism for testing the strength of the hierarchy so that, for instance, the illness of a dominant animal can quickly lead to its being replaced by a subordinate. Being a subordinate monkey is thus not a passive state, and carries persistent risks of being attacked (Dixson and Herbert, 1977).

Being a subordinate monkey has widespread effects on both behaviour and physiology. Subordinate males, for example, are much less likely than dominants to mate (Fig. 4.1); if the group is confined to a large cage, they will spend much of their time in unfavourable positions (far away from the source of food); they show high levels of visual monitoring of other animals (particularly dominant males); they appear much more alert and aroused then the more relaxed dominants; and, of course, they may be attacked from time to time – though in a well-established group, overt aggression may be low. Nevertheless, the threat of aggression is always present. There are also several important endocrine consequences of being a subordinate – a potent form of social stress (Herbert, 1987). Mason (1972) pointed out, many years ago, that the response to such chronic stressors

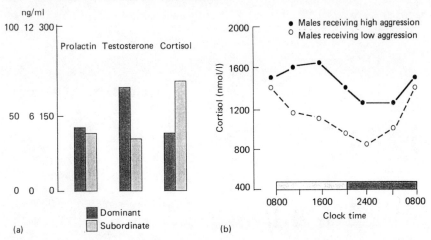

Fig. 4.2   *The effects of social rank, and hence persistent social stress, on hormone levels in groups of talapoin monkeys. (a) Differences between dominant and subordinate males in three stress-associated hormones. Prolactin shows no change, but testosterone is lowered and cortisol raised in subordinate males. (b) Circadian rhythms in cortisol in males receiving either high or low levels of aggression from other members of the group. Not only are cortisol levels raised in the first group but there are alterations in the shape of the daily rhythm of cortisol.*

involved many hormones. Subordinate male talapoin monkeys, housed in heterosexual groups, have lower levels of testosterone than dominant males. Prolactin (another well-recognized stress hormone) may be raised in them, though this is not always found (Fig. 4.2). Most attention has been focused on cortisol. It is useful to discuss this hormone in the context of the way that persistent threat can alter peripheral hormones and, as a consequence, brain function.

CORTICOIDS AND THE RESPONSE TO AGGRESSION

Most workers studying groups of primates find that subordinates have the highest levels of cortisol (Fig 4.2), though there have been exceptions. Cortisol in the blood is bound to corticoid-binding globulin (CBG). The binding affinity of this protein, and its concentration, is such that, under basal conditions, about 90–95% of cortisol is bound to it. The free fraction (thus about 5%) is generally considered to be biologically available; this is the fraction that can pass across the blood–brain barrier into the cerebral extracellular fluid (ECF). The concentration of cortisol, therefore, in the fluid surrounding the neurons will depend upon blood levels, since increasing them will alter the absolute value of the free fraction. However, as blood levels of cortisol rise to those seen during stress (including persistent aggressive interactions, or the threat of such actions) there will come a point at which the binding capacity of CBG is exceeded. At this point, any additional cortisol will be entirely free; thus the amount entering the brain will show a rapid increase, no longer predictable from measuring the total level of cortisol in the blood (Herbert *et al.*, 1986). There is a second factor leading to a non-linear relation between blood and brain levels of cortisol. The clearance of cortisol from the cerebrospinal fluid (and hence, it must be presumed, the ECF) is much slower than from the blood. (Martensz *et al.*, 1983). Thus, even transient increases in intracerebral cortisol will persist for longer than they would have done in the blood. These findings are given added point by reports of at least two populations of corticoid receptors in the brain. The first, with relatively high affinity, are largely saturated at basal cortisol levels. But the second, with a lower affinity, are only about 50% saturated under basal conditions, but become fully saturated (i.e. active) as intracerebral corticoids rise into the stress range. Thus we can expect animals with persistently elevated corticoids to show corticoid-dependent neural responses distinct from those under non-stressed conditions.

Whilst change in absolute levels of corticoids is most important, it is not the only significant change that distinguishes subordinates (or animals under other types of stress). Corticoid secretion, in common with many other functions, shows well-marked circadian rhythmicity. This means that there is a time (the evening in primates) when the brain and other tissues are relatively corticoid-deficient. This period may be important, though this supposition is based on an analogy drawn from studies on other steroids such as oestradiol and progesterone. For example, in order for an oestradiol surge to elicit a Luteinizing Hormone surge in the female monkey (the normal stimulus), there must be a period of relative oestradiol deficiency. If oestradiol remains persistently high, then Luteinizing Hormone surges are not observed. Similarly, progesterone, added to oestradiol, can promote the appearance of sexual receptivity in the female rat. But if progesterone remains high, then oestrus is inhibited. Studies on subordinate monkeys have shown that not only do they have elevated cortisol, but that the form of the daily rhythm is altered (Fig. 4.2; Martensz *et al.*, 1987). Though we are unable at present to say what this means in terms of altered brain function, there must be considerable suspicion that both elevated corticoids and altered circadian rhythms – particularly if present chronically and magnified in the brain by the different dynamics of cortisol in the cerebral compartment – may have important consequences for neural activity. Neuronal degeneration has been reported to be increased in the pyramidal cells of the hippocampus by high doses of corticoids in rats (Sapolsky and McEwen, 1986) and subordinate monkeys are said to show a similar phenomenon. There may be other, perhaps more reversible, alterations in neuronal activity during states of hypercortisolaemia.

BRAIN MECHANISMS AND AGGRESSION: WHAT ARE WE LOOKING FOR?

This discussion suggests that the form of the neural systems concerned with aggressive behaviour might be rather different from those regulating, say, sexual activity or eating. Aggressive behaviour (or response to aggression in another) is a form of motor output which is clearly identifiable. So it might be plausible to postulate a specific neural mechanism responsible for this behaviour pattern. All behaviour (at a motor or output level) is, of course, organized by mechanisms in the cortex, brainstem and spinal cord. Since behaviours of different categories (including aggression) are fairly stereotyped, there must be some system that organizes the motor pattern to deliver the optimal sequence of aggressive actions, or response to aggression in another. This might not be limited to muscular action: both endocrine and autonomic outputs are well-recognized to be part of any definable behaviour pattern, particularly aggression. So the first mechanism is one that coordinates this tripartite behavioural output. There must be a second mechanism, however, which is common to, or linked with, the other behaviours of which aggression is a part. Since aggression is always an optional component, this mechanism is concerned with determining whether the stimuli or circumstances that are controlling the parent behaviour call for an aggressive component to be added – that is, a tactical decision. There might also be a third system, not entirely separate from the second: this would be concerned with reactions to aggression in another, and also makes tactical decisions – for example, whether to retaliate or submit. Finally, submission (or subordination) is a separable motor defence system, coordinating its own defined motor, endocrine and autonomic output pattern. As for all behaviour, there must be essential interactions between these neural systems and those concerned with cognitive analysis of the current environment, or social or other forms of learning.

A MODULAR VIEW OF THE BRAIN: AGGRESSION AND THE AMYGDALA

Efforts to fit defined parts of the brain to this scheme have to take into account the various ways of classifying neural systems. The traditional one is to identify anatomically defined parts of the brain that have a common or connected function and call this a system: hence the motor system and, more relevantly, the limbic system. Within these systems are anatomical components that have defined subfunctions: the basal ganglia, cerebellum and motor cortex etc. in the motor system; the hypothalamus, amygdala, septum and so on in the limbic system. The extensive connections between the components of a given system support the experimental data showing that they may be concerned with the same sort of function. However, there is a strict limit to the usefulness of this view of the brain. It is not clear, for example, where the motor system begins or ends, and the limbic system overlaps both anatomically and functionally with other systems, including the motor system. This is understandable, because it is obvious that the brain operates as a functional unit and that dividing it into systems, though a representation of neural organization, is also a descriptive convenience. However, there is no doubt that various parts of the limbic system have been implicated experimentally in aggressive behaviour, particularly the amygdala.

The anatomical features of the amygdala make it a prime candidate for modulating interactions between the neocortical and limbic systems. Profuse connections link it with the temporal lobe cortex on the one hand, and with the medial limbic structures such as the hypothalamus and ventral striatum and the brainstem on the other (Price *et al.*, 1987). The amygdala is made up of a number of constituent nuclei, usually divided into three groups: the basolateral receive most of the cortical input, and project to the ventral striatum and thalamus, as well as to the more medially placed amygdala nuclei (Fig. 4.3). The central nucleus is connected reciprocally with the hypothalamus and brainstem, as well as parts of the cortex. The corticomedial group has a major input from the olfactory system, and a large projection to the hypothalamus. These anatomical findings have resulted in efforts to ascribe different functions to subdivisions of the amygdala.

A traditional method of investigating regional brain function is by making lesions. Whilst this method can be (and has been) criticized, and undoubtedly has limitations, it has given vast amounts of information. Since the 1930s it has been known that lesions of the amygdala in monkeys and humans produce calming or 'taming' effects. Objects which would normally elicit a hostile, aggressive or fearful response no longer do so following bilateral amygdalotomy (Mark *et al.*, 1975). Conversely, electrical stimulation of the amygdala can precipitate aggressive responses, particularly in the presence of stimuli which might, under normal conditions, also induce aggression (Kaada, 1972). In the case of lesions, many experiments tested the animals' postoperative responses to fear-inducing stimuli such as a stick, or the experimenter, and this would not qualify as aggressive behaviour in the sense used in this chapter. In contrast to studies in primates, those in rats – using the more relevant stimulus of an intruder male – have not been very successful in showing changes in agonistic behaviour after bilateral damage to the whole amygdala (e.g. Blanchard and Takahashi, 1988). There is a parallel literature implicating the amygdala in sexual behaviour. Amygdaloid lesions

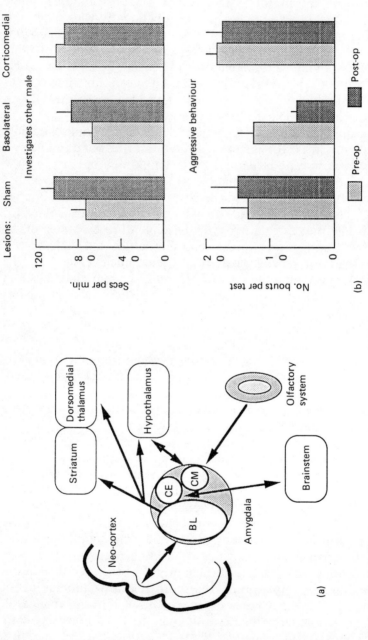

Fig. 4.3 *The role of the amygdala in aggression. (a) The anatomical arrangement of the amygdala showing the three principal subdivisions. BL = Basolateral nuclei; CM = corticomedial nuclei; CE = central nucleus. Each subdivision has a distinct pattern of input and output, though the extensive connections between the nuclei are not shown. (b) The effect of selective amygdala lesions on aggressive interactions between male rats. Basolateral lesions decrease aggression. Corticomedial lesions have no effect, though they decrease sexual interaction (data not shown).*

may induce hypersexuality (i.e sexual behaviour towards inappropriate or unusual objects) in primates, though this has not been reproduced in rodents, in which decreased sexual behaviour is more commonly seen. Recently, experiments using neurotoxin-induced (i.e. neuronally specific) lesions have shown that basolateral damage interferes with intermale aggressive behaviour, whereas corticomedial lesions decrease sexual behaviour with a female (McGregor and Herbert, 1992a; Fig. 4.3) and more reflexive events such as 'startle' have been abolished by damaging the central nuclei (Davis, 1990), suggesting that there may be some correlation of function with anatomy within the amygdala.

One of the more consistent findings following amygdaloid lesions has been apparent reductions in fear. A number of authors (e.g. Weiskrantz, 1956) have suggested that the amygdala links cognitive and limbic function, allowing affective or emotional value to be assigned to stimuli, partly on the basis of learned associations. If the amygdala contains the neural representation of fear or the mechanism whereby external stimuli are recognized as fearful, then it might have a general role in aggression. Any aggressive interaction is liable to generate fear in either (or both) the aggressor or the recipient. Furthermore, the ability for situations to engender a fearful state may act powerfully to bias an animal towards or away from using aggression as a tactic (Hansen and Ferreira, 1986). Since aggression is part of many other behaviours, the amygdala would be an essential part of all these behavioural complexes. This does not imply that assigning fearfulness to a stimulus is the only function of the amygdala. Thus, regional lesions may interfere with other associations between stimuli and value (e.g. the rewarding properties of food or sex; Everitt *et al.*, 1989), or have their restricted effects because they interfere with one channel of sensory input – for example, olfaction is particularly important in the sexual behaviour of rodents (Lehman *et al.*, 1980), whereas visual or other stimuli may be more significant for interactions between males. Together with the anatomical relations of the amygdala, the evidence suggests that the amygdala has an essential role in assigning value or significance to neo- or allocortically derived information, and modulating behavioural responses accordingly, by output directed towards the hypothalamus and brainstem. Thus, we may postulate that the amygdala is essential for the tactical decisions about whether or not to use, or respond to, aggressive behaviour.

Two other modules of the limbic system should be mentioned, though briefly. Stimulation of the hypothalamus (particularly the ventromedial area) can elicit aggressive behaviour (Flynn, 1967; Mancia and Zanchetti, 1980), and although lesions (somewhat paradoxically) may have similar effects, they can reduce intermale aggression (Albert *et al.*, 1987). The hypothalamus regulates a wide variety of homeostatic and procreative behaviours, and it is not clear how its role in aggressive behaviour fits in. For example, testosterone can heighten male aggression in the context of sexual behaviour; whether this depends upon the hormone acting on the same neurons that regulate sexual interaction, or whether there is a separate hormone-sensitive site for aggression in the medial hypothalamus (Albert *et al.*, 1987b) is not clear. If the former is true, presumably another set of neurons control aggressive responses in the context of food acquisition, itself regulated by a distinct part of the ventromedial hypothalamus. Alternatively, the hypothalmus could contain a mechanism 'downstream' from the amygdala for organizing the complex aggressive response pattern, and this could be recruited in a variety of behavioural contexts. Lesions of the septum also increase aggression (Dominguez and Longo, 1970), but such lesions also increase responses to a wide variety of stimuli, including aversive and sexual ones (Albert and Chew, 1980), and may represent damage to a response suppression system (Dickinson, 1974).

A NEUROCHEMICAL VIEW OF THE BRAIN: SEROTONIN AND PEPTIDES

Immunohistochemistry and associated techniques have led to a different view of the way the brain is organized. Neuronal systems are now characterized not only by their topography or connections, but also by their content of substances, particularly amino acids, amines and peptides. Neurons can be classed into chemical categories because they express genes that enable them to make particular neurochemicals. In some cases, these properties are so widespread that it would not be credible to suggest that all the neurons belonging to the same neurochemical class made up a functionally correlated and identifiable single system. For example, glutamate and gamma-aminobutyric acid (GABA) are produced widely in the central nervous system. The role of such neurons may reside in their anatomical connections and location, rather than in the fact that they make and use glutamate or GABA, though which transmitter they use will determine their role in each part of the brain. The same may be true for some short chain peptides such as enkephalins, because these peptides are also dispersed quite widely in the brain, and seem (in most cases) to be found in short-axoned neurons (type II).

The monoamine-containing systems, such as dopamine, noradrenaline and serotonin (SHT), are quite different. From relatively few, circumscribed neurons in the brainstem or basal diencephalon, these project to widespread (though defined) areas of the cranial and caudal central nervous system. The essential property of the monoaminergic systems is that each clearly affects the function of a considerable part of the brain. Their actions are not easily incorporated into a strictly modular view of the brain – or of the limbic system, since this part of the brain receives a particularly rich monoaminergic innervation. There is much evidence from both human and animal studies that brain 5HT pathways are involved in the mediation of anxiety and the behavioural and endocrine response to stress (Joseph and Kennett, 1983). Recent investigations have suggested a high degree of anatomical and functional specialization in brain 5HT pathways (Wilson and Molliver, 1991a, b). Projections from the dorsal raphe nucleus, particularly those innervating the amygdala, are involved in the genesis of conditioned avoidance behaviours via postsynaptic $5HT_2$ receptors (Hensman *et al.*, 1991). Projections from the median raphe to the hippocampus appear to mediate resilience and adaption to stress (Deakin, 1989) and postsynaptic 5HT receptors have been implicated in these behavioural effects. The postulated selectivity in the receptors activated by the two components of the raphe system is paralleled by morphological and pharmacological differences: the terminals from the dorsal and medial raphe have distinct appearances in immunohistological preparations, and react differently to amphetamine-related neurotoxins (Wilson and Molliver, 1991a). There is particular interest in the role of 5HT in aggressive behaviour in humans. Low cerebrospinal fluid 5-hydroxyindolacetic acid levels have been associated with suicide and destructive or aggressive behaviour (Brown and Linnoila, 1990), suggesting alterations in central 5HT. 5HT levels seem lower in the brains of patients with Alzheimer's disease who had been aggressive than those who were not (Procter *et al.*, unpublished results).

Recent studies on monkeys have shown 5HT to be involved also in the formation of dominance hierarchies. Males treated with drugs that would be expected to increase 5HT levels became dominant, whereas those that were given drugs that reduced 5HT were rendered subordinate. These effects could be reversed by altering the type of drug given (Raleigh *et al.*, 1991). There was an interesting inverse relation between these changes in social status and aggressive behaviour – monkeys treated with 5HT-enhancing drugs became less aggressive (though more dominant) and vice versa.

Perhaps not surprisingly, in view of its distribution in the brain, 5HT has been implicated both experimentally and clinically in a wide variety of behaviours. For example, lowering 5HT in rats can increase sexual, aggressive and ingestive responses (Everitt *et al.*, 1975; Stricker, 1983) as well as many other behaviours and the secretion of many hormones. These conclusions are, for the most part, based on procedures that deplete most of the cranial serotoninergic system. These data present a problem: whilst it seems reasonable to equate lowered 5HT with dyscontrol syndromes in humans, the experimental evidence does not explain why this should necessarily take the form of increased aggressivity. Neither does current clinical practice: in some individuals, alterations in patterns of food intake, or sexual behaviour (e.g. paraphilias) or depressive disorder may be as likely – all are treated by drugs that act on cerebral 5HT systems. If lowered 5HT is to accentuate aggressive responses, then some second factor seems to be needed, which biases or encourages the dyscontrol in the direction of aggression. Two possibilities suggest themselves at the level of neural systems. The first is limited to the 5HT system: there may be either regional alterations in 5HT receptor activity (e.g. in the amygdala), or a subset of the 5HT system (say, that originating from the dorsal raphe or even part of the dorsal raphe; see Wilson and Molliver, 1991b) may become hypoactive. Alternatively, the state of some other system (e.g. one containing neuropeptides – see below) or region of the brain (e.g. the amygdala) may be responsible for predisposing individuals who develop low 5HT to react aggressively to a variety of stimuli; the latter reconciles modular and chemical views of the brain. The two postulated mechanisms may overlap: for example, alterations in neuropeptides may result in local changes in 5HT receptors. Whatever the mechanism, it seems, on the basis of present information, that an 'and' condition may need to be fulfilled if low 5HT is to result in heightened aggressivity, of whatever kind. This second condition might represent the activity of a specific neural system; alternatively, more global characteristics, such as social learning or personality, may be involved.

The neuropeptides represent another feature of the chemical architecture of the brain, and one that is much more complicated than the monoamines. Peptidergic systems differ so much between themselves that there is a danger of overgeneralizing their features. There is a range of peptides that have well-established functions in the peripheral endocrine system but also highly significant actions on behaviour and on the autonomic nervous system. This triadic control is not unique to peptides – a similar case can be made for the monoamines (e.g. noradrenaline and 5HT). Peptides also share with the amines the property of being distributed across the conventional modules of the limbic system (as well as, in some cases, outside it). Peptides may represent a more specific level of control than other widely dispersed systems such as the monoamines, and this resides in the chemical nature of the peptides themselves. Peptides in the brain, as in other physiological contexts such as the immune system, may carry significant information in their molecules, and this is the reason that their molecular structure is so complex (compared to the monoamines) and modifiable by both genomic and post-translational events. It seems plausible that their function is the amalgamated result of the circumstances under which they are activated (or inhibited), their regional distribution (or anatomical addressing) and their biochemical actions (chemical addressing), which will depend upon the distribution and state of their receptors. Peptides are now known to be concerned both with the response to aggression and with its expression.

PRO-OPIOMELANOCORTIN (POMC) PEPTIDES: *β*-ENDORPHIN

The evidence points to the POMC peptides as significant components of the response to persistent stressors of various kinds, including the threat of aggressive interaction (Herbert, 1987, 1989a) The major group of neurons that synthesize β-endorphin lies in and around the hypothalamic arcuate nucleus (Finley *et al.*, 1981). There is a second group in the region of the nucleus of the solitary tract in the brainstem. The hypothalamic group projects to wide areas of the limbic system. An interior projection terminates in the dorsomedial and anterior hypothalamus, preoptic area, bed nucleus of the stria terminalis, diagonal band and septum, as well as part of the nucleus accumbens. More lateral fibres enter the amygdala, particularly the central and medial nuclei, though a few are found in the basolateral nuclei. A group of fibres runs first dorsally and then caudally to enter the brainstem, ending in the periaqueductal grey and nuclei of the reticular formation, including the aminergic neurons and the solitary tract nucleus. It seems probable that changes in the function of the major arcuate POMC group will result in a distributed pattern of altered neural activity.

The social structure of captive groups of talapoin monkeys is described above. Only the most socially dominant males copulate with the females. Subordinates not only make few, if any, attempts to mate, but even if the dominant males are removed their sexual behaviour takes extended periods to recover (Dixson and Herbert, 1977; Yodyinguad *et al.*, 1982). When the two categories of males are caged with sexually active females, blood levels of testosterone in subordinates are lower than dominant animals (Fig. 4.2; Martensz *et al.*, 1987). However, injecting subordinates with testosterone does not restore their sexual activity; in other words, they have become insensitive to their own steroid. Injecting dominant males with opiate-blockers (e.g. naltrexone or naloxone) releases Luteinizing Hormone, but fails to do so in subordinates (Meller *et al.*, 1980; Martensz *et al.*, 1986). The suspicion that endogenous opiates may be involved in the process whereby social rank – and hence the threat of aggressive behaviour – regulates reproduction is strengthened by the finding that β-endorphin levels in the cerebrospinal fluid of subordinates are about three times as high as in dominant males (Fig. 4.4; Martensz *et al.*, 1986).

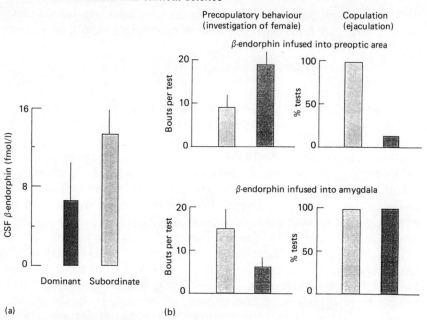

Fig. 4.4 *Opiate peptides and aggression. (a) The levels of β-endorphin in the cerebrospinal fluid (CSF) are increased in subordinate male monkeys. (b) β-endorphin infused into the preoptic area of the hypothalamus of male rats inhibits copulation but has either no effect (or increases) precopulatory behaviour. The same peptide infused into the amygdala depresses precopulatory behaviour but has no effect on copulation, though the latency for this to occur is prolonged (data not shown).*

The behavioural effects of β-endorphin and other members of the POMC family of peptides have been investigated in more detail in the rat. The questions asked were whether β-endorphin had the postulated effect on sexual behaviour, and if its action varied according to the site at which it was administered (whether there was anatomical addressing). β-endorphin infused into the preoptic area (POA) of male rats, a region well-known to be concerned with the expression of masculine patterns of sexual behaviour, abolished the male's ability to mount, intromit and ejaculate (Hughes *et al.*, 1987 see Fig 4.4). Similar infusions into the ventromedial hypothalamus did not, thus establishing site-specificity for this behavioural effect within the hypothalamus. However, even after β-endorphin infusions into the POA, the males continued to investigate the females, and pursue them in the characteristic manner of males before they copulate. This suggested that the infusions were interfering with only a part of sexual behaviour. This was confirmed in two ways: males trained to perform an operant response for access to females continued to do so after POA β-endorphin, even though they no longer copulated (Hughes *et*

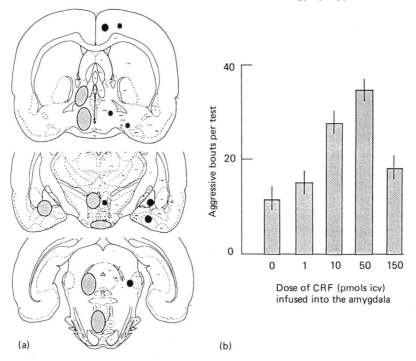

(a)　　　　　　　　　　　(b)

Fig. 4.5 *Corticotropin-releasing factor (CRF) and aggression. (a) The distribution of CRF in the rat brain. The right sections show the location of the major CRF-containing neurons; the left shows the position of the major terminal fields. (b) CRF infused into the amygdala of male rats increases their aggressive behaviour towards other, unfamiliar male rats.*

al., 1990), and if the β-endorphin infusions were delayed until after the male had made his first mount, they became ineffective (Stavy and Herbert, 1989). Does β-endorphin play a role in precopulatory behaviour? Infusions into the amygdala showed the converse effects of those in the POA. Precopulatory behaviour was reduced, but copulation itself was left unaltered (McGregor and Herbert, 1992b; Fig 4.4 and Fig 4.5). However, intermale aggression was not altered by these infusion, although infusing corticotropin-releasing factor (CRF) – another peptide implicated in aggression (see below) – into the amygdala increased intermale aggressive behaviour (Elkabir *et al.*, 1990; Fig. 4.5). β-endorphin in the cerebrospinal fluid of subordinate monkeys may represent a neurochemical link between aggression or the threat of aggression, and the behavioural and endocrine response to such conditions.

Taken together, these experiments lead to the following conclusions about the behavioural effects of these peptides. A given peptide may have its principal action on a given category of behaviour: β-endorphin on sexual behaviour, oxytocin on maternal behaviour

(Pedersen *et al.*, 1990), neuropeptide (NPY) on eating (Kalra and Kalra, 1990) etc., and these effects may correspond to other actions of the same peptide, for example the way it controls peripheral hormone levels. Within each peptide–behaviour category, the exact effect the peptide has depends upon its site of action – this is a property of the structure concerned (i.e. amygdala, hypothalamus) rather than the peptide. Finally, the amygdala is not concerned solely with aggressive behaviour, since selectively altering its neurochemical environment (rather than the more general procedures of lesioning and electrical stimulation) shows that separable effects on other patterns of behaviour (e.g. sexual) can be obtained.

CORTICOTROPIN-RELEASING FACTOR AND AGGRESSION

CRF, already mentioned above, is another peptide that could be implicated in some forms of aggression. Clinical interest in CRF centres on its role in major depressive disorder (Gold *et al.*, 1988); experimentally, it has been found to have a behavioural role that – as for several other peptides – correlates with its established endocrine function, in this case as a regulator of adrenocorticotrophic hormone (and hence the adrenal cortex) in the response to stressors. The behavioural and metabolic states of the two conditions may be comparable (Gold *et al.*, 1988). It has already been noted that stressors, such as pain or isolation, effectively induce aggression under experimental conditions. CRF is found in many areas outside the hypothalamic paraventricular nucleus and median eminence – structures directly concerned with adrenocorticotrophic hormone regulation; these include other areas of the limbic system (e.g. amygdala), brainstem nuclei associated with autonomic function, as well as the cerebral cortex (particularly the cingulate and prefrontal regions; Sakanaka *et al.*, 1987). The cell bodies of CRF neurons are thus not concentrated into localized packets like the POMC system described above. Hypotheses invoking hyperactivity of cerebral CRF-containing systems need to take these anatomical facts into consideration. Intracerebroventricular infusions of CRF potentiate certain stress-induced behaviours, such as fighting, as well as startle responses and other behaviours that may correspond to anxiety (Sherman and Kalin, 1987; Tazi *et al.*, 1987).

Most experimental information on CRF is based on intracerebroventricular infusions, but two sites of action have been studied. Electrophysiological and other techniques have focused on the locus ceruleus, a major noradrenaline-containing group of neurons in the medulla; CRF activates the locus, an action which has been correlated with its arousing effect on behaviour (Valentino and Foote, 1988). A second site is the amygdala. Infusions of CRF into the amygdala increased agonistic encounters between males kept in isolation and then paired with a second, strange, male (Elkabir *et al.*, 1990). However, intracerebroventricular infusions did not have this effect, suggesting that altered activity of this peptide within localized parts of the limbic system might have effects that differed from more general release into the cerebrospinal fluid (note that cerebrospinal fluid levels of CRF have been found to be elevated in depression – Nemeroff *et al.*, 1984). But there may be additive or synergistic effects of more than one peptide on aggressive behaviour. Vasopressin (AVP) has long been known to synergize with CRF to regulate the pituitary's secretion of adrenocorticotrophic hormone; recent findings show a similar potentiation by AVP of the aggressive-promoting action of intra-amygdaloid CRF (Elkabir *et al.*, 1990). It is tempting to speculate that certain sex differences in behaviour, including aggression and the response to stress, might be associated with corresponding sex differences in the distribution of AVP in the brain (Herbert and Fuller, 1989, De Vries, 1990).

CELLULAR RESPONSES TO NEUROPEPTIDES: MAPPING AGGRESSION IN THE BRAIN

The recent recognition that stimulated neurons express immediate-early gene (IEG) products looks set to offer a new dimension to the study of activity patterns in the central nervous system. Immunohistochemical and *in situ* methods show that IEGs, particularly *c-fos*, response to transynaptic stimuli. Originally identified as part of the response to growth factors in non-neural tissue, they are now known to be activated in the brain by either neurotransmitters or electrical stimulation (Curran and Morgan, 1987), or by peripheral sensory stimuli (Hunt *et al.*, 1987). Furthermore, IEG expression shows both temporal and anatomical specificity with respect to the locus and nature of the stimulus (Sheng and Greenberg, 1990). This technique has been used to map the neuronal responses in the limbic system to CRF (Arnold *et al.*, 1992). Intracerebroventricular infusions of CRF activate *c-fos* protein in a restricted population of neurons, including the ventrolateral septum, the central nucleus of the amygdala, the bed nucleus of the stria terminalis and the paraventricular nucleus (Fig. 4.6). Restraint stress also activates *c-fos*; the paraventricular pattern is somewhat more extensive, but the central nucleus of the amygdala is not activated. Cecatelli *et al.* (1989) have also shown that stress activates *c-fos* in the paraventricular nucleus, and by using double-staining techniques, that many of these cells are CRF-positive. In the

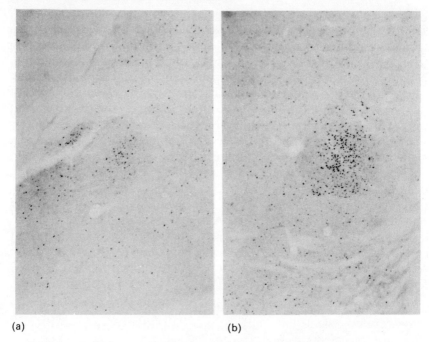

(a)   (b)

Fig. 4.6   *The effect of corticotropin-releasing factor (CRF) on the expression of an immediate-early gene. (a) The low expression of* c-fos *in the central muscles of the amagydala in rats following control infusions of cerebrospinal fluid (CSF). (b) The increased expression of nuclear* c-fos *protein following intracerebroventricular infusions of CRF.*

future we may anticipate that this method will enable us to map changes in regional brain activity during behavioural interactions – including aggression – and the results of altering the intracerebral environment using the range of steroids, amines and peptides discussed in this paper.

IMPLICATIONS FOR CLINICAL STRATEGY

Laboratory work, if it is valuable, ought to point the direction of future clinical strategies. This paper has considered only some of the neural and endocrine factors known to be implicated in aggression. The fact that there are so many others (e.g. other hormones such as testosterone, other amines such as noradrenaline, other parts of the brain such as the cingulate cortex) in part reflects the use of aggression in so many different contexts and for so many purposes. However, some correlations between the experimental literature and clinical concerns are evident. The classification of aggression needs careful attention, though work on humans (e.g. children) has already shown greater awareness of the problems than many experimental designs. If we believe that there are regional brain areas (e.g. the amygdala) that can, under some circumstances, play a central role in determining why some people may respond aggressively to situations which would not, in most others, elicit this response, then attention must be given (perhaps using current imaging techniques) to activity in this part of the brain under the conditions that evoke aggression. The implication is that there may be local abnormalities in some of those showing aggressive states which may be directly treatable. However, if we suspect that disorders in specific neurochemical systems may be responsible for defined types of aggressive disorders, then the strategy will be different; the hunt will be on for defined neurochemical correlates of aggression, and firm correspondence between these changes and aggressive syndromes. This offers, of course, the potential for developing rational pharmacological treatments These considerations need to take into account the variegated nature of aggression: there is unlikely to be a single cause of clinically significant aggressive disorders, and it seems likely that future diagnostic procedures and treatment strategies will reflect this.

ACKNOWLEDGEMENTS

The work of my laboratory is supported by grants from the Medical Research Council and the Wellcome Trust.

REFERENCES

Albert D.J., Chew G.I. (1980). The septal forebrain and the inhibitory modulation of attack and defense in the rat: a review. *Behavioral and Neural Biology*; **30**: 357–88.

Albert D.J. Dyson E.M., Walsh M.L., Gorzalka B.B. (1987a). Intermale social aggression in rats: suppression by medial hypothalamic lesions independently of enhanced defensiveness or decreased testicular testosterone. *Physiology and Behavior*; **39**: 693–8.

Albert D.J. Dyson E.M., Walsh M.L. (1987b). Intermale social aggression: reinstatement in castrated rats by implants of testosterone in the medial hypothalamus. *Physiology and Behavior*; **39**: 555–60.

Arnold F.J.L., de Lucas Bueno M., Shiers H., Hancock D.C., Evan G.I. (1992) Expression of *c-fos* in regions of the basal limbic forebrain following intracerebroventricular corticotropin releasing factor in unstressed or stressed male rats. *Neuroscience*; **51**: 377–90.

Attili G., Hinde R.A. (1986). Categories of aggression and their motivational heterogeneity. *Ethology and Sociobiology*: **7**: 17–27.

Blanchard D.C., Takahashi S.N. (1988). No change in intermale aggression after amygdala lesions which reduce freezing. *Physiology and Behavior*; **42**: 613–16.

Brown G.L., Linnoila M.I. (1990). CSF serotonin metabolite (5-HIAA) studies in depression, impulsivity and violence. *Journal of Clinical Psychology*; **51**: 31–41.

Cecatelli S. Villar M.J. Goldstein M., Hokfelt H. (1989). Expression of *c-fos* immunoreactivity in transmitter-characterized neurons after stress. *Proceedings of the National Academy of Sciences of the USA*; **86**: 9569–73.

Curran T., Morgan J.I. (1987). Memories of *fos*. *Bioessays*; **7**: 255–8.

Davis M. (1990). Animal models of anxiety based on classical conditioning: the conditioned emotional response (CER) and the fear-potentiated startle effect. *Pharmacology and Therapeutics*; **47**: 147–65.

Deakin J.F.W. (1989). 5HT receptor subtypes in depression. In: *Behavioural Pharmacology of 5HT* (Bevan P., Cosh R., Archer J., eds), pp. 179–204. New Jersey: Erlbaum.

De Vries G. (1990) Sex differences in neurotransmitter systems. *Journal of Neuroendocrinology*; **2**: 1–12.

Dickinson A. (1974). Response suppression and facilitation by aversive stimuli following septal lesions in rats: a review and model. *Physiology and Psychology*; **2**: 444–56.

Dixson A.F., Herbert J. (1977). Testosterone aggressive behaviour and dominance rank in captive male talapoin monkeys. *Physiology and Behavior*; **18**: 539–43.

Dominguez M., Longo V.G. (1970). Effects of p-chlorophenylalanine, a-methyl-paratyrosine and of other indole- and catechol-amine depletors on the hyperirritability syndrome of septal rats *Physiology and Behavior* **5**: 607–10.

Elkabir D.R., Wyatt M.E. Vellucci S.V., Herbert J. (1990). The effects of separate or combined infusions of corticotrophin-releasing factor and vasopressin with intraventricularly or into the amygdala on aggressive and investigative behaviour in the rat. *Regulatory Peptides* **28**: 199–214.

Everitt B.J. Fuxe K., Jonsson G. (1975). The effects of 5,7-dihydroxytrypyamine lesions of ascending 5-hydroxytryptamine pathways on the sexual and aggressive behaviour of female rats. *Journal of Pharmacology (Paris)*; **6**: 25–32.

Everitt B.J. Cador M., Robbins T.W. (1989). Interactions between the amygdala and ventral striatum in stimulus-reward associations; studies using a second-order schedule of sexual reinforcement. *Neuroscience*; **30**: 63–75.

Finley J. Lindstrom P., Petrusz P. (1981). Immunocytochemical localisation of β-endorphin containing neurons in the rat brain. *Neuroendocrinology*; **33**: 28–42.

Flynn J.P. (1967). The neural basis of aggression in cats. In: *Neurophysiology and Emotion* (Glass D.C., ed.), pp. 40–69. New York: Rockefeller UP.

Gold P.W. Goodwin F.K., Chrousos G.P. (1988). Clinical and biochemical manifestations of depression. Relation to the neurobiology of stress. *New England Journal of Medicine*; **391**: 413–20.

Hansen S., Ferreira A. (1986). Food intake, aggression and fear behaviour in the mother rat: control by neural systems concerned with milk ejection and maternal behaviour. *Behavioural Neuroscience*; **100**: 64–70.

Hensman R. Guimares F.J. Wang M. Deakin J.K.W. (1991). Effects of ritanserin on aversive classical conditioning in humans. *Psychopharmacology*; **104**: 220–4.

Herbert J. (1987). Neuroendocrine responses to social stress. In: *Neuroendocrine Responses to Stress* (Grossman A. ed.). London: Baillière Tindall.

Herbert J. (1989a). Specific roles for β-endorphin in reproduction and sexual behaviour. In: *Brain Opioid Systems in Reproduction* (Dyer R.G., Bicknell R.J., eds), pp. 167–86. Oxford: Oxford University Press.

Herbert J. (1989b). The physiology of aggression. In: *Aggression and War* (Groebel J., Hinde R.A., eds). Cambridge: Cambridge University Press.

Herbert J., Keverne E.B., Yodyinguad U. (1986). Modulation by social status of the relationship between cerebrospinal fluid and serum cortisol levels in male talapoin monkeys. *Neuroendocrinology*; **42**: 436–42.

Herbert J., Fuller L. (1989). Sex differences in the neuroendocrine responses to stress with particular reference to the cardiovascular system. In: *The Circulation in the Female. From the Cradle to the Grave.* (Ginsburg J., ed.), pp. 143–60. Carnforth: Parthenon Publishing.

Hinde R.A. (1974) *Biological Bases of Human Social Behaviour* New York: McGraw-Hill.

Hughes A.M. Everitt B.J., Herbert J. (1987). Selective effects of beta-endorphin infused into the hypothalamus, preoptic area and bed nucleus of the stria terminalis on the sexual and ingestive behaviour of male rats. *Neuroscience*; **23**: 1063–73.

Hughes A.M. Everitt B.J., Herbert J. (1990). Comparative effects of preoptic area infusions of opioid peptides, lesions and castration on sexual behaviour in male rats: studies of instrumental behaviour, conditioned place preference and partner preference. *Psychopharmacology*; **102**: 243–56.

Hunt S.P. Pini A., Evan G. (1987). Induction of *c-fos*-like protein in spinal cord neurons following sensory stimulation. *Nature*; **328**: 632–4.

Joseph M.H., Kennett G.A. (1983), Corticoisteroid responses to stress depends upon increased tryptophan availability. *Psychopharmacology*; **79**: 79–81.

Kaada B.R. (1972). Stimulation and regional ablation of the amygdaloid complex with reference to functional representations. In: *Neurobiology of the Amygdala* (Elefteriou B.E., ed.), pp. 205–81. New York: Plenum.

Kalra, S.P., Kalra P.S. (1990) Neuropeptide Y: a novel peptidergic signal. In: *Behavioural Aspects of Neuroendocrinology* (Ganten D., Pfaff D.W., eds), pp. 191–222. Berlin: Springer.

Karczmar A.G., Scudder C.L. (1969). Aggression and neurochemical changes in different strains and genera of mice. In: *Aggressive Behaviour* (Garratini S., Sigg E.B., eds). Amsterdam: Excerpta Medica.

Keverne E.B., Leonard R.A., Scruton D.M. (1978). Visual monitoring in social groups of talapiun monkeys (*Miopithecus talapoin*). *Animal Behaviour*; **26**: 933–44.

Lehman M.N., Winanas S.S., Powers J.B. 1980). Medial nucleus of the amygdala mediates chemosensory control of male hamster sexual behaviour. *Science*: **210**: 557–60.

Mancia G., Zanchetti A. (1980). Hypothalamic control of autonomic functions. In: *Handbook of the Hypothalamus* (Morgane P.J., Panksepp J., eds), vol. 3. pp. 147–202. New York: Marcel Dekker.

Mark V.H., Sweet W.H. & Ervin W.H. (1975). Depp temporal lobe stimulation and destructive lesions in episodically violent temporal lobe epileptics. In: *Neural Bases of Violence and Aggression* (Foelds W.S., Sweet W.H., eds), pp. 379–391. St Louis: Warren Grenn.

Martensz N.D., Herbert J., Stacey P.M. (1983). Factors regulating levels of cortisol in cerebrospinal fluid of monkeys during acute and chronic hypercortisolaemia. *Neuroendocrinology*; **36**: 39–48.

Martensz N.D., Vellucci S.V., Keverne E.B., Herbert J. (1986). Beta-endorphin levels in the cerebrospinal fluid of male talapoin monkeys in social groups related to dominance status and the luteinizing hormone response to naloxone. *Neuroscience*; **18**: 651–8.

Martensz N.D., Vellucci S.V., Fuller L.M., Everitt B.J., Keverne E.B., Herbert J. (1987). Relation between aggressive behaviour and circadian rhythms in cortisol and testosterone in social groups of talapoin monkeys. *Journal of Endocrinology*; **115**: 107–20.

Mason J.W. (1972). Organisation of psychoendocrine mechanisms. In: *Handbook of Psychophysiology* (Greenfield N.S., Sterbach R.A., eds), pp. 3–91. New York: Holt, Rinehart and Winston.

McGregor A.M., Herbert J. (1992a). Differential effects of excito-toxic basolateral and corticomedial lesions of the amygdala on the behavioural and endocrine responses to either sexual or aggression-promoting stimuli in the male rat. *Brain Research*; **574**: 9–20.

McGregor A.M., Herbert J. (1992b). Specific effects of beta-endorphin infused into the amygdala on sexual behaviour in the male rat. *Neuroscience*; **46**: 165–72.

Meller R.E., Keverne E.B., Herbert J. (1980). Behavioural and endocrine effects of naltrexone in male talapoin monkeys. *Pharmacology Biochemistry and Behavior*; **23**: 883–7.

Moyer K.E. (1968). Kinds of aggression and their physiological basis. *Community Behavior and Biology*; **2**: 65–87.

Nemeroff C.B., Wilderlov E., Bissette G. (1984). Elevated concentrations of CSF corticotropin-releasing factor-like immunoreactivity in depressed patients. *Science*; **226**: 1342–4.

Pedersen C.A., Caldwell J.D. & Brooks P.J. (1990). Neuropeptide control of parental and reproductive behaviour. In: *Behavioural Aspects of Neuroendocrinology* (Ganten D., Pfaff D.W., eds), pp. 81–114. Berlin: Springer.

Price J.L., Russchen F.T., Amaral D.G. (1987). The limbic region III. The amygdaloid complex In: *Handbook of Chemical Neuroanatomy* (Bjorklund A., Hokfelt T., Swanson L.W., eds). Amsterdam: Elsevier. pp. 279–388.

Raleigh M.J., McGuire M.T., Bramner G.L. Pollack D.B., Yuwiler A. (1991). Serotoninergic mechanisms promote dominance acquisition in adult male vervet monkeys. *Brain Research*; **559**: 181–90.

Sakanaka M., Shibasaki T., Lederis K. (1987). Corticotropin releasing factor-like immunoreactivity in the rat brain revealed by a modified cobalt glucose oxidase-diaminobenzidine method. *Journal of Comparative Neurology*; **260**: 256–98.

Sapolsky R.M., McEwen B.S. (1986). Adrenal steroids and the hippocampus involvement in stress and ageing. In: *The Hippocampus* (Isaacson R., Pribram K.H., eds), vol. 3. pp. 257–80. New York: Plenum.

Sheng M., Greenberg M.E. (1990). The regulation and function of *c-fos* and other immediate early genes in the nervous system. *Neuron*; **4**: 477–83.

Sherman J.E., Kalin N.H. (1987). The effects of icv-CRF on novelty-induced behaviour. *Pharmacology, Biochemistry and Behavior* **26**: 699–703.

Stavy M., Herbert J. (1989). Differential effects of β-endorphin infused into the hypothalamic preoptic area at various phases of the male rat's sexual behaviour. *Neuroscience*; **30**: 433–42.

Stricker E.M. (1983). Brain neurochemistry and the control of food intake. In: *Handbook of Behavioural Neurobiology* (Satinoff E., Teitelbaum P., eds), vol. 6, pp. 329–66. New York: Academic Press.

Tazi A., Dantzer R., Le Moal M., Rivier J., Vale W., Koob GF (1987). Corticotropin releasing factor antagonist blocks stress-induced fighting in rats. *Regulatory Peptide*; **18**: 37–2.

Valentino R.J., Foote S.L. (1988). Corticotropin-releasing hormone increases tonic but not sensory-evoked activity of the noradrenergic locus coeruleus neurons in unanaesthetised rats. *Journal of Neuroscience*; **8**: 1016–25.

Weiskrantz L. (1956). Behavioural changes associated with ablation of the amygdaloid complex in monkeys. *Journal Comparative Physiology and Psychology*; **49**: 181–212.

Wilson A.P., Boelkins R.C. (1970). Evidence for seasonal variation in aggressive behaviour by *Macaca mulatta*. *Animal Behavior*; **18**: 719–24.

Wilson M.A., Molliver M.E. (1991a). The organisation of serotoninergic projections to cerebral cortex in primates: regional distribution of axon terminals. *Neuroscience*: **44**: 537–53.

Wilson M.A., Molliver M.E. (1991b). The organisation of serotoninergic projections to cerebral cortex in primates: retrograde transport studies. *Neuroscience*; **44**: 555–70.

Yodyginguad U., Eberhart J.A., Keverne E.B. (1982). Effects of rank and novel females on behaviour and hormones in male talapoin monkeys. *Physiology and Behavior*; **28**: 995–1005.

5 Serotonin and impulsive aggression: relationship to alcoholism

EMIL F. COCCARO, RICHARD J. KAVOUSSI and
SCOTT STEHLE

Evidence for a trivariate relationship among indices of central serotonergic (5HT) system function, suicidal and/or impulsive aggressive behaviours and history of alcoholism has been accumulating over the past few decades. Specifically, indices of reduced central 5HT system function have been shown to correlate in many, though not all, studies with measures of impulsive aggressive behaviour and with the presence, or a history, of alcoholism. The primacy of one variable over the others is not known. However, the cumulative weight of evidence at this time suggests that individuals with evidence of reduced central 5HT system function are at risk for the display of suicidal and/or impulsive aggressive behaviour and/or the development of alcoholism.

This chapter will first review the evidence for a role of the central 5HT system in suicidal and/or impulsive aggressive behaviours and then review the evidence for a 5HT abnormality in alcoholism and for suicidal and impulsive aggressive behaviour as an important behavioural correlate of this biological abnormality.

SEROTONIN AND SUICIDAL AND IMPULSIVE AGGRESSIVE BEHAVIOUR

Studies in patients with major depression

The first study to suggest a link between central 5HT function and suicidal behaviour was that of Asberg et al. (1976). These investigators reported that a history of suicidal behaviour in a sample of depressed patients was significantly greater among those patients with reduced cerebrospinal fluid concentrations of the 5HT metabolite 5-hydroxyindolacetic acid (CSF 5-HIAA). Since levels of 5HT itself were also reported to be low in the brains of suicide victims in three of four previous studies (Coccaro and Astill, 1990), this finding suggested that patients with a history of suicide attempts also had low brain levels of 5HT. Most interesting of all was the observation that patients with a history of a violent suicide attempt or patients who eventually died by suicide (at follow-up) belonged exclusively to the subgroup with reduced CSF 5-HIAA concentration; patients utilizing non-violent means appeared to be equally distributed between the reduced and non-reduced CSF 5-HIAA groups. This finding suggested further that reduced CSF 5-HIAA concentration was more specifically correlated with violent (or medically lethal) suicidal behaviour. This hypothesis was further supported by experimental data from animal studies which demonstrated a relationship between reduced central 5HT activity and aggression (see Coccaro, 1989 for review).

The observation that psychiatric patients with history of suicidal behaviour have reduced CSF 5-HIAA concentrations, compared with comparable patients who do not, has been replicated many times by other investigators (see Coccaro and Astill, 1990 for review). The observation that violent suicidal behaviour correlates specifically with this biological index has also been replicated but not with the same consistency. Reasons for this probably relate to the fact that while violent individuals often display suicidal behaviour, suicidal individuals (especially patients with depression and little comorbid personality disturbance) do not necessarily display violent behaviour (Coccaro *et al.*, 1990a).

Studies in patients with personality disorder and with other psychiatric diagnoses

The first studies to demonstrate a relationship between an index of reduced central 5HT function and history of aggression (i.e. violence) and of suicidal behaviour were those of Brown *et al.* (1979, 1982). In two studies of personality-disordered individuals, Brown and his colleagues demonstrated a strong inverse relationship between CSF 5-HIAA concentration and a history of actual aggressive behaviour ($r = -0.78$) and of suicide attempts. As expected from this relationship, individuals with history of a prior suicide attempt also had a greater history of actually committing aggressive acts (Brown *et al.*, 1982). These data were the first to demonstrate an interactive relationship between reduced CSF 5-HIAA concentration and increased history (risk) of suicidal and aggressive behaviour. In these subjects, history of these behaviours could be considered the behavioural correlate of reduced central 5HT system function.

Linnoila *et al.* (1983) refined these relationships in a landmark study which reported that 'impulsive', but not 'premeditated', aggressive behaviour was specifically associated with reduced concentrations of CSF 5-HIAA. In this study, all individuals had committed one or more serious aggressive acts. However, only 'impulsive' violent offenders with a (*DSM-II*) diagnosis of either antisocial or explosive personality disorder had reduced CSF 5-HIAA concentration; the CSF 5-HIAA of 'non-impulsive' violent offenders (with a diagnosis of either passive–aggressive or paranoid personality disorder) was not reduced in magnitude. Similar to the Brown *et al.* (1979, 1982) studies, violent offenders with a history of at least one suicide attempt had reduced CSF 5-HIAA concentrations compared to those individuals without a history of suicide attempts.

The notion that indices of reduced central 5HT system function are related to 'impulsive' aggressive and/or suicidal behaviour is supported by a number of other studies in several patient populations. Specifically, van Praag (1983) reported that suicidal behaviour in schizophrenic patients with reduced CSF 5-HIAA is frequently associated with sudden command suicidal hallucinations. Similarly, van Praag (1986) reported that depressed patients with histories of suicide attempts and reduced CSF 5-HIAA concentration typically have a life history characterized by anger and personality disturbance associated with getting into arguments and fights. In another study, adolescents with conduct disorder demonstrated an inverse relationship between platelet tritiated imipramine binding ([3H]IMI), a putative index of presynaptic 5HT function, and impulsive aggressive behaviours (Stoff *et al.*, 1987). Similarly, [3H]IMI binding correlates inversely with clinical assessments of impulsivity in a recently reported sample of patients with histories of self-mutilation (Simeon *et al.*, 1992). Similar relationships appear to exist for non-psychiatric samples as well. In one small study of healthy volunteers, Roy *et al.* (1988) reported an inverse relationship between 'outwardly directed hostility' (or 'irritability', see below) and CSF 5-HIAA concentration.

Behavioural irritability as the core behavioural correlate of central 5HT system function

A recently reported study by the author and his colleagues (Coccaro *et al.*, 1989) suggested further that the core behavioural correlate of central 5HT system function may be defined as the threshold at which individuals respond aggressively to adverse events. This behavioural trait can be characterized as irritability. In these studies, the prolactin response to acute challenge with the 5HT releaser/uptake inhibitor, fenfluramine, correlated inversely with past history of suicide attempt and with measures of irritability and aggressiveness, the latter of which were also correlated. Since irritability also correlated with a measure of impulsiveness, it was suggested that irritability may be the common thread running through many of the previous studies associating reduced central 5HT system function with suicidality, aggressivity and/or impulsiveness. Support for this notion was found upon closer examination of the data which revealed that an inverse relationship between irritability and PRL[FEN] existed in subjects regardless of whether PRL[FEN] values were categorically reduced or in the normal range. A similar inverse relationship with aggressivity was only found for subjects with reduced PRL[FEN] values. This suggested that while irritability (i.e. the threshold for responding aggressively) was modulated by 5HT across its full range of function, assaultive behaviour only became manifest when 5HT function was categorically reduced in nature.

ALCOHOLISM AND CENTRAL 5HT SYSTEM FUNCTION

Early studies of CSF 5-HIAA concentration

A relationship between alcoholism and abnormalities in central 5HT system function has been suggested since 1974 when Takahashi and colleagues reported reduced CSF 5-HIAA concentrations in alcoholics with florid withdrawal symptoms compared with healthy non-alcoholic controls (alcoholics without severe withdrawal symptoms did not have reduced CSF 5-HIAA concentrations). Repeat assessment of CSF 5-HIAA levels in these alcoholics, 4 weeks later, revealed a persistently low CSF 5-HIAA concentration. This observation suggested the possibility that a subgroup of alcoholics (i.e. those with the more severe disorder, as evidenced by severe withdrawal symptoms when abstinent) had a reduction in central 5HT system function which persists well into the drug-free state. A second study by Ballenger *et al.* (1979) similarly found a reduction in CSF 5-HIAA concentration in alcoholics, compared with non-alcoholic (personality-disordered) control subjects when studied 4 weeks into the abstinence phase. Curiously, CSF 5-HIAA concentrations in alcoholics examined at 48 hours post-withdrawal were no different from those of controls (Fig. 5.1). This suggested the possibility that CSF 5-HIAA concentrations in alcoholics are reduced in the drug-free state but are 'pharmacologically' elevated by alcohol in these subjects when they are consuming alcohol. An inverse relationship between CSF 5-HIAA concentration and days abstinent in a group of alcoholics (Banki, 1981) supports this hypothesis. Ballenger *et al.* (1979) further suggested that a subgroup of alcoholics have a deficit in central 5HT system function which alcohol temporarily corrects, and that this deficit drives the alcoholic to seek and consume alcohol. Reduced CSF 5-HIAA concentrations in alcoholics have also been replicated in studies by Borg *et al.* (1985).

Chronic alcohol consumption could be associated with a reduction in CSF 5-HIAA concentration simply due to the toxic effects of

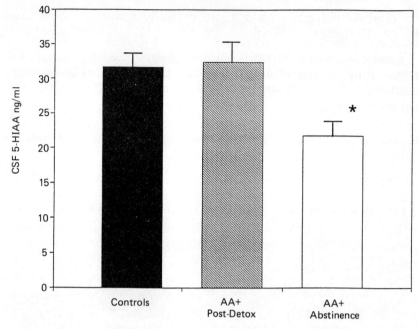

Fig. 5.1   *Cerebrospinal fluid 5-hydroxyindolacetic acid (CSF 5-HIAA) concentration in alcoholic patients immediately post-detoxification (AA + Post-Detox) and 4 weeks into abstinence (AA + Abstinence) compared to non-alcoholic controls (controls: personality-disordered individuals). *P < 0·01 for the comparison between AA + Abstinence and Controls; P < 0·001 for the comparison between AA + Abstinence and AA + Post-Detox. Drawn from data in Ballenger et al. (1979).*

alcohol. However, several lines of evidence suggest a more primary association with central 5-HT function itself:

1. Destruction of the midbrain raphe (the brain region with the largest concentration of 5HT), which results a great decrease in brain 5HT, results in increased alcohol intake in rats (Melchoir *et al.*, 1976; Ho *et al.*, 1974).
2. Strains of rats bred to prefer alcohol to water (alcohol-preferring rats) have been reported to have abnormalities in a variety of brain 5HT indices (i.e. reduced regional brain 5-HT concentration: Murphy *et al.*, 1982; reduced brain 5HT uptake: Daoust *et al.*, 1985; increased brain $5HT_1$-like receptors: Wong *et al.*, 1988).
3. Chronic alcohol consumption by these alcohol-preferring rats is not associated with any change in brain 5HT compared to similar alcohol-preferring rats who have not been treated chronically with alcohol (Murphy *et al.*, 1983).
4. Depressed non-alcoholic patients with family histories of alcoholism have reduced CSF 5-HIAA concentration relative to corres-

ponding patients with a negative family history of alcoholism (Rosenthal *et al.*, 1980).

These data, though limited, suggest that reduced indices of 5HT system function in alcoholics may be primary (e.g. constitutional/ genetic) rather than secondary to an acquired, toxic effect of excessive alcohol exposure.

Relationship between alcoholism and suicidal and impulsive aggressive behaviour

If there is a direct relationship between alcoholism and reduced central 5HT system function, it is logical to expect the presence of a relationship between alcoholism and behaviours frequently associated with evidence of reduced central 5HT system function, specifically suicidal and impulsive aggressive behaviour. An increased risk of suicidal behaviour among alcoholics has been reported in at least four studies to date (Kessel and Grossman, 1961; Kendell and Staton, 1988; Gillis, 1969; Miles, 1977). This risk is estimated to be nearly 60–85-fold higher than among the general population. In one meta-analysis of 15 follow-up studies, Miles (1977) suggested that up to 15% of alcoholics die from suicide. Similarly, alcoholics appear to manifest greater irritability and aggressivity than non-alcoholic controls. In one study of suicidal patients (Virkkunen, 1971) alcoholic patients were more frequently rated as having 'outwardly directed aggressiveness' than non-alcoholic patients. Similarly, alcoholic patients with later suicidal behaviour have been reported as more irritable, dysphoric, and/or aggressive during initial evaluation (i.e. prior to the development of suicidal behaviour) than those who did not develop suicidal behaviour (Berglund, 1984). Hence, there is developing evidence suggesting that a subgroup of alcoholics appear to manifest the type of behaviours typically associated with evidence of reduced 5HT system function.

Subtypes of alcoholism

Alcoholism, like all other behavioural disorders, is a clinically hetero-geneous disorder. The studies reviewed briefly up to this point suggest further that there may be a subgroup of alcoholic patients with an abnormality in central 5HT system function which may, in turn, account for (or be associated with) an increased risk for suicidal and impulsive aggressive behaviour in a substantial subgroup of such patients. Convergent validity for this hypothesis comes from adoption and phenomenological data which suggest that there are at least two forms of alcoholism (see Cloninger, 1987 for review). One form is male-linked with high penetrance and one form is not male-linked and has low penetrance. The latter form is referred to as type I while the former is referred to as type II. Type I alcoholism is passed on to both males and females (i.e. not male-linked) and is of low penetrance (i.e. requires an adverse environment; e.g. alcoholic adoptive parent) for expression. Its age of onset is greater than 25 years of age. Alcohol consumption tends to be non-impulsive in nature and appears to be linked to alcohol's potential anxiolytic effects. In contrast, type II alcoholism is largely passed on from father to son (i.e. male-linked) and is of high penetrance (appears regardless of the environment; e.g. even in the presence of non-alcoholic adoptive parents). Its age of onset is relatively early, occurring before the age of 25, frequently in the early teenage years. Alcohol consumption is impulsive and unrestrained in nature and appears to be linked to alcohol's potential for euphoriogenic effects. As expected, it is alcoholics in this group that tend to be impulsive, verbally aggressive, and to have features of antisocial personality disorder (von Knorring *et al.*, 1987). Moreover, it is alcoholics with type II alcoholism who appear to have reduced indices of central 5HT system function (see below).

Relationship between alcoholism and central 5HT system function and its related behaviours: new studies

Evidence of a trivariate relationship between alcoholism, suicidal and/ or impulsive aggressive behaviour, and reduced central 5HT system function has been accumulating over the past decade. Linnoila *et al.* (1983) reported an association between reduced CSF 5-HIAA concentrations among a group of hospitalized violent offenders with comorbid alcoholism, and impulsive violent behaviour specifically. CSF 5-HIAA concentrations among the non-impulsive violent offenders tended to be similar to those reported for healthy controls in similar studies. In a later assessment of an expanded series of alcoholic violent offenders, Linnoila *et al.* (1989) reported that alcoholic violent offenders with an alcoholic father had reduced CSF 5-HIAA concentration ($P < 0.01$) and a greater incidence of comorbid history of intermittent explosive disorder ($P < 0.10$) compared to alcoholic violent offenders with a non-alcoholic father. In addition, nearly 90% of the subjects with an alcoholic father were characterized as being impulsively violent, compared to less than 60% among those without an alcoholic father ($P < 0.02$; Fig. 5.2). Hence, among alcoholics, abnormalities in central 5 HT system function may be specific to individuals with type II alcoholism.

Similar findings were reported by Buydens-Branchey *et al.* (1989) and Coccaro *et al.* (1989). Buydens-Branchey *et al.* (1989) reported a reduced tryptophan : neutral amino acid ratio (T : NAA ratio) in patients with early-onset alcoholism (type II). A reduced T : NAA ratio suggests reduced transport of the 5HT precursor, tryptophan,

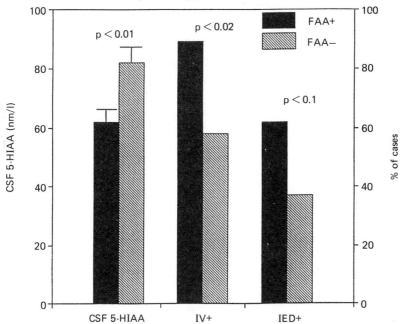

Fig. 5.2 *Cerebrospinal fluid 5-hydroxyindolacetic acid (CSF 5-HIAA) concentration and percentage of cases rated as impulsively violent (IV +) or as meeting DSM-III criteria for intermittent explosive disorder (IED +) in a sample of violent offenders and impulsive arsonists categorized as having familial alcoholism (FAA + versus FAA −). This figure demonstrates that familial (e.g. type II) alcoholics have reduced CSF 5-HIAA and a greater frequency of impulsive violence. Drawn from data in Linnoila* et al. *(1989).*

into the brain and a lower availability of the precursor for 5HT synthesis. In addition to a reduced T : NAA ratio, early-onset alcoholics with histories of aggressive behaviour had among the lowest T : NAA ratios noted, again pointing to a trivariate relationship between reduced 5HT function and aggression and (type II) alcoholism.

In another study, Coccaro *et al.* (1989) reported that *DSM-III* personality-disordered patients with a past history of alcohol abuse demonstrated a significantly reduced PRL response to fenfluramine challenge compared to corresponding patients without history of alcohol abuse. A battery of assessments of aggressiveness and impulsiveness revealed significant differences between the personality-disorder patients with past histories of alcohol abuse and those without (Fig. 5.3). Further analysis revealed that reduced PRL responses to fenfluramine were accounted for almost entirely by the greater scores of impulsive aggression among the patients with a past history of alcohol abuse (Fig. 5.4).

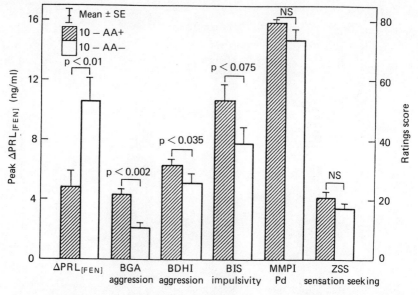

Fig. 5.3 *Mean peak delta prolactin responses to fenfluramine challenge (PRL[FEN]) and ratings of aggression (BGA = Brown–Goodwin assessment for history of lifetime aggression; BDHI = aggression factor for the Buss–Durkee hostility inventory); impulsivity (BIS = Barratt 7B impulsiveness scale); Minnesota multiphasic personality inventory (MMPI) psychopathic deviance; sensation-seeking (ZSS = Zuckerman sensation-seeking scale) in personality-disorder patients with (AA +) and without (AA −) a past history of alcohol abuse. This figure demonstrates a significant reduction in PRL[FEN] values, and elevations in rating of aggression and impulsiveness, in AA + compared with AA − subjects. Absence of differences between these groups in MMPI Pd and ZSS scores suggests a degree of specificity for the relationship between reduced PRL[FEN] values and elevated ratings of aggression and impulsiveness in AA + subjects.*

Site of abnormality in central 5HT system function in alcoholics.

The specific nature of the putative abnormality in central 5HT system function is unknown. Reduced CSF 5-HIAA concentrations suggest reduced synthesis and release of central 5HT and/or reduced numbers of 5HT neurons in the brain (Stanley *et al.*, 1985). However, since postsynaptic 5HT receptors may upregulate to compensate for decreased synaptic availability of 5HT, the functional state of 5HT neurotransmission is in question. On the other hand, reduced PRL responses to fenfluramine, whose action reflects on both pre- and postsynaptic 5HT function, suggest reduced overall function of 5HT synapses in the limbic hypothalamus. Recent studies in alcoholics, or personality-disordered individuals with substance abuse histories (largely alcohol abuse), with other 5HT probes [e.g. 5HT precursor 5-hydroxytryptophan (5-HTP) and 5HT postsynaptic agonists m-CPP and MK-212] similarly yield evidence of a central 5HT abnor-

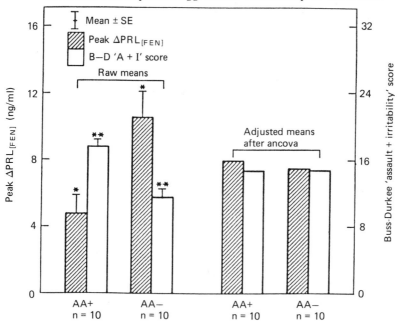

Fig. 5.4 *Mean peak delta prolactin responses to fenfluramine challenge (PRL[FEN]) and the sum score of the Buss–Durkee hostility inventory subscales assault and irritability (BDHI A + I; this score yields a Pearson correlation* (r) *of* −0.77 *with PRL[FEN] values; Coccaro et al., 1989) in personality-disorder patients with (AA+) and without (AA−) a past history of alcohol abuse. Left: raw data; right data after ANCOVA with BDHI A + I scores as covariate. This figure demonstrates that differences between AA+ and AA− subjects in PRL[FEN] values are eliminated when a measure of irritable, impulsive aggression (which itself correlates with PRL[FEN] to a very high degree) is factored out. Reproduced from Coccaro et al. (1990a).*

mality. Reduced cortisol responses to 5-HTP (Lee and Meltzer, 1991) and reduced prolactin responses to m-CPP (Moss *et al.*, 1990) and MK-212 (Lee and Meltzer, 1991) suggest that decreased synaptic function is present at postsynaptic 5HT receptors sites in the limbic hypothalamus as well. This is in contrast to what has been found for a laboratory model of alcoholism (i.e. alcohol-preferrring rats) where increased, not decreased, 5HT receptor binding was found (Wong *et al.*, 1988). It is possible that this difference is due to the fact that there are multiple receptor subtypes for 5HT. Accordingly, the identity of the specific 5HT receptor subtype(s) reflected in these human studies may be different from the $5HT_1$-like group of receptors reported in alcohol-preferring animals. At this time, basic studies with the probes utilized (Koenig *et al.*, 1987, 1988; Seibyl *et al.*, 1989; Lee *et al.*, 1991) suggest that both $5HT_{1c}$ (m-CPP, MK-212) and $5HT_2$ (MK-212,

5-HTP) type receptors may be abnormal in these types of patients. ($5HT_{1c}$ receptors are similar in many ways to $5HT_2$ receptors and appear to be quite different from other $5HT_1$-like receptors; see Coccaro *et al.*, 1990b for review).

In addition, there may be altered sensitivity of $5HT_{1c}/5HT_2$ receptors in brain areas related to the affective response to alcohol. In a recent study of behavioural responses to intravenous m-CPP in alcoholics (Benkelfat *et al.*, 1991), m-CPP but not placebo challenge was associated with a euphoric 'high' (11 of 21 patients: 52%) and/or a craving to drink alcohol (7 of 21 patients: 33%). Given that m-CPP administration is more often associated with anxiogenic responses (Murphy *et al.*, 1989), these data suggest that a subgroup of altered 5HT receptors may mediate affective responses that reinforce drinking patterns by providing the euphorigenic responses to alcohol observed in type II alcoholics. Whether this response reflects a subsensitive (as would follow from the neuroendocrine data) or a supersensitive $5HT_{1c}/5HT_2$ receptor is unknown at this time. However, anxiogenic responses to m-CPP are usually interpreted as the result of stimulating a supersensitive 5HT receptor (e.g. when seen in anxiety-disordered patients: Zohar *et al.*, 1987; Kahn *et al.*, 1990) or of overstimulating a normosensitive 5HT receptor (e.g. when seen in healthy volunteers: Murphy *et al.*, 1989).

It is possible that there are multiple abnormalities in central 5HT system function in individuals with alcoholism. One set of abnormalities may relate to suicidal and/or impulsive aggressive behaviours while another (e.g. involving different brain regions and/or 5HT receptor types) may relate to the regulation of mood in these individuals. Further research involving the psychopharmacological dissection of the central 5HT system will be necessary to determine the answer to these and many other important questions regarding the role of central 5HT system function in individuals with alcoholism.

REFERENCES

Asberg M., Traksman L., Thoren P. (1976). 5-HIAA in the cerebrospinal fluid: a biochemical suicide predictor? *Archives of General Psychiatry*; **33**: 1193–7.

Ballenger J.C., Goodwin F.K., Major L.F. *et al.* (1979). Alcohol and central serotonin metabolism in man. *Archives of General Psychiatry*; 36: 224–7.

Banki C.M. (1981). Factors influencing monoamine metabolites and tryptophan in patients with alcohol dependence. *Journal of Neural Transmission*; **50**: 223–32.

Benkelfat C., Murphy D.L., Hill J.L. *et al.* (1991). Ethanollike properties of the serotonergic partial agonist m-chlorophenylpiperazine in chronic alcoholic patients. *Archives of General Psychiatry*; **48**: 383.

Berglund M. (1984). Suicide in alcoholism, a prospective study of 88 alcoholics: multidimensional diagnosis at first admission. *Archives of General Psychiatry*; **41**: 888–91.

Borg S., Kuande H., Liljeberg P. *et al.* (1985). 5-Hydroxyindolacetic acid in cerebrospinal fluid in alcoholic patients under different clinical conditions. *Alcohol*; **2**: 415–18.

Brown G.L., Goodwin F.K., Ballenger J.C. *et al.* (1979). Aggression in humans correlates with cerebrospinal fluid amine metabolites. *Psychiatry Research*; **1**: 131–9.

Brown G.L., Ebert M.H., Goyer P.F. *et al.* (1982). Aggression, suicide, and serotonin: relationships to CSF amine metabolites. *American Journal of Psychiatry*; **139**: 741–6.

Buydens-Branchey L., Branchey M.H., Noumair D. *et al.* (1989). Age of alcoholism onset. II. Relationship to susceptibility to serotonin precursor availability. *Archives of General Psychiatry*; **46**: 231–6.

Cloninger C.R. (1987). Neurogenetic adaptive mechanisms in alcoholism. *Science*; **236**: 410–16.

Coccaro E.F. (1989). Central serotonin and impulsive aggression. *British Journal of Psychiatry*; **155** (suppl 8): 52–62.

Coccaro E.F., Astill J.L. (1990). Central serotonin function in parasuicide. *Progress in Neuro-psychopharmacology and Biological Psychiatry*; **14**: 663–74.

Coccaro E.F., Siever L.J., Klar H. *et al.* (1989). Serotonergic studies in affective and personality disorder patients: correlates with suicidal and impulsive aggression. *Archives of General Psychiatry*; **43**: 587–99.

Coccaro E.F., Siever L.J., Owen K.R. *et al.* (1990a). Serotonin function in mood and personality disorder. In: *Serotonin in Major Psychiatric Disorders* (Coccaro E.F., Murphy D.L., eds), pp. 71–97, Washington, DC: American Psychiatric Press.

Coccaro E.F., Gabriel S., Siever L.J. (1990b). Buspirone challenge: preliminary evidence for a role for central 5-HT-1a receptor function in impulsive aggressive behavior in humans. *Psychopharmacology Bulletin*; **26**: 393–405.

Daoust M., Chretien P., Moore N. *et al.* (1985). Isolation and striatal (3H) serotonin uptake: role in the voluntary intake of ethanol by rats. *Pharmacology, Biochemistry and Behavior*; **22**: 205–8.

Gillis L. (1969). The mortality rate and causes of death of treated chronic alcoholics. *South African Medical Journal*; **42**: 230–2.

Ho A.K.S., Tsai C.S., Chen R.C.A. *et al.* (1974). Experimental studies on alcoholism: I. Increase in alcohol preference by 5,6-dihydroxytryptamine and brain acetylcholine. *Psychopharmacologia*; **40**: 101–7.

Kahn R.S., Asnis G.M., van Praag H.M. *et al.* (1990). Behavioral indicators of serotonin receptor hypersensitivity in patients with panic disorder. *Psychiatry Research*; **25**: 101–4.

Kendell R., Staton M. (1988). The fate of untreated alcoholics. *Quarterly Journal of Studies on Alcohol*; **27**: 30–41.

Kessel N., Grossman G. (1961). Suicide in alcoholics. *British Medical Journal*; **2**: 1671–2.

Koenig J.I., Gudelsky G.A., Meltzer H.Y. (1987). Stimulation of corticosterone and beta-endorphin secretion by selective 5-HT receptor subtype activation. *European Journal of Pharmacology*; **137**: 1–8.

Koenig J. I., Meltzer H. Y., Gudelsky G. A. (1988). Hormone response to selective serotonergic stimulation in the rat. In: *5-HT Agonists as Psychoactive Drugs*, (Rech R. H., Gudelsky G. A., eds), pp. 283–98. Ann Arbor, MI: NPP Books.

Lee M. A., Meltzer H. Y. (1991). Neuroendocrine responses to serotonergic agents in alcoholics. *Biological Psychiatry*; **30**: 1017–30.

Lee M. A., Nash F., Barnes M. *et al.* (1991). Inhibitory effect of ritanserin on the 5-hydroxytryptophan-mediated cortisol, ACTH and prolactin secretion in human. *Psychopharmacology*; **103**: 258–64.

Linnoila M., Virrkunen M., Scheinin M. *et al.* (1983). Low cerebrospinal fluid 5-hydroxyindolacetic acid concentration differentiates impulsive from nonimpulsive violent behaviour. *Life Sciences* **33**: 2609–14.

Linnoila M., De Jong J., Virrkunen M. (1989). Family history of alcoholism in violent offenders and impulsive fire setters. *Archives of General Psychiatry*; **46**: 613–16.

Melchoir C. L., Myers R. D. (1976). Genetic differences in ethanol drinking of the rat following injection of 6-OHDA, 5,6,-DHT, or 5,7,-DHT into the cerebral ventricles. *Pharmacology, Biochemistry and Behavior*; **5**: 63–72.

Miles C. (1977). Conditions predisposing to suicide: a review. *Journal of Nervous and Mental Disease*; **164**: 231–46.

Moss H. B., Yao J. K. Panzak G. L. (1990). Serotonergic responsivity and behavioural dimensions in antisocial personality disorder with substance abuse. *Biological Psychiatry*; **28**: 325–38.

Murphy D. L. Mueller E. A. Hill J. L. *et al.* (1989). Comparative anxiogenic, neuroendocrine, and other physiologic effects of m-chlorophrenylpiperazine given intravenously or orally to healthy volunteers. *Psychopharmacology*; **98**: 275–82.

Murphy J.M., McBride W.J., Lumeng L. *et al.* (1982). Regional brain levels of monoamines in alcohol-preferring and -nonpreferring rats. *Pharmacology, Biochemistry & Behavior*; **16**: 145–9.

Murphy J.M., McBride W.J., Lumeng L. *et al.* (1983). Monoamine and metabolite levels in CNS regions of the P line of alcohol-preferring rats after acute and chronic ethanol treatment. *Pharmacology, Biochemistry & Behavior*; **19**: 849–56.

Rosenthal N.E., Davenport Y., Cowdry R.W. *et al.* (1980) Monoamine metabolites in cerebrospinal fluid of depressive subtypes. *Psychiatry Research*; **2**: 113–19.

Roy A., Virrkunen M., Linnoila M. (1987). Reduced central serotonin turnover in a subgroup of alcoholics? *Progress in Neuropsychopharmacology and Biological Psychiatry*; **11**: 173–7.

Roy A. Adinoff B., Linnoila M. (1988). Acting out hostility in normal volunteers: negative correlation of 5-HIAA in cerebrospinal fluid levels. *Psychiatry Research*; **24**: 187–94.

Seibyl J.P., Krystal J.H., Price L.H. *et al.* (1989). Neuroendocrine and behavioral responses to m-CPP in unmedicated schizophrenics and healthy subjects. Abstracts of the 28th Annual Meeting of the American College of Neuropsychopharmacology, p 121.

Simeon D., Stanley B., Francis A. *et al.* (1992). Self-mutilation in personality disorders: psychological and biological correlates. *American Journal of Psychiatry*; **149**: 221–6.

Stanley M.S., Traksman-Bendz L., Dorovini-Zis K. (1985). Correlations between aminergic metabolites simultaneously obtained from human CSF and brain. *Life Sciences*; **37**: 1279–86.
Stoff D.M., Pollack L., Vitiello B. *et al.* (1987). Reduction of (^{3}H)-imipramine binding sites on platelets of conduct-disordered children. *Neuropsychopharmacology*; **1**: 55–62.
Takahashi S., Yamane H., Kondo H. *et al.* (1974). CSF monoamine metabolites in alcoholism, a comparative study with depression. *Folis Psychiatrica Neurologica Japan*; **28**: 347–54.
van Praag H.M. (1983). CSF 5-HIAA and suicide in non-depressed schizophrenics. *Lancet*; **i**: 977–8.
van Praag H.M. (1986). (Auto) aggression and CSF 5-HIAA in depression and schizophrenia. *Psychopharmacology Bulletin*; **22**: 669–73.
Virkkunen M. (1971). Alcoholism and suicide in Helsinki. *Psychiatrica Fennica* 201–7.
von Knorring I., von Knorring A., Smifan L. *et al.* (1987). Personality traits in subtypes of alcoholics. *Journal of Studies on Alcohol*; **48**: 523–7.
Wong D.T., Lumeng L., Threlkeld P.G. *et al.* (1988). Serotonergic and adrenergic receptors in alcohol-prefering and non-preferring rats. *Journal of Neural Transmission*; **71**: 207–18.
Zohar J., Mueller E.A., Insel T.R. *et al.* (1987). Serotonergic responsivity in obsessive-compulsive disorder: comparison of patients and healthy controls. *Archives of General Psychiatry*; **44**: 946–51.

ACKNOWLEDGEMENTS

This work was supported in part by NIMH grants RO1 MH46948 and KO2 MH00951 and by a grant from the Harry F. Guggenheim Foundation.

6 *Aggression and epilepsy**

PETER FENWICK

INTRODUCTION

The psychosocial consequences of aggression in our society are only too clear to see. Both at a personal and a national level aggression destroys relationships, inhibits trust and is in danger of leading to the destruction of humanity. It is thus essential that we come to understand more precisely those brain structures which underpin aggression and whose function and malfunction can lead to such unhappy consequences.

Patients with epilepsy provide an excellent model with which to determine the relationship between cerebral damage and aggression in humans. Ictal discharges arising in those brain structures which are thought to mediate aggression may well give clues to the mechanism by which aggression arises in non-pathological states and may also lead to an understanding of how aggression could be controlled.

Unfortunately, aggression and violent behaviour in people with epilepsy, as in anyone else, are the end-result of a multitude of different factors, and it is thus unlikely that any single pathological process could account in a simple way for all incidences of aggressive behaviour.

NEUROPHYSIOLOGY OF AGGRESSION: ORIGINAL STUDIES

It is not the aim of this chapter to deal in a comprehensive way with the neurophysiology of aggression. However, it is essential to review current thinking in this area.

Studies of aggression in animals point to several sites within the limbic system and hypothalamus which potentially can enhance, modify or reduce aggression. It has been suggested that aggression is not a simple unitary emotion and that it may have several components. Moyer (1971) has suggested a neural basis of aggression based on a survey of research in this area. The literature is large and

* Reprinted from Fenwick (1986) by permission of John Wiley and Sons Ltd.

confusing, and his formulation is only one of a number that have been suggested. His theory does, however, have the advantage of being based on the neurophysiology of the brain. He has shown that aggression falls into a number of different categories, which he has defined as predatory, territorial, intermale, maternal, defensive, fear-induced, irritable and instrumental. Each category has either a specific outward behaviour or a definite stimulus which determines it. Predatory aggression is quiet, organized and lethal. Territorial, intermale, maternal and defensive we are not concerned with. Fear-induced aggression, which is the aggression seen in a cornered animal, irritable aggression, the true rage produced by frustration or pain, and instrumental aggression, the learning of an aggressive response in different circumstances which call for displayed anger, are the closest to the spontaneous aggressive behaviour shown by humans.

Moyer gives some neurophysiological evidence for the different aggression circuits. Predatory aggression is located in the lateral hypothalamus, for if this area is stimulated in a cat, it will ignore the experimenter and quietly stalk and kill a rat (Wasman and Flynn, 1962). Stimulation of the medial hypothalamus will produce marked sympathetic arousal, spitting and hissing with unsheathed claws; the cat will attack the experimenter and if a rat is present will ignore it (Egger and Flynn, 1963). There is some suggestion that these circuits use acetylcholine as a neurotransmitter (Smith *et al.*, 1970). Yasuko-chi (1960) has suggested that fear-induced aggression in cornered animals arises from the anterior hypothalamus and the dorsal hypothalamus (Romaniuk, 1965). Irritable aggression is claimed by Moyer to involve the ventromedial nucleus of the hypothalamus and has been evoked by both stimulation and lesions in this area.

The relationship of the amygdala to aggression is a complex one as there is evidence that it may play both an inhibitory and an excitatory role (Gloor *et al.*, 1982a; see Chapter 4). In animals the amygdala is involved with the predatory fear-induced and irritable aggression responses. Amygdalectomy abolishes predatory aggression in cats (Summers and Kaelber, 1962). This reduces fear-induced aggression in monkeys, rats and cats (Shealy and Peele, 1957), but it has also been noted by other workers to increase irritable aggression (Schreiner and Kling, 1953). This dual role illustrates the different functions which underlie the amygdala. Moyer (1971) has suggested that there are eight identifiable nuclei in the amygdala, each of which is involved in the localization of aggression. Here we are only concerned with irritable aggression which is facilitated from the medial nuclei and inhibited from the central nuclei. The rhinencephalic structures, hippocampus and cingulate gyrus (limbic system, Papez circuit) are also involved in emotion (Fig. 6.1). Hippocampal lesions appear to increase irritable aggression in cats (Green *et al.*, 1957), and Maclean and Delgado (1953) have confirmed this with cholinergic stimulation

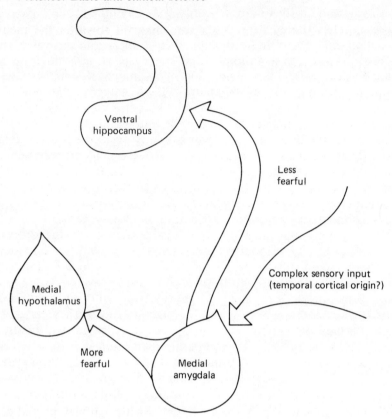

Fig. 6.1 *Summary of data acquired by evoked potential techniques which indicate different preferential routes of conduction of evoked excitatory neural activity from the amygdala to the ventromedial hypothalamus (VMH, or medial hypothalamus in the figure), and from the amygdala to the ventral hippocampus. More fearful cats display enhanced conduction from the amygdala to the VMH. Less fearful cats show the strongest conduction from the amygdala to the ventral hippocampus. From Adamec and Stark-Adamec (1983).*

of the hippocampus. In dogs and cats, Brutkowski *et al.*, (1961) and Kennard (1955) have shown that destruction of the cingulate gyrus has led to an increase in irritable aggression. This is clearly species-specific as cingulectomy has led to the calming of violence in humans (Le Beau, 1952; Tow and Whitty, 1953) and makes monkeys tamer and more docile (Kennard, 1955).

An extension of these findings is suggested in a model proposed by Flynn *et al.* (1970). They argued that the basomedial amygdala exerts some tonic inhibitory control over hypothalamically mediated attack behaviour. Adamec and Stark-Adamec (1983) have extended this model and introduced the idea of kindling and neuroresponsiveness. They suggest that cats with higher discharge rates of the basal amygdala were most defensive in their behaviour and least aggressive when activity of their amygdala was directed towards the medial hypothalamus. They found that more aggressive cats showed higher discharge rates of the ventral hippocampus. Prekindling of the amygdala led to an increase in discharge rates to the medial hypothalamus and inhibition of amygdala discharges to the ventral hippocampus with a consequent increase in the defensiveness and reduction in aggressiveness of the cat (Fig. 6.1).

Adamec and Stark-Adamec (1983) present data that support the idea that kindling may lead to a permanent change in synaptic transmission between hippocampus, hypothalamus and amygdala, resulting in permanent changes in behaviour of the animal. They show that kindled animals, depending on the area kindled, become either more aggressive or defensive and that their change in behaviour induced by kindling is stable over a long period of time. Further studies have confimed these early findings and additional work (Adamec, 1989) has shown how specific such kindling-induced changes can be. Engel, for example (personal communication), has produced unilaterally amygdala-kindled cats where the animals scratch only if stroked on the contralateral side to the kindled amygdala. Adamec and Stark-Adamec (1983) argue that kindling-induced behaviour changes could occur in humans, though they acknowledge that the evidence is less secure. They support the extension of their work to humans with the evidence, amongst others, of Herman (1982) who showed different Minnesota multiphasic personality inventory profiles for patients with complex partial seizures. The differences were dependent on whether or not the seizure started with an aura of fear – showing limbic system involvement. Further work with different patient groups has again shown limbic involvement in seizure spread to be an important variable in the causation of anxiety and fear (Adamec *et al.*, 1989). Other evidence for a change in limbic system functioning in patients with epilepsy comes from that of Halgren *et al.* (1978) and Gloor *et al.* (1982a) who showed that human emotions can be altered by direct electrical limbic system stimulation.

If kindling-induced changes causing aggressive behaviour can be shown to occur in humans, and this is not found to be species-specific, then the argument with regard to aggression would be as follows. Discharging epileptic lesions situated in the limbic system but specifically involving the amygdala, ventral hippocampus and medial hypothalamus would modify the functioning of these structures in such a way that the individuals would become more or less aggressive, – more aggressive if the functioning of the amygdala towards the ventral hippocampus was enhanced; less aggressive and more fearful if the activity of the amygdala towards the medial hypothalamus was enhanced. The idea that there is limbic system malfunction in epilepsy leading to an alteration in limbic system tone so that behaviour is altered in a specific way (the limbic hyperconnection syndrome) is already part of the epilepsy literature (Waxman and Geschwind, 1975; Bear, 1979). However, evidence for this proposal remains scanty and will be reviewed below. Added to this idea of an alteration in limbic system functioning is the idea of 'periods' in development. Taylor (1981) has consistently stressed the point that damage to the brain will have different effects depending on when during development the damage occurs. Thus the theory would also include the developmental concept that the timing of the onset of the epilepsy was crucial and that the changes in limbic function would be different in those with an early or a late onset to their epilepsy.

NEUROPHYSIOLOGICAL AND SURGICAL STUDIES IN HUMANS

Intracranial stimulation in humans has provided some evidence that there are specific brain areas which are involved in the mediation of aggression, and others which, when stimulated, will cause calming. Heath (1963) showed that electrodes implanted in the centromedian thalamus led to very high self-stimulation rates. The subjective experience of the stimulated patient was the feeling that he could not remember a thought. Repeated stimulation rapidly led to an aroused angry state. The angry state quickly subsided on stimulation of other electrodes implanted in the septum. A second patient 'was stimulated in the septal region during a period when he was exhibiting agitated and violent, psychotic behaviour. The stimulus was introduced without his knowledge. Almost instantly his behavioural state changed from one of disorganisation, rage, and persecution to one of happiness and mild euphoria'. Mark and Ervin (1970) report the case of a patient who became aggressive and behaved violently during a partial complex seizure. Electrodes implanted in the amygdala showed that abnormal behaviour coincided with an amygdala ictal discharge. Hitchcock and Cairns (1973) found that stimulation of the amygdala induced both rage and escape attempts. Heath and Mickle (1960) demonstrated that a wide range of responses followed electrical stimulation, one of which was aggressive behaviour.

Since those early studies the idea of aggression arising when specific neural pathways in human beings are stimulated or invaded by seizure discharges has fallen out of fashion. The main reason for this is that it has become recognized that the factors involved in aggression are very complex, ranging from the sociological to the psychological so that biological studies are subject to many non-specific variables. It has been pointed out that amygdala stimulation in humans very rarely leads to the expression of violence (Gloor, 1972), and there is considerable evidence that the results of stimulation depend not only on the brain region which was stimulated but also on the mental content of the patient and other non-specific factors at the time of stimulation (Higgins *et al.*, 1956). Chapman (1958) was unable to evoke aggressive behaviour with periamygdaloid and temporal lobe stimulation. Gloor (1978) disscused the paradoxical effect of amygdala stimulation in which direct stimulation and ictal discharges normally led to the sensation of fear, whereas the abnormally facilitated response to an external stimulus was seldom fear but rather an outburst of fighting.

A recent report by Wieser (1983) again emphasizes the importance of the amygdala in aggressive behaviour. He reports 2 patients, one with implanted electrodes, whose behaviour became aggressive when seizure discharges invaded the amygdala region:

> One of them...with socially disabling behaviour disorders and frequent rage attacks sometimes initiated by fear and gastric sensation displayed at the beginning of such seizures in the EEG scalp recording a flattening of the EEG activity well localised in the left fronto-temporal derivation...We decided to perform a selective left amygdalohippocampectomy. Now, with a follow up of $2\frac{1}{2}$ years since this operation, the patient continues to be seizure free, has experienced no further rage attacks and is attested to be a calm pupil.

In the second patient, 'Prior to EEG exploration these rage attacks were not believed to be of epileptic origin and the patient was mistakenly diagnosed as an 'aggressive psychopath'...The neurological examination showed a left temporobasal cyst communicating with the temporal horn'. Depth electrodes showed amygdala spiking with initially no surface changes. Removal of the cyst resulted in a marked improvement in behaviour.

Amygdalectomy in humans

The above evidence, both in animals and in humans, suggests that the amygdala is involved in the mediation of aggression. Although animal experiments cannot be directly extrapolated to humans there is nevertheless evidence to suggest that neurosurgical intervention in humans can lessen aggressive behaviour. Narabayashi *et al.* (1963) reported the results of amygdalectomy in a series of 60 patients. Their patients were drawn from three different populations:

1. those who had temporal lobe epilepsy;
2. those who had other seizures and aggressive behaviour; and
3. those without epilepsy who had disorders of behaviour and were 'feeble-minded'.

Their results were encouraging, as following amygdalectomy 29 patients – nearly 50% – were greatly improved, becoming calm and showing improved social adaptation. Twenty-two patients were moderately improved, being easier to control, calmer and with better concentration. A further 7 were slightly improved and only 2 showed no change. The significance of this report is difficult to assess, however, as none of the ratings were carried out blind and no baseline data were recorded. Hitchcock and Cairns (1973) described a series of 16 epileptic patients and 2 others who received amygdalectomy by thermal coagulation. Five of these showed a decrease in violent behaviour and the authors concluded that overall there was a clinically significant reduction in antisocial or maladaptive behaviour.

Mark *et al.* (1975) reported on 6 patients who had received bilateral amygdala lesions. In 3 subjects the rage attacks ceased, and 1 showed a decrease. Two patients experienced no relief from their aggressive episodes. These patients were followed up for 3 years and those with a positive outcome did not relapse. Unfortunately, again, quantifiable data were not presented.

Not all studies have shown beneficial effects. That of Kim and Umbach (1973), for example, failed to find a decrease in aggressive behaviour following amygdala lesions, but this may in part have been due to the rather different patient population involved. However, negative results have also been obtained by Nadvornick *et al.* (1973) who used a patient population similar to that employed in the more successful studies.

The posterior hypothalmus has been suggested from animal studies to be involved in the mediation of aggression. Building on this observation, Sano *et al.* (1970) induced lesions in the posterior hypothalamus in 44 patients. They were successful in reducing aggression, as 12 patients had excellent results. They had 'no violent, aggressive or restless behaviour, they were calm, placid and required no care or supervision'. Twenty-eight, although still occasionally irritable, were usually calm and tractable and did not require constant care. Only 2 patients were unchanged.

It may be remembered that in the study of Heath (1963), stimulation of the central median nucleus of the thalamus led rapidly to increasing rage and frustration of the patient. Andy (1970) argued that thalamotomy, with destruction of this area, was likely to reduce aggressive behaviour. Five patients had surgical lesions in this area and attenuation of aggressive behaviour was reported in all subjects.

The evidence, therefore, is conflicting, as amygdalectomy has been found to be helpful only in some studies. It is, however, far too early to say that neurosurgery has no place in the treatment of aggressive behaviour, as many of the populations studied included large numbers of brain-damaged and mentally subnormal patients. What is clear, however, is that amygdalectomy can in some cases be helpful, but the criteria needed to select patients who will benefit are not yet sufficiently understood.

These findings suggest that the amygdala, hippocampus and the hypothalamus are all involved in the mediation of aggression in humans. It is thus logical to assume that abnormal seizure discharges traversing these structures and interfering with their function may well result in aggressive behaviour.

AGGRESSIVE BEHAVIOUR IN EPILEPSY

Prevalence of aggression in patients with epilepsy

Gastaut *et al.* (1955) reported paroxysmal rages in 50% of their group of patients with temporal lobe epilepsy. This figure, however, is unusually high. Currie and co-workers (1970), in a survey of 666 patients with temporal lobe epilepsy of mixed aetiology and type at the London Hospital, found aggression reported in 7%. Rodin (1973), looking at a population from the Michigan Epilepsy Centre, reported pathological aggression in only 4.8% of 700 cases. The majority of the aggressive group were young men with below-average intelligence and when compared to a control group without aggressive outbursts and matched for age, sex and IQ, those with aggression had a higher rate of psychiatric problems and there was more evidence of organic damage in the central nervous system. Bingley (1958) looked at 90 patients from both neurological and neurosurgical clinics of a general hospital in Sweden and found that 17% of patients with temporal lobe epilepsy showed aggressive behaviour. Patients attending neurology clinics have been shown by Pond and Bidwell's study (1966) to be selected by the presence of psychiatric disorder. Bingley's study (1958) is likely to have had the true prevalence rate of aggressive behaviour elevated by this factor.

Falconer (1973) from the Maudsley Neurosurgical Unit reported a high prevalence of aggressive behaviour in patients with severe epilepsy who were assessed for temporal lobectomy. In those patients who had a predominantly unilateral spike focus (mainly left-sided), pathological outbursts of aggressive behaviour occurred in 38% of 50 cases. Many of these individuals were well-adjusted. A further 14% showed milder or more persistent aggressiveness associated with a paranoid outlook. These patients had been originally described by James (1960), Serafetinides (1965) and Taylor (1969). There is no doubt that this is a special group of patients with severe epilepsy, referred to a specialist epilepsy unit with a particular interest in the psychiatric aspects of epilepsy. Thus the population contained a high rate of psychiatric disorder and severe drug-resistant epilepsy. In many of these patients there was evidence of brain damage and an early onset to their epilepsy, both of which could be expected to lead to aggressive behaviour due to poor impulse control and disordered social development.

It has been argued that as aggressive behaviour is a common reason for imprisonment, prevalence rates for patients with epilepsy in prisons should be higher. A methodologically comprehensive survey carried out on the total population of Iceland by Gudmundson (1966) found 1169 epileptics. Of these, 271 were over 16 years of age and had police records. Thirty-three of these patients had been convicted of criminal offences. The overall rate of criminal offences was three times higher in the epileptic population than in the general community. Gunn (1977), after a survey of prisoners in England and Wales, found the prevalence of epilepsy to be 7.2 per 1000, which is well in excess of the 4.5 per 1000 of the College of General Practitioners' survey of people with epilepsy in England and Wales (1960). A recent prospective study by Britten *et al.* (1984), using the Medical Research Council's National Survey of Health and Development, which is a longitudinal study of a national sample of children born one week in March 1946, shows an overall prevalence rate of about 9.5 per 1000. This sample showed higher prevalence rates in socioeconomic groups III and IV. This would suggest that Gunn's figures show a lower, rather than higher, prevalence in the prison population, and it certainly indicates that a connection between crime and epilepsy is unlikely. Channon (1982) has repeated Gunn's survey using a questionnaire sent to prison doctors, and found a prevalence rate of 7.6 people with epilepsy per 1000 prison population – again a rate which is similar to Britten's Medical Research Council birth cohort study. Several studies from the USA (Norvik *et al.*, 1977; Derro, 1978; King and Young, 1978) have also found higher prevalence rates in prison populations. These studies suffer, however, from the disadvantage that anticonvulsant medication or examination by prison doctors were used as the methods of detecting epilepsy and thus may be inaccurate.

A methodologically sound study by Whitman *et al.* (1984) identified 162 men with possible epilepsy during the prevalence period when 3652 men entered the prison. After adjusting these figures for confirmation of the diagnosis, a prevalence rate was found some four times higher than that for a similar age group in the study by Rodin (1973). They add that almost one-half of the prisoners with epilepsy had a post-traumatic aetiology, a figure that they point out was surprisingly high, and they finally conclude:

Thus our prison study, along with other studies of more general populations, indicates that epilepsy is directly related to socioeconomic status. These sociologic factors, rather than any intrinsic relationships between the biologic aspects of epilepsy and aggressiveness, largely explain the high prevalence of epilepsy in prisons.

Many different studies show an increased prevalence of patients with epilepsy in the prison services of the UK, Sweden and America. However, this increased prevalence is likely to be due to many non-specific factors. Firstly, prisoners are selected from populations of socioeconomic class III and IV, in which there is already a higher prevalence of epilepsy. Secondly, some studies have found a higher prevalence of post-traumatic epilepsy in prison populations, which again suggests that these prisoners came from a violent subculture. Thirdly, there is a weak link between aggressive behaviour and committal to prison. Fourthly, there is no difference in the number or nature of violent crimes committed by prisoners with epilepsy and those without. Finally, those studies which have specifically compared violent with non-violent prisoners (Gunn and Bonn, 1971) found no differences in the prevalence of epilepsy.

Relationship of aggressive behaviour to seizure occurrence and type

It has been suggested that aggressiveness is more frequently reported in patients with seizures and especially those with temporal lobe seizures. It is convenient to classify aggressive behaviour into that which occurs during the seizure and postictally and that which is interictal, occurring between seizures in a setting of clear consciousness.

Ictal aggression

Aggressive episodes of disordered behaviour which have as their basis an ictal discharge have already been mentioned above. There is evidence that temporal lobe discharges which involve the hippocampus, amygdala and hypothalamus are particularly likely to lead to episodes of violent behaviour. These episodes have characteristics that would be expected if they were due to seizure activity. There is a disorder of consciousness, and the aggressive activity is usually carried out in a disordered, uncoordinated and non-directed way. The most comprehensive study is by Delgado-Escueta *et al.* (1981) who collected 5400 video-taped seizures from different units throughout the world and rated them according to the degree of ictal violence. They found only 13 cases of violent behaviour. Most of these were postictal and in a confusional setting; only 3 had attacked people. They conclude that frank ictal violence is very rare. Although this study is methodologically sound, the authors have unfortunately failed to recognize that the form an epileptic seizure takes is dependent on not only the spread of the discharge through the brain, but also on the thought content of the patient at the time of the seizure. There are numerous examples in the literature of the interaction between the patient's intended action and the modification of this by the seizure. It is thus not surprising that Delgado-Escueta and coworkers (1981) should find an absence of ictal aggression in the clinical situation of a videotape recording laboratory. Aggression occurs in the community but to a much lesser extent in hospital.

This point is well brought out in a study by King and Ajmone Marsan (1977) who studied 270 epileptic patients with temporal lobe foci and observed complex partial seizures in 199 of these. Twenty of these patients had a history of interictal violent behaviour, fighting, striking people and throwing objects, but in no case did interictal violence occur in hospital. However, 9 of the 199 patients for whom well-observed seizures had been recorded had peri-ictal behaviour that could be defined as violent. In most of these it was postictal and confusional in nature. This point is again emphasized by Rodin (1973), who between 1959 and 1964 satisfactorily recorded in hospital 150 patients with seizures. At no time did any patient – with one possible exception – show clear evidence of ictal aggression. Although this was interpreted by Rodin and subsequent workers as suggesting that ictal violence is rare, part of the reason for the finding could be due to the recording situation in hospital. Further evidence can only be obtained by portable recording devices used at home.

However, the number of cases of ictal aggression published in the literature is small. One reason for this is the difficulty in being certain that the event described is ictal in origin, as it has not previously been possible to monitor patients continuously in the community (Lewis and Pincus, 1983).

Other examples of ictal aggression have already been mentioned (see above). Knox (1968) in a systematic study of the relationship between epileptic automatism and violence found only 1 patient out of a total of 434 epileptic outpatients who had acted in an aggressive and violent fashion. In a survey of epileptic offenders in prisons and Borstals in England and Wales (Gunn and Fenton, 1969, 1971; Gunn, 1979) there were only 2 persons out of a total of 158 whose crime was probably committed during or following a seizure. One of these was a possible postictal automatism and the other occurred in a postictal phase. In a survey of Broadmoor Hospital, a special hospital for violent psychiatric offenders, of the 29 male epileptics who had committed offences, in only 2 was there a definite relationship between their crimes and their seizures: both had behaved violently in a postictal confusional state. Further cases of ictal aggression have been described by Stevenson (1963), Brewer (1971), Gunn (1978), Milne (1979), Cope and Donovan (1979) and Simon and de Silva (1981). Although in some of the above studies the evidence that direct ictal behaviour was the sole responsible cause for the aggressive act is dubious, the evidence supports the conclusion that ictal violence does, rarely, occur. (For a fuller review see Treiman and Delgado-Escueta, 1983.)

Two further cases have come before the British courts. The first was a brain-damaged man with complex partial seizures who during a witnessed automatism attacked and severely injured an 80-year-old neighbour (Fenwick, 1984; Fenwick and Fenwick, 1985). The second was a man who also suffered from temporal lobe epilepsy and during a presumed automatism killed a woman neighbour with a chisel.

Lewis *et al.* (1982), in a study of children in a reform school, found 5 of the 78 violent boys had committed violent acts during an ictus. They state (Lewis and Pincus, 1983): 'Clearly, most violence in this group was not caused by epilepsy but neither was the association [with ictal discharge] exceedingly rare'.

Despite this positive evidence that ictal violence does occur, contrary views do exist in the literature. Penfield and Jasper, in 1954, state, regarding anger: 'So far as our experience goes, neither localised epileptic discharge, nor electrical stimulation, is capable of awakening any such emotion'. Gloor (1967) reports never having seen a case of ictal rage. Later evidence suggests that this may be due to selection of cases rather than to a non-association of ictal violence and epilepsy.

Interictal aggression

The literature on interictal aggression is confused. In many studies the definition of aggression is unclear and the relationship of the aggressive behaviour to the underlying personality is seldom described. Mungus (1983) points out that violent behaviour is not a unitary syndrome and by means of cluster analysis he was able to define five homogeneous subgroups derived from 138 neuropsychiatric outpatients who attended University College of Los Angeles Neurobehavioral Clinic. Seizure disorders were only related to two of these categories, and these showed a high frequency of impulsive, violent acts. Owing to sample size, specific seizure type was not investigated. There was no relationship between temporal lobe abnormalities and any of the five categories. Thus they found that violent behaviour was not a unitary measure and seizures were not related to all types of violence.

Violent individuals tend to come from violent families with a long history of violent behaviour since childhood. They are most frequently males under the age of 40 and a large number show 'soft' neurological signs and abnormal electroencephalograms (EEGs). Cognitively, they are frequently impaired, with a higher proportion of left-handers, and many show poor attention span and occasionally focal cognitive deficits. They tend to come from the lower socioeconomic groups where there are higher levels of perinatal mortality, infections and trauma. When these factors are taken into account, many of the associations of aggression and violence with epilepsy become weaker (Stevens and Herman, 1981).

A positive association between epilepsy and aggression has been shown by several studies. Nuffield (1961) developed an aggression score for 322 children with temporal lobe petit mal and grand mal epilepsy, classified by use of the EEG. He found that the temporal lobe epileptics had aggression scores which were nearly four times those of the patients who had petit mal. This paper has been criticized by Kaufman *et al.* (1980) on the basis of evidence that EEG abnormalities tend not to be consistent from recording to recording and that mixed forms of abnormality are the rule rather than the exception. A further criticism from Stevens and Herman (1981) is that many of the patients also suffered from grand mal seizures. The association which was found by Nuffield could be with grand mal seizures rather than with temporal lobe epilepsy.

Currie *et al.* (1971), in a retrospective study of 666 patients with temporal lobe epilepsy attending the London Hospital, showed that aggressive affect on examination of the mental state was relatively rare. Only 16 of their patients showed rage attacks, while another 5 had violent outbursts. Without a control from other patients in a neurology clinic it is difficult to know whether or not the prevalence of aggression is raised, and there was no information given as to what proportion of these patients suffered from grand mal seizures.

Lindsay *et al.* (1979) describe a population of 100 epileptic patients in a 30-year prospective study. Of these 100 patients, 36 had rages in childhood. These rages carried a poor adult prognosis in terms of both social and psychiatric outcome. The boys were more prone to overt physical violence than the girls. This study has been frequently quoted to support the relationship of temporal lobe epilepsy to aggression. However, this investigation is not definitive because a large proportion of the patients who showed aggressive behaviour also had coexistent brain damage. Only 12 of these children had pure temporal lobe epilepsy without associated brain damage or grand mal seizures and none of these 12 had significant psychological problems, or a history of rage outbursts. This suggests that non-specific factors unrelated to the temporal lobe epilepsy were involved. Overall, 85% of the original group of children had psychological problems in childhood, whereas after 15 years, 75% of those who had survived were psychologically normal. This suggests that the psychiatric morbidity noted in childhood was related not so much to the epilepsy, but to an interaction between the epilepsy and those psychosocial factors which lead to a high prevalence of psychiatric morbidity.

Both Stafford-Clarke and Taylor (1949) and Hill and Pond (1952) studied the EEGs of alleged murderers. Non-specific abnormalities were common, but not more so than in other studies of prison populations. In those patients who had claimed epilepsy as a defence, only a third had specific abnormalities which were thought to be epileptic in nature. Williams (1969) in a study of 333 habitually aggressive prisoners found that 65% showed abnormal EEGs compared to 12% of the normal population. Although these patients did not necessarily have temporal lobe epilepsy, he felt there was a relationship between temporal lobe epilepsy, pathology and aggression. It should be noted that many of these patients had other weak indicators of associated brain damage and thus the suggested relationship between temporal lobe epilepsy and aggression is confounded by these other variables.

Riley and Niedermeyer (1978) studied the EEGs of 212 patients who were referred for acts of violence and outbursts of aggression without provocation, and found that 6.6% had slightly abnormal EEGs and that none of these were characteristic of epilepsy. They suggested that there was no definite relationship between aggressive behaviour and EEG abnormalities and certainly there was nothing to suggest that epilepsy was involved.

It would be surprising if discharges in the medial temporal structures did not lead to some alteration in aggressive behaviour. One of the difficulties is separating the epilepsy from social and drug factors which may be involved. However, if it can be shown that the patient's personality and behaviour prior to the onset of seizures were normal, then the development of aggressive behaviour after the onset of the epilepsy is a persuasive argument for the causative role of the seizures and interictal discharges.

Devinsky and Bear (1984) describe 5 patients whose behaviour became aggressive following the development of limbic epileptic foci. They argue that the possible mechanism is an alteration in limbic activity, due to the interictal epileptic discharges, with possibly a reduction of orbital prefrontal control over the aggressive behaviour.

Berkovic *et al.* (1988) have described aggressive behaviour in 3 out of 4 patients with hypothalamic hamartomas. One patient had bouts of uncontrolled violent rage lasting for hours. They began without provocation and appeared not to be related to his seizure disorder. He had been expelled from school for striking a teacher, and had chased his parents with knives. In the group as a whole the behaviour disorders were independent of the subjects' epilepsy, and were possibly related to their cognitive deterioration. Hypothalamic hamartomas are frequently associated with severe epilepsy and gelastic (laughing) seizures. 'The behavioural abnormalities of this hypothalamic syndrome. . .might be multifactorial due to psychosocial difficulties, hospitalisation, mental retardation, epilepsy, or the effect of drugs. Episodes of severe rage may be related to the lesion but have rarely been directly observed.' The authors go on to point out that sham rage can be produced in animals by lesions in the hypothalamus and that lesions of the basal hyothalamus are a recognized cause of episodic rage in humans.

Although there is evidence (Nuffield, 1961; Currie *et al.*, 1971;

Lindsay *et al.*, 1979) that temporal lobe epilepsy may have a special relationship to violence, methodological difficulties and patient selection weaken the correlations found between interictal aggression and temporal lobe seizures. When adequate control groups are used, many of the differences which were apparently significant disappear (Kligman and Goldberg, 1975; Stevens and Herman, 1981).

This point was brought out by Herzberg and Fenwick (1989) in a study of patients with temporal lobe epilepsy and aggressive behaviour. They found that those factors which correlated with violent behaviour were non-specific and not directly related to the severity of the epilepsy, but more related to social factors and brain damage. Important causative factors were a behaviour disorder in childhood ($P=0.03$), residential schooling ($P=0.007$), fewer educational qualifications ($P=0.002$) and unskilled jobs ($P=0.04$). There was also a slightly lower IQ in the violent group and a tendency to have more computed tomography scan and EEG abnormalities.

Differential diagnosis of seizure-related aggression

Close and detailed questioning of the patient by the physician is essential if seizure-related aggression is to be distinguished from non-epileptic aggressive episodes. The following factors are especially important.

Behaviour before the episode

In a seizure-related aggressive episode, the patient's behaviour before the incident will have seemed normal and there will be no specific triggers. The attack may occur when the patient is with people or alone, whether he or she is in a dangerous position or comfortably sitting down. The moment of the attack is unlikely to have apparent psychological significance for the patient.

An aggressive outburst due to temper is quite different. It usually occurs in the presence of other people, who are usually emotionally important to the patient. The episode tends to occur at a psychologically significant time, and often in a significant place, for example, when the family are gathered round the tea-table. Although temper outbursts are often described as occuring out of the blue, close questioning usually reveals some tension or unhappiness which suddenly bursts forth as an episode of frustration.

The onset of the episode

In a seizure-related aggressive episode, the onset is sudden, over a matter of seconds. One moment the patient is normal; the next he or she is showing aggressive, violent behaviour, which is inappropriate to the circumstances, and can occur anywhere. Detailed enquiry will usually reveal that the onset was characteristic of a partial complex seizure. Witnesses should be asked about stopping, staring, simple motor automatisms and confusion.

In an aggressive outburst due to temper, close questioning will reveal a slow, gradual onset, usually over minutes to hours, although the final explosion of temper may be rapid. The patient is usually aware of his or her thought content and recognizes that this is negative. There is always a trigger, usually in relation to a significant or caring adult, although sometimes it is in response to a situation outside the family. Detailed questioning will show that the temper appears fairly low-key at first, and that the patient, over a matter of minutes, slowly works up to a crescendo.

The nature of the episode itself

A seizure-related episode will last from 1 to 3 min, and should have the characteristics of automatisms and partial complex seizures. Behaviour will be confused, and inappropriate to the situation, and make no psychological sense. Articles may be picked up at random and broken, and violence will be directed towards anyone who happens to be within reach rather than anyone who stands in a particular relationship to the patient. The aggressive behaviour reaches its zenith within a few seconds and then, if it is ictal, subsides. Postictal violence may last longer and the acts may be more complex. However, it will always be seen to be inappropriate and out of character. Memory is usually absent for this period.

In contrast, a temper episode shows a definite pattern. Once started it may proceed in waves, each wave having a trigger, often the soothing attempts of people present. Violence is directed and clearly psychologically determined. Walls may be struck but not people, significant possessions of the patient or of close adults will be broken. In a severe episode, memory is frequently lost for the time the patient is most highly aroused. The attack may continue for minutes to 10s of minutes, and at its height the patient will seem out of control and will not respond to commands.

The offset of the episode

In a seizure-related episode the patient may return immediately to full consciousness, or may return to normality slowly, over a matter of minutes as the confusional element of the episode disappears. After the episode the patient is puzzled by what has happened and behaves appropriately.

Recovery as temper subsides may take many minutes. The patient is clearly in touch and there is no evidence of waning confusion. As the arousal diminishes, and the patient realises the havoc he or she has wrought, he or she becomes guilty, self-recriminatory and apologetic.

Treatment and management of seizure-related aggression

The principles of treatment and management of aggressive episodes will depend on the cause of the episode. Ictally related episodes are treated by seizure control. Patients showing confusional aggression should be nursed in a situation where they cannot damage themselves or other patients. In severe cases it may be necessary to tell other patients on the ward that the patient is liable to be aggressive after a seizure and should be given space while he or she is confused. Direct ictal aggression is fortunately rare, and will require the isolation of the patient until seizure control has been established.

Interictal aggression is more difficult to manage as it has multiple causes. The patient should be admitted to a hospital unit that can cope with and understands aggressive outbursts. A specialist neuro-psychiatric epilepsy unit is ideal. Here the psychological meaning and precipitants of the outburst can be investigated, and the patient's relationships to family, work etc. studied.

Postictal psychoses require special nursing care because of the danger of impulsive self-destructive behaviour. Patients should be nursed in a secure environment and adequate supervision and antipsychotic medication are essential. Haloperidol, in the author's experience, is the drug of choice, as it provides rapid improvement of the psychosis with minimal epileptogenic effects.

CONCLUSIONS

At least part of the public prejudice with which people who have epilepsy have to contend is due to the stereotypical view of epileptics as aggressive. However, the facts do not confirm this. The experienced physician is best placed to distinguish between an epileptic aggressive act and a temper outburst, and to instruct colleagues accordingly.

There is little doubt that violent episodes in patients with epilepsy do not occur at random. An epileptic discharge traversing the amygdala will have a very different effect on a patient when he or she is in hospital than when aroused in an argument. It is in this latter situation that the onset of the seizure may lead to aggressive acts and, unfortunately, bring the patient before the courts.

A better understanding of the nature of aggression and its relationship to epilepsy is essential if the stereotype of the aggressive epileptic patient is to be finally abandoned, and if epileptic patients in medical wards are to receive the care they require.

Despite all the above evidence that temporal lobe epilepsy may have a special relationship to violence, methodological difficulties and patient selection weaken the correlations found between interictal aggression and temporal lobe epilepsy. However, what is clear is that a relationship does exist between aggressive behaviour and epilepsy. A recent review of the literature comes to the conclusion that the relationship is probably due to non-specific factors which are common in both violent populations and patients with epilepsy, the most significant of which is likely to be the associated brain damage (Treiman, 1991).

REFERENCES

Adamec R. (1990). The role of the amygdala and medial hypothalamus in spontaneous aggression and defense. *Aggressive Behaviour*; **16**: 207–22.

Adamec R. E., Stark-Adameck C. (1983). Limbic kindling and animal behaviour: implications for human psychopathology associated with complex partial seizures. *Biological Psychiatry*; **18**: 269–293.

Adamec R., Perry D., Stark-Adamec C. Epilepsy and psychopathology: the contribution of auras to our undertanding of the nature and pathophysiological basis of psychopathology associated with epilepsy in humans. *Epilepsia*; (in press).

Andrulonis P. A., Glueck B. C., Strobel C. F., Vogel N. G. (1982). Borderline personality subcategories. *Journal of Nervous and Mental Disease*; **170**: 670–9.

Andy D. J. (1970). Thalamotomy in hyperactive and aggressive behaviour. *Confinia Neurologica*, **32**: 322–5.

Bear D. M. (1979). Temporal lobe epilepsy: a syndrome of sensory-limbic hyper-connection. *Cortex*; **15**: 357–84.

Berkovic S., Andermann F., Melanson F., Ethier R., Feindell W., Gloor P. (1988). Hypothalamic hamatomas and ictal laughter: evolution of a characteristic epileptic syndrome and diagnostic value of magnetic resonance imaging. *Annals of Neurology*; **23**: 429–39.

Bingley T. (1958). Mental symptoms in temporal lobe epilepsy and temporal lobe gliomas with special reference to laterality of lesion and the relationship between handedness and brainedness. *Acta Psychiatrica Scandinavica*; **33** (suppl. 120): 1–151.

Brewer C. (1971). Homicide during a psychomotor seizure. *Medical Journal of Australia*; **1**: 857–9.

Britten N., Wadsworth M., Fenwick P. (1984). Stigma in patients with early epilepsy: a national longitudinal study. *Journal of Epidemiology and Community Health*; **38** 291–5.

Brutkowski S., Fonberg E., Mempel E. (1961). Angry behaviour in dogs following bilateral lesions in the genual portion of the rostral cingulate gyrus. *Acta Biologici Experimentalis*; **21**: 199–205.

Channon S. (1982). The resettlement of epileptic offenders. In: *Abnormal Offenders, Delinquency, and the Criminal Justice System*, vol. 1. (Gunn J., Farrington D.P., eds), pp. 339–73. Chichester: John Wiley.

Chapman W. P. (1958). Studies of the periamygdaloid area in relation to human behaviour. *Association of Research in Nervous and Mental Disease*; **36**: 258–77.

College of General Practitioners (1960). A survey of the epileptics in general practice. *British Medical Journal*; **2**: 416–22.

Cope, R. Donovan, W. (1979). A case of insane automatism? *British Journal of Psychiatry*; **135**: 574–5.

Currie S., Heathfield W., Henson R., Scott D. (1971). Clinical course and prognosis of temporal lobe epilepsy: a survey of 666 patients. *Brain*; **94**: 173–90.

Delgado-Escueta A., Mattson R., King L. (1981). The nature of aggression during epileptic seizures. *New England Journal of Medicine*; **305**: 711–16.

Derro R. (1978). Admission health evaluation of a city-county workhouse. *Minnesota Medicine*; **61**: 333–7.

Devinsky O., Bear D. (1984). Varieties of aggressive behaviour in temporal lobe epilepsy. *American Journal of Psychiatry*; **141**: 651–6.

Egger M. D., Flynn J. P. (1963). Effects of electrical stimulation of the amygdala. *Journal of Neurophysiology*; **26**: 705–20.

Falconer M. (1973). Reversibility by temporal lobe resection of the behavioural abnormalities of temporal lobe epilepsy. *New England Journal of Medicine*; **289**: 451–5.

Fenwick P. (1984). Epilepsy and the law. *British Medical Journal*; **288**: 1938–9.

Fenwick P. (1986). Aggression and epilepsy. In: *Aspects of Epilepsy and Psychiatry* (Bolwig H., Trimble M., eds), pp. 62–98. Chichester: John Wiley.

Fenwick P., Fenwick E. (eds) (1985). *Epilepsy and the Law—A Medical Symposium on the Current Law*, pp. 3–8. London: Royal Society of Medicine.

Fenwick P., Howard R., Fenton G. (1983). Review of cortical excitability, neurohumeral transmission and the dyscontrol syndrome. In: *Advances in Epileptology: XIVth Epilepsy International Symposium* (Parsonage M. *et al.*, eds), pp. 181–91. New York: Raven Press.

Flynn J. P., Howard W., Edwards S. (1970). Neural mechanisms involved in a cat's attack on a rat. In: *The Neural Control of Behaviour* (Whalen R. E., Thompson R. F., Verzeano M., Weinberger N. M., eds), pp. 210–40. New York: Academic Press.

Gastaut H., Morrin G., Lesevre N. (1955). Etudes du comportement des épileptiques psychomoteurs dans l'interval de leurs crises. *Annals of Medical Psychology*; **113**: 1–29.

Gloor P. (1967). Discussion of brain mechanisms related to aggressive behaviour, by B. Kaada. In: *Aggression and Defence: Neural Mechanisms and Social Patterns*, vol. 5: *Brain Function*. (Clemente C., Lindsay D., eds). Los Angeles: University of California Press.

Gloor P. (1972). Temporal lobe epilepsy: its possible contribution to the understanding of the functional significance of the amygdala and of its interaction with neocortical-temporal mechanisms. In: *The Neurobiology of the Amygdala* (Eletheriou B., ed.), pp. 423–58. New York: Plenum Press.

Gloor P. (1978). Inputs and outputs of the amygdala: what the amygdala is trying to tell the rest of the brain. In: *Limbic Mechanisms: the Continuing Evolution of the Limbic System Concept* (Livingstone K.E., Hornykiewicz O., eds), pp. 189–209. New York: Plenum Press.

Gloor P., Olivier A., Quesney L. F., Andermann F., Horowitz S. (1982a). The role of the limbic system in experimental phenomena of temporal lobe epilepsy. *Annals of Neurology*; **12**: 129–44.

Gloor P., Metrakos J., Metrakos K., Andermann E., and Van Gelder N. (1982b). Neurophysiological, genetic, and biochemical nature of the epileptic diathesis. *Electroencephalography and Clinical Neurophysiology* (suppl. 35): 45–56.

Green J. D., Clement C. D., De Groot J. (1957). Rhinencephalic lesions and behaviour in cats. *Journal of Comparative Neurology*; **108**: 505–36.

Gudmundson G. (1966). Epilepsy in Iceland: a clinical and epidemiological investigation. *Acta Neurologica Scandinavica*; **23** (suppl. 25); 100–14.

Gunn J. (1977). *Epileptics in Prison*. London: Academic Press.

Gunn J. (1978). Epileptic homicide: a case report. *British Journal of Psychiatry*; **132**: 510–13.

Gunn J. (1979). Forensic psychiatry. In: *Recent Advances in Clinical Psychiatry* (Granville-Grossman K., ed.) Edinburgh: Churchill Livingstone.

Gunn J., Bonn J. (1971). Criminality and violence in epileptic prisoners. *British Journal of Psychiatry*; **118**: 337–43.

Gunn J., Fenton G. (1969). Epilepsy in prisons: a diagnostic survey. *British Medical Journal*; **4**: 326–8.

Gunn J., Fenton G. (1971). Epilepsy, automatism and crime. *Lancet*; **i**: 1173–6.

Halgren E., Walter R. D., Cherlow D. G., Crandall P. H. (1978). Mental phenomena evoked by electrical stimulation of the human hippocampal formation and amygdala. *Brain*; **101**: 83–117.

Heath R. G. (1963). Electrical self stimulation of the brain in man. *American Journal of Psychiatry*; **120**: 571–7.

Heath R. G., Mickle W. A. (1960). Evaluation of seven years experience with depth electrode studies in human patients. In: *Electrical Studies of the Unanaesthetised Brain* (Ramey E.R., O'Doherty D., eds), pp. 214–47. New York: Paul B. Hober.

Herman B. P. (1982). Interictal psychopathology in patients with ictal fear. A quantitative investigation. *Neurology*: **32**; 7–11.

Herman B. P., Riel P. (1981). Interictal personality and behavioural traits in temporal lobe and generalised epilepsy. *Cortex*; **17**: 125–8.

Herman B. P., Dikmen S., Schwartz M. S., Karnes W. E. (1982). Interictal psychopathology in patients with ictal fear: a quantitative investigation. *Neurology*; **32**: 7–11.

Herzberg J. L., Fenwick P. B. C. (1989). The aetiology of agression in temporal lobe epilepsy. *British Journal of Psychiatry*; **153**: 50–5.

Higgins J. W., Mahl G.F., Delgado J., Hamlin H. (1956). Behavioural changes during intracerebral electrical stimulation. *American Medical Association Archives of Neurology and Psychiatry*; **76**: 399–419.

Hill D., Pond D. (1952). Reflections on a hundred capital cases submitted to EEG. *Journal of Mental Science*; **98**: 23–43.

Hitchcock E., Cairns V. (1973). Amygdalotomy. *Postgraduate Medical Journal*; **49**; 894–904.

James I. (1960). Temporal lobectomy for psychomotor epilepsy. *Journal of Mental Science*; **106**: 543–58.

Kaufman K., Harris R., Shaffer D. (1980). Problems in the categorization of child and adolescent EEGs. *Journal of Child Psychology and Psychiatry*; **21**: 333–42.

Kennard M. A. (1955). Effects of bilateral ablation of cingulate area on behaviour of cats. *Journal of Neurophysiology*; **18**: 159–69.

Kim Y., Umbach W. (1973). Combined stereotactic lesions for treatment of behavioural disorders and severe pain. In: *Surgical Approaches in Psychiatry* (Laitinen L., Livingstone K., eds), pp. 182–8. Baltimore: University Park.

King D., Ajmone Marsan C. (1977). Clinical features and ictal patterns in epileptic patients with EEG temporal lobe foci. *Annals of Neurology*; **2**: 138–47.

King D., Young Q. (1978). Increased prevalence of seizure disorders among prisoners. *Journal of the American Medical Association*; **239**: 2674–5.

Kligman D., Goldberg D. T. (1975). Temporal lobe epilepsy and aggression. *Journal of Nervous and Mental Disease*; **160**: 324–41.

Knox S. (1968). Epileptic automatisms and violence. *Medicine, Science and the Law*; **8**: 96–104.

Le Beau J. (1952). The cingular and pre-cingular areas in psychosurgery (agitated behaviour, obsessive compulsive states, epilepsy). *Acta Psychiatrica et Neurologica, Copenhagen*; **27**: 305–16.

Lewis D., Pincus J. (1983). Psychomotor epilepsy and violence. *American Journal of Psychiatry*; **140**: 646–8.

Lewis D., Pincus, J., Shanok S., Glaser G. (1982). Psychomotor epilepsy and violence in a group of incarcerated adolescent boys. *American Journal of Psychiatry*; **139**: 882–7.

Lindsay J., Oundstead C., Richards P. (1979). Long-term outcome in children with temporal lobe seizures. (3) Psychiatric aspects in childhood and adult life. *Developmental Medicine and Child Neurology*; **21**: 630–6.

Maclean P. D., Delgado J. (1953). Electrical and chemical stimulation of front temporal portion of limbic system in waking animal. *Electroencephalography and Clinical Neurophysiology*; **5**: 91–100.

Mark V. H., Ervin F. (1970). *Violence and the Brain*. New York: Harper & Row.

Mark V. H., Sweet W., Ervin F. (1975). Deep temporal lobe stimulation and destructive lesions in episodically violent temporal lobe epileptics. In: *Neural Bases of Violence and Aggression* (Fields W., Sweet W., eds), pp. 379–91. St Louis: Warren H. Greem.

Milne H. (1979). Epileptic homicide: drug induced. *British Journal of Psychiatry*; **134**: 547–8.

Moyer K. E. (1971). *The Physiology of Hostility*. Chicago: Markham.

Mungus D. (1983). An empirical analysis of specific syndromes of violent behaviour. *Journal of Nervous and Mental Disease*; **171**: 354–61.

Nadvorick P., Pogady J., Sramka M. (1973). The result of stereotactic treatment of the aggressive syndrome. In: *Surgical Approaches in Psychiatry* (Laitinen L., Livingstone K., eds) pp. 125–8. Baltimore: University Park.

Narabayashi H., Nagao T., Yosluda M., Nagahata M. (1963). Stereotaxic amygdalotomy for behaviour disorders. *Archives of Neurology*; **9**: 1–16.

Norvik L., Dellapenna R., Schwartz M. *et al.* (1977). Health status of the New York city prison population. *Medical Care*; **15**: 205–17.

Nuffield E. (1961). Neurophysiology and behaviour disorders in epileptic chidren. *Journal of Mental Science*; **107**: 438–58.

Penfield W., & Jasper H. H. (1954). *Epilepsy and the Functional Anatomy of the Human Brain*, pp. 113–43. Boston: Little, Brown.

Pond D., Bidwell B. (1960). A survey of epilepsy in 14 general practices. II Social and psychological aspects. *Epilepsia*; **1**: 285–99.

Pontius A. (1984). Specific stimulus evoked violent action in psychotic trigger reaction: a seizure-like imbalance between frontal lobe and limbic systems. *Perceptual and Motor Skills*; **59**: 299–333.

Riley T., Niedermeyer E. (1978). Rage attacks and episodic violent behaviour electroencephalographic findings and general consideration. *Journal of Clinical Electroencephalography*; **9**: 113–39.

Rodin E. (1973). Psychomotor epilepsy and aggressive behaviour. *Archives of General Psychiatry*; **28**: 210–13.

Romaniuk A. (1965). Representation of aggression and flight reactions in the hypothalamus of the cat. *Acta Biologicae Experimentalis Sinica, Warsaw*; **25**: 177–86.

Sano K., Mayanagi Y., Sekino H. E., Ajashiwa M., Ishyima B. (1970). Results of stimulation and destruction of the posterior hypothalamus in man. *Journal of Neurosurgery*; **33**: 689–707.

Schreiner L., Kling A. (1953). Behavioural changes following rhinencephalic injury in cat. *Journal of Neurophysiology*; **16**: 643–59.

Sem-Jacobson C. W. (1968). Vegetative changes in response to electrical brain stimulation. *Electroencephalography and Clinical Neurophysiology*; **24**: 88.

Serafetinides E. (1965). Aggressiveness in temporal lobe epilepsy and its relation to cerebral dysfunction and environmental factors. *Epilepsia*; **6**: 33–47.

Shealy C., Peele T. (1957). Studies on amygdaloid nucleus of cat. *Journal of Neurophysiology*; **20**: 125–39.

Simon R., de Silva M. (1981). Intercranial tumour coexistent with uncinate seizures in violent behaviour. *Journal of the American Medical Association*; **245**: 1247–8.

Smith D. E., King M. D., Hoebelb G. (1970). Lateral hypothalamic controls of killing: evidence for a thalinergic mechanism. *Science*; **167**: 900–1.

Stafford-Clarke D., Taylor F. (1949). Clinical and electroencephalographic studies of prisoners charged with murder. *Journal of Neurology, Neurosurgery and Psychiatry*; **12**: 325–9.

Stevens J. R. (1975). Interictal clinical manifestations of complex partial seizures. *Advances in Neurology*; **11**: 85–107.

Stevens J. R., Herman B. (1981). Temporal lobe epilepsy, psychopathology and violence: the state of the evidence. *Neurology (New York)*; **31**: 1127–32.

Stevenson H. (1963). Psychomotor epilepsy associated with criminal behaviour. *Medical Journal of Australia*; **50**: 784–5.

Summers T. B., Kaelber W. W. (1962). Amygdalectomy: effects in cats and a survey of its present status. *American Journal of Physiology*; **203**: 1117–19.

Taylor D. (1969). Aggression and epilepsy. *Journal of Psychosomatic Research*; **13**: 229–36.

Taylor D. (1981). Brain lesions, surgery, seizures, and mental symptoms. In: *Epilepsy and Psychiatry* (Reynolds E., Trimble M., eds), pp. 227–41. Edinburgh: Churchill Livingstone.

Tow P. M., Whitty C. W. (1953). Personality changes after operations in the cingulate gyrus in man. *Journal of Neurology, Neurosurgery and Psychiatry*; **16**: 186–93.

Treiman D.M. (1991). Psychobiology of ictal aggression. In: *Advances in Neurology 55*. (Smith D.B., Treiman D.M., Trimble M.R. eds), pp. 341–56. New York: Raven Press.

Treiman D., Delgado-Escueta A. (1983). Violence and epilepsy: a critical review. Chapter 11. In: *Recent Advances in Epilepsy 1*. (Pedley T., Meldrum B. eds), pp. 179–209. Edinburgh: Churchill Livingstone.

Wasman M., Flynn J. P. (1962). Directed attack elicited from hypothalmus. *Archives of Neurology Chicago*; **6**: 220–7.

Waxman S. G., Geschwind N. (1975). The interictal behaviour syndrome of temporal lobe epilepsy. *Archives of General Psychiatry*; **32**: 1580–6.

Whitman S., Colman T., Borg B. *et al.* (1980). Epidemiological insights into the socioeconomic correlates of epilepsy. In: *A Multidisciplinary Handbook of Epilepsy* (Herman B. P., ed.), pp. 243–71. Springfield, IL: Charles C. Thomas.

Whitman S., Coonley-Hoganson R., Desai B. (1984). Comparative head trauma experiences in two socioeconomically different Chicago-area communities: a population study. *American Journal of Epidemiology*; **119**: 570–80.

Wieser H. G. (1983). Depth recorded limbic seizures and psychopathology. *Neuroscience and Behavioural Reviews*; **7**: 427–40.

Williams D. (1969). Neural factors related to habitual aggression. *Brain*; **92**: 503–20.

Yasukochi G. (1960). Emotional responses elicited by electrical stimulation of the hypothalamus in cats. *Folia Psychiatrica et Neurologica Japonica*; **14**: 260–7.

Part 3 *Clinical science*

7 *Psychopathic disorder, personality disorders and aggression*

RONALD BLACKBURN

INTRODUCTION

Psychopathic personality is often regarded as embodying the relationship between abnormal personality and aggression. The category of *psychopathic disorder* of the 1983 Mental Health Act for England and Wales is defined as 'a persistent disorder or disability of mind. . .which results in abnormally aggressive or seriously irresponsible conduct on the part of the person concerned'. This is, of course, a legal and not a clinical category, but clinical conceptions also emphasize aggression. McCord and McCord (1964), for example, describe the psychopath as 'an asocial, aggressive, highly impulsive person, who feels little or no guilt, and is unable to form lasting bonds of affection with other human beings'. Aggression is also among the traits of the antisocial and borderline personality disorders of *DSM-III* (American Psychiatric Association, 1987). Although Cleckley's influential concept of psychopathy does not include aggression among the defining criteria, prisoners who meet these criteria are more likely to have committed violent offences, and to be violent when in prison (Hare and McPherson, 1984). An understanding of the psychological attributes of psychopaths might therefore be expected to shed some light on how individual characteristics contribute to violence.

There is, however, continuing disagreement as to whether the concept of the psychopath as a discrete category of antisocial person is anything more than a stereotype, and hence whether it serves any useful scientific or clinical purpose. I have argued elsewhere that it does not (Blackburn, 1988), for essentially three reasons. First, current uses of the term confound moral judgement with personality description. Second, those to whom the label is applied are not a homogeneous group. Third, concepts of psychopathy have developed within an atheoretical, positivist tradition, and lack a theoretically grounded scheme for identifying personality variation. In this chapter, I will outline one such scheme, and describe some empirical findings which I believe support its utility in understanding the contribution of the person to violence.

Acts and dispositions

It is important at the outset to distinguish between *acts* and personal *dispositions*. An act is an intentional, goal-directed behaviour performed by a person in a specific situational context. A violent act, for example, can be construed as the forceful infliction of physical injury by one person on another. A disposition is a tendency or capacity to perform particular kinds of act. Performance of those acts requires a context, but the disposition is nevertheless possessed by the person, whether or not the act is performed. To take an analogy, salt has the disposition of being soluble in water. It possesses that property whether or not it gets wet. Similarly, aggressiveness can be regarded as a disposition to inflict harm, which people possess in varying degrees, whether or not that disposition is realized in acts of criminal violence.

Dispositions and acts call for different kinds of causal explanation. We may attempt to explain an aggressive disposition in terms of distal factors, such as genetic endowment, early family environment or experiences with peers. These, however, do not explain the occurrence of an act of aggression, which depends on more proximal factors such as recent life events or situational factors. In the open world, these may often be fortuitous. Studies of homicides, for example, suggest that they are often unpredicted altercations which go further than intended, the outcome depending on the victim – offender interaction and the availability of a weapon (Block, 1977).

Violent acts, then, require more than violent actors. One implication is that the relation between aggressive dispositions and the performance of violent acts is a loose one. There are people with marked aggressive tendencies which will not necessarily eventuate in a violent crime. This has been ignored in much of the research on the prediction of dangerousness, which has not distinguished the assessment of violent tendencies from the forecasting of violent acts (Gordon, 1977). Clinicians should reasonably be expected to do the former, but it is unreasonable to expect them to do the latter with more than modest accuracy. Conversely, violent crimes may often be committed by people who are not habitually aggressive. Again, the failure to distinguish acts and dispositions has resulted in a considerable amount of flawed research. Studies still appear which attempt to establish the attributes of violent people by taking a sample of prisoners or offender-patients defined solely by reference to a single conviction for violence. Many of these, however, will have committed their offence because of situational factors or temporary state rather than a propensity for violence. On the other hand, some will have contributed directly to a violent outcome by the tendencies they bring to the situation. These more habitually aggressive people are more likely to create the conditions for an act of violence, and are also more likely to be labelled psychopaths.

Populations of violent offenders are therefore likely to be heterogeneous in personality, and this has been demonstrated in research with violent mentally disordered offenders in the English special hospitals which I will describe shortly. However, before considering this research, I will briefly consider why the concept of psychopathic personality is problematic.

PSYCHOPATHIC DISORDER AND PERSONALITY DISORDER

Current concepts of psychopathy and personality disorder

There is currently no agreed concept of psychopathic personality. Although etymologically psychopathic simply means psychologically damaged, it has long been used to denote a type of socially damaging person, but the term no longer appears in clinical classifications. It is represented in *DSM-III* by *antisocial personality disorder* (APD), which is one of 11 categories of personality disorder. However, this is quite concretely defined by criteria such as history of delinquency, fighting, child neglect or inconsistent work behaviour, and cannot be assumed to be very closely related to the English legal category of psychopathic disorder. In the UK, psychopathic disorder and personality disorder are often used interchangeably, but as Pichot (1978) and Millon (1981) note, these terms have had different meanings in European and Anglo-American psychiatry.

In Germany, Schneider (1950) followed Kraepelin in describing a 10-fold typology of psychopathic personalities. He explicitly excluded antisocial behaviour from the criteria for abnormal personality, which he construed in statistical terms as a deviation from average. Psychopathic personalities were abnormal personalities who cause suffering to themselves or others. As Pichot (1978) observes, it is paradoxical that this generic concept of psychopathic personalities corresponds to the broad class of personality disorders adopted in psychiatry, whereas in the UK and USA the notion of psychopath has been confined to a narrow category of antisocial person.

Schneider's concept was never widely adopted in the UK, where the 19th century notion of *moral insanity* resulted in the statutory category of *moral imbecile* in the 1913 Mental Deficiency Act, and eventually in the category of *psychopathic disorder* of the English Mental Health Act. Although the term psychopathic is adopted from the German, this category bears no resemblance to Schneider's concept. The definition in fact contains no reference to personality, the only defining features being the aggressive conduct from which a 'mental disability' is inferred. As the Butler Committee (Home Office/ Department of Health and Social Security, 1975) noted: 'The class of persons to whom the term "psychopathic disorder" relates is not a single category identifiable by any medical, biological, or psychological criteria'.

One other concept of note is that of Cleckley (1976). Cleckley rejected Schneider's generic concept of personality disorder, seeing most categories as neurotic or psychotic disorders, but he proposed a 'distinct clinical entity' of psychopathic personality defined by criteria such as superficial charm, lack of remorse, egocentricity and interpersonal unresponsiveness. Cleckley's concept provides the basis for Hare's psychopathy checklist (PCL), which is used widely in research in North America, and which overlaps with the antisocial personality disorder category of *DSM-III* (Hare, 1985). The PCL has been derived empirically, and is the most valid measure of psychopathy currently in use. However, the relationship between Cleckley's concept and the classes of personality disorder remains unclear. As I will indicate shortly, Cleckley's concept, as represented by Hare's PCL, may be more readily understood as one dimension of personality disorder, rather than a discrete category.

I have suggested previously that much of the confusion surrounding the concept of psychopathy arises from a logical confounding of the universes of personality disorder and social deviance, which classify people in different ways (Blackburn, 1988). For example, *DSM-III* classifies personality disorders in terms of personality *traits*, which are defined as 'enduring patterns of perceiving, relating to, and thinking about the environment and oneself'. Traits constitute personality disorder when they are 'inflexible and maladaptive' and result in social dysfunction or subjective distress. However, committing a crime, failing to honour financial obligations or abusing drugs are not personality traits. Rather are they departures from sociocultural or moral norms of what constitutes acceptable conduct. While socially deviant behaviour may well be a *consequence* of personality disorder or even mental illness, antisocial behaviour *per se* cannot logically be used to define a disorder of personality. The legal category of psychopathic disorder clearly fails on this point. The *DSM-III* classification of personality disorders is also inconsistent, defining the category of antisocial personality disorder almost exclusively in terms of socially deviant behaviours. Millon (1981) calls this an 'accusatory judgment'. He proposes that the concept should be replaced by that of the aggressive personality, defined by traits of hostile affectivity, social rebelliousnes, vindictiveness, and disregard for danger. I concur with this view, but as I will show, there is more than one type of aggressive personality. This brings me to the empirical objections to the notion of a unitary category of antisocial personality.

An empirical classification of personality deviation

My own research has been conducted with forensic psychiatric patients detained in the English special hospitals because of their presumed dangerousness. My earliest studies with this population were initially concerned with testing Megargee's hypothesis that those who have committed an act of extreme violence can be divided into overcontrolled and undercontrolled personality types (Megargee, 1966). Megargee proposed that undercontrolled offenders are those with weak inhibitions, who respond aggressively with some regularity, and are likely to be identified as psychopathic personalities. Overcontrolled offenders, in contrast, have strong inhibitions, and aggress only when instigation (anger arousal) is sufficiently intense to overcome inhibitions. They are therefore expected to attack others rarely, but with extreme intensity if they do so, and should hence be found more commonly among those who have been extremely assaultive or homicidal. Supporting his hypothesis, Megargee (1966) found that boys with a record of extreme assault were rated as more controlled and unaggressive, and showed greater control and conventionality on personality tests than moderately assaultive and non-violent delinquents. I obtained further support in a study of mentally disordered offenders (Blackburn, 1968). Extreme assaultives were significantly more controlled, inhibited and defensive on psychological tests than moderate assaultives, and were less likely to have a prior criminal record or to be diagnosed as psychopathic personality.

The overcontrol hypothesis sheds some light on why typically timid and *unaggressive* individuals are found among violent offenders, but rests on a questionable energy model, in which anger arousal accumulates with repeated provocation. Current theorizing would predict that anger is most likely to be maintained by the cognitive rehearsal of grievances, resulting in a bias to respond more readily to further provocation (Zillmann, 1979). Nevertheless, our subsequent research supports the useless of the overcontrolled – undercontrolled distinction.

In one study, I carried out a cluster analysis of Minnesota Multiphasic Personality Inventory profiles of patients who had committed homicide (Blackburn, 1971). This supported Megargee's hypothesis, but in fact indicated two overcontrolled and two undercontrolled types. In subsequent work, I have used a questionnaire which focuses on traits particularly relevant to personality disorder, the SHAPS (Special Hospitals Assessment of Personality and Socialization; Blackburn, 1982a). The 10 SHAPS scales can be reduced to two factor dimensions, one of which is defined by scales of impulsivity, aggression, hostility and negatively by the lie scale (defensive denial), and has been labelled *aggression* or *psychopathy*. The second factor is defined by shyness, social anxiety, and lack of self-esteem, and is labelled *withdrawal versus sociability*.

Cluster analyses of SHAPS profiles have consistently reproduced the earlier fourfold typology. This emerged from a study of those in the legal category of psychopathic disorder (Blackburn, 1975), but it also accounts for the main patterns of personality deviation in the special hospital population as a whole (Blackburn, 1986). The four classes have been described as:

1. *Primary psychopaths* (P; impulsive, aggressive, hostile, extraverted, self-confident, low-to-average anxiety).
2. *Secondary psychopaths* (S; hostile, impulsive, aggressive, socially anxious, withdrawn, moody, low in self-esteem).
3. *Controlled* (C; defensive, controlled, sociable, very low anxiety).
4. *Inhibited* (I; shy, withdrawn, controlled, moderately anxious, low self-esteem).

The first two groups share personality characteristics consistent with descriptions of psychopathic personality in some of the clinical literature, and for present purposes I will stick to these labels. The four groups represent combinations of extremes on the two factor dimensions. P and S are those who score at the aggressive extreme of the first factor of aggression, but who occupy opposite positions on the withdrawal factor. The C and I groups score at a low level on the aggression factor, but again are opposite on the withdrawal–sociability dimension. This typology seems robust, having been replicated in research in the English prison system on 'normal' murderers (McGurk, 1978), violent offenders (Henderson, 1982), and also unselected prisoners (McGurk and McGurk, 1979). It clearly represents the main personality types identifiable through self-report measures among violent offenders in prison and forensic psychiatric populations.

Several studies in the special hospitals have established differences between the four groups on behavioural, emotional, psychophysiological and cognitive variables (Blackburn, 1982b). While I have not examined relation to criminal record in any detail, the mean age at first conviction is significantly lower for P and S, tending to be in the early teens, suggesting greater criminality in these groups. There are, however, differences between the groups in the pattern of offences (Blackburn, 1984). P is most likely to have previous history of violent crimes, I the least. S and I, on the other hand, are more likely to have been admitted following a sexual crime. In research in American prisons, Heilbrun and Heilbrun (1985) have also found that secondary psychopaths who are low in intelligence tend to be more violent than other prisoners within the prison setting (Heilbrun and Heilbrun,

Table 7.1 Mental Health Act classification and MCMI patterns of four patient clusters

	SHAPS groups			
	Primary psychopath	*Secondary psychopath*	*Controlled*	*Inhibited*
Mental Health Act Category				
Mental illness	15	17	36	22
Psychopathic disorder	16	12	6	6
Mental illness/psychopathic disorder	0	3	1	2
MCMI high scores	Narcissistic Antisocial Histrionic	Passive–aggressive Avoidant Schizoid Paranoid Antisocial	Compulsive Dependent	Avoidant Schizoid Dependent Schizotypal Passive–aggressive

SHAPS = Special Hospital Assessment of Personality and Socialization; MCMI = Millon Clinical Multiaxial Inventory.

1985). These findings therefore suggest that this empirical typology has some validity in discriminating classes of personality deviation among offenders. They are also consistent with the view that there is no single type of deviant personality which predominates among violent offenders.

We are currently examining some data obtained from a representative sample of 136 patients resident at one special hospital. Cluster analysis of the SHAPS yields the four groups identified previously. Confirming previous findings (Blackburn, 1986), the typology shows some relation to Mental Health Act classification. P and S make up a higher proportion of the psychopathic disorder category, but the same four types are also found among those classified as mentally ill (Table 7.1). We have also looked at the relation of the typology to the current categories of personality disorder, as assessed by the Millon Clinical Multiaxial Inventory (MCMI: Millon, 1983). There are marked differences between the groups on most of the MCMI scales, but of particular interest is the difference between P and S. Both groups meet Millon's criteria for antisocial personality, but where P patients are also narcissistic, S are passive–aggressive, avoidant and paranoid. This provides further support for the view that psychopaths are not a homogeneous group.

Before discussing further research with this sample, I would like to describe a cognitive interpersonal theory which provides a fertile basis for a clinically relevant classification of personality deviation, and which I believe clarifies the relationship of personality disorder to aggression.

A COGNITIVE INTERPERSONAL MODEL OF PERSONALITY DISORDER

Personality disorder and the interpersonal circle

The theory originated in the 1950s with the work of Sullivan (1953) and Leary (1957). Sullivan's social psychiatry was an attempt to integrate psychoanalysis with social psychology. He argued that the traditional focus on the problems of the individual is misplaced, and that we should examine what goes on in a person's interactions. He saw most psychiatric problems as the outcome of early distortions in relationships which are perpetuated into adult life. His views about psychopathology are echoed in attachment theory, and their implications for psychological treatment have been developed more recently by Carson (1979), Kiesler (1983), and Safran (1990). Leary's research extended these ideas to develop an interpersonal theory of personality, which has had a lasting impact on psychology (Wiggins, 1982).

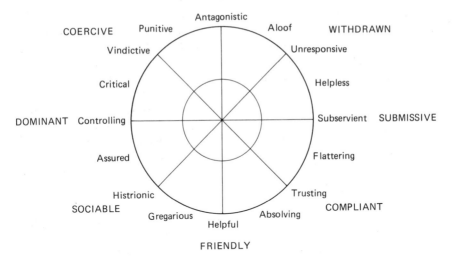

Fig. 7.1 *The interpersonal circle.*

The descriptive scheme resulting from Leary's work is the *interpersonal circle*. Figure 7.1 shows a simplified version of this. When interpersonal behaviours occurring across a sample of interactions are examined, their intercorrelations typically produce a circular array around a two-dimensional space, known mathematically as a circumplex. The two dimensions most commonly defining the space relate first to the degree of power or control in an interaction (dominance versus submission), and second, the degree of affiliation (hostile versus friendly). Most kinds of interaction reflect different blends of these two, which accounts for the circular relationships. Thus, a trusting interaction entails a combination of submission and friendliness; a vindictive interaction a combination of dominance and hostility. Behaviours close to each other around the circle are similar, while those opposite are negatively related.

The two-dimensional space can be defined by any two independent axes without changing the relationships. For example, dimensions of aggression or coercion and withdrawal are alternative ways of defining the space. In fact, dimensions of aggression and withdrawal appear consistently in studies of disturbed behaviour, although the use of different labels has served to obscure similarities. These are the main dimensions appearing in analyses of child behaviour disorders (Achenbach and Edelbrock, 1978) and delinquency (Quay, 1987), and as I have noted, they are the main dimensions emerging from the SHAPS. While some investigators choose to work with the four quadrants of hostile–dominant, friendly–submissive, and so on, some have developed descriptive systems differentiating 32 behaviours. In my current research, I focus on the eight points of dominance, coercion, hostility, etc., as indicated in the outer part of the figure. I prefer the concept of coercion to that of aggression, following Tedeschi (1983), who proposes the alternative notion of *coercive power*, a form of social influence involving the use of threats or punishments to gain compliance. This conception emphasizes the interpersonal context of aggression, and implies that behaviour labelled aggression is reinforced by power and control. It also clarifies the distinctions between aggression, dominance and assertion, which often prove troublesome. All involve influence through the exercise of power, but entail varying degrees of hostility. This is reflected in the interpersonal circle, in which coercion represents a combination of dominance and hostility.

This system now has a firmly established empirical basis (Wiggins, 1982). The elements may be individual acts, emotions or problem behaviours, but the system also applies to the traits of personality, and Leary developed the notion of *interpersonal style*. He suggests that adaptive behaviour requires that people be able to produce behaviour represented at all parts of the circle, according to situational demands, and hence that they have an adequate range of interpersonal skills. However, as a result of early experiences, people will tend to acquire a distinctive style which emphasizes a particular area of the circle, and this is the basis for individual differences. The inner circle of Figure 7.1 represents the normal range. The more a style exceeds this, the narrower is the range of interactions on which the person relies. This follows from the circumplex structure in which segments of the circle are positively associated with adjacent segments, and negatively associated with opposite segments. A person with an extreme dominant style, for example, is someone whose interactions are marked by a high frequency of dominant exchanges. Such a person will also show coercive and sociable characteristics quite often, but submissive, withdrawn or compliant behaviour infrequently. The individual's behaviour will hence be rigid, inflexible and maladaptive.

Leary's notion is consistent with the *DSM-III* concept of personality disorders as inflexible traits. Several workers from Leary onwards have therefore suggested that the interpersonal circle provides a basis for describing personality disorder, and that it could provide an alternative classification (e.g. Widiger and Frances, 1985; Blackburn, 1988; Wiggins and Pincus, 1989). In these terms, the classes of personality disorder would be represented by styles at different parts of the circle. Such a scheme makes it explicit that there is a continuity between normality and abnormality (i.e. from the centre of the circle outwards), and that different styles shade into each other around the circle, rather than being tightly defined categories.

Interpersonal styles in behaviour ratings

We have recently been examining how far interpersonal styles can be detected in the daily behaviour of special hospital patients, as assessed by nurse ratings. We developed a set of items which sample the interpersonal circle (CIRCLE: Chart of Interpersonal Reactions in Closed Living Environments). These are grouped into eight scales to mark the octants around the circle. The circular relationship between the scales in a sample of 210 patients is entirely in accord with the circumplex model, and this instrument therefore provides a means of testing hypotheses derived from interpersonal theory.

One question is the relation of personality disorder categories to interpersonal style. Figure 7.2 shows the relationship of the MCMI measures of personality disorder to the interpersonal circle as defined by dominant and friendly ratings. The figure is a plot of the scales against the first two principal components. The position of most categories is consistent with the interpersonal characteristics inferred from *DSM-III* criteria. It will be noted that the antisocial or aggressive category falls within the coercive segment of the circle, consistent with Millon's concept. One implication of these results is that some of the current categories are so similar to each other as to be redundant, and a smaller number of categories spaced more evenly around the circle would provide a more discriminating system.

In one study of Rampton patients, we found that nurse ratings of Cleckley's criteria of psychopathy fall in the hostile segment of the circle (Blackburn and Maybury, 1985). Using different measures with Canadian prisoners, Hare has also found that his PCL aligns with the coercive axis of the interpersonal circle (Harpur *et al.*, 1989). There is thus some convergence in these results, which suggests that psychopathy may be broadly equated with the coercive–compliant axis of the interpersonal circle.

However, the location of an individual in the circle requires reference to two axes. For example, some coercive individuals will be sociable, but others withdrawn. This is implied by the differentiation of primary and secondary psychopaths on SHAPS data. P, for example, would appear to represent styles falling in the quadrant between coercive and sociable, S between coercion and withdrawal. Figure 7.3 shows the rating scale profiles of the four SHAPS groups in standard score form ($+1.0$ to -1.0), the inner circle representing the mean (0.0) for the total sample. They provide significant support for the assumption that these groups represent distinguishable interpersonal styles. P are characterized by a dominant–sociable style, and score highest on coercion. This pattern coincides with their self-reported extraversion, narcissism and aggressive traits. S, who describe themselves as antisocial but also as avoidant and passive–aggressive, are also coercive, but differ from P in being more submissive and

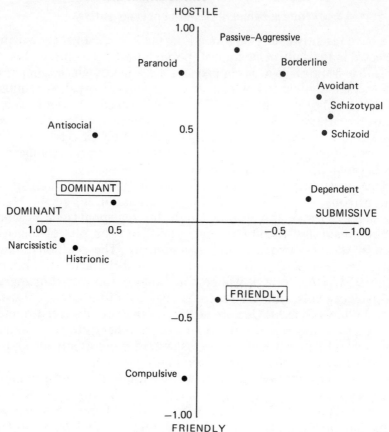

Fig. 7.2   *Relation of Millon Clinical Multiaxial Inventory (MCMI) personality disorder scales to the interpersonal circle.*

Reproduced with permission from Criminal Behaviour and Mental Health. *Vol 2, No. 2.*

withdrawn. The interpersonal characteristics of the C and I groups are also consistent with their self-report patterns.

Interpersonal style, cognition and the persistence of personality disorder

Reference to the interpersonal circle, then, appears to resolve some of the diagnostic dilemmas about psychopathy. Psychopaths may be construed as those showing a more extreme coercive style, but they are not a homogeneous group. There seem to be two groups, differentiated by their interpersonal behaviour and also by the categories of personality disorder into which they fall. A central question is the implications of this differentiation for explanation and treatment.

Current views assume that persisting aggression originates primar-

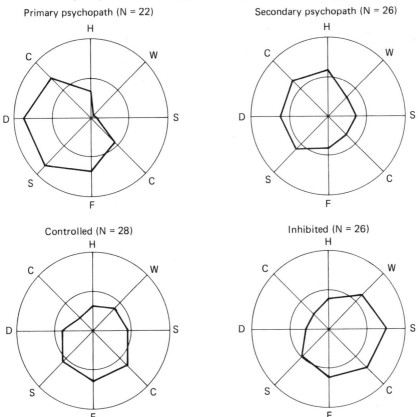

Fig. 7.3 *Profiles of four patient groups on Chart of Interpersonal Reactions in Closed Living Environments (CIRCLE) ratings of interpersonal style.*

ily in family modelling and reinforcement. The assumption that aggression becomes more likely following the experience of successful aggression or observation of aggressive models is now well-established by experimental and observational studies, such as the work of Patterson (1982). Longitudinal studies such as those of Huesmann *et al.* (1984) also show that family histories of aggressive children and delinquents are characterized by higher rates of parental deviance, marital conflict, parental indifference and lack of supervision, and violent adults frequently report a history of witnessing violence and experiencing physical abuse in childhood.

However, exposure to such conditions is not sufficient to account for the perpetuation of an aggressive style of interaction across the life-course. Social cognitive analyses provide the basis for recent attempts to account for consistency. Caspi *et al.* (1989) found that children who exhibited explosive tempers in childhood were judged more undercontrolled and irritable 20 years later, and had shown a life-course pattern of educational, occupational and marital failure consistent with a recurring maladaptive coercive style. They identify two forms of person–environment interaction which promote continuity. *Cumulative continuity* arises when a person's disposition leads to the selection of environments which sustain the disposition. For example, dropping out of school because of poorly controlled temper may restrict career options to frustrating occupational roles which evoke further patterns of ill-tempered behaviour. In *interactional continuity* the immediate and recurring consequences of coercive exchanges short-circuit the learning of more controlled forms of interaction. This can be understood in terms of expectancy confirmation processes, and Carson (1979) has developed a theory of social exchange which proposes a causal relation between expectancies, interpersonal style and the behaviour of others.

According to interpersonal theory, a particular behaviour 'pulls' a reaction from the other person, within a limited range of possibilities, and this is governed by principles of *complementarity* (Kiesler, 1983). Along the dominance–submission axis, this is held to be reciprocal, i.e. a dominant response pulls a submissive reaction, while along the hostile–friendly axis, the relation is corresponding or congruent, i.e. a hostile response invites a hostile reaction, and a friendly overture elicits a friendly reaction. These will be combined for different behaviours around the circle. For example, hostile–dominant · behaviour is likely to elicit a hostile–submissive reaction. The effect of a rigid interpersonal style will be for the person to produce many anticomplementary reactions which are aversive to other people.

Carson (1979) attempts to account for how people elicit and construe signals coming from each other. He assumes that people have a need for cognitive congruence or the avoidance of dissonance, and that this is maintained by eliciting behaviour from the other which accords with the concept of the self and one's role in the interaction. As he puts it: 'The overriding goal of most persons in their social relations seems to be very much a matter of maintaining their selves as going concerns'. A particular overture involves verbal and non-verbal behaviour which sends a message about the relationship, not necessarily at a conscious level. It invites a complementary response from the other which, if forthcoming, provides feedback confirming the relationship. In this way, people engage in negotiated self-confirmation in their interactions.

This analysis is extended to rigid interpersonal styles. Early interactions create expectations of how others are likely to react to oneself, and these expectations subsequently become self-fulfilling prophecies. Behaviour is directed to others to elicit a complementary reaction which then confirms the expectations. Thus, a hostile person expects hostile reactions from others and behaves in a way which gets them. People with strong expectations are thus likely to create interactions which minimize the chance of disconfirming experiences. Thus, the competitive style of the aggressive and narcissistic personality will reflect expectations of hostile–submission, and a relative lack of skills for eliciting friendly–dominant or friendly–submissive responses. Such expectations are likely to come about as a consequence of deficits in certain kinds of experience.

The notion of the self-fulfilling prophecy, namely that people behave in ways which fulfil our expectations of them, now has substantial support in social psychology (Jones, 1986). There is some related work with aggressive children by Dodge and his colleagues (Dodge, 1986), which suggests that hyperaggressive boys have an attributional bias to interpret non-hostile behaviour as hostile, and that such boys are more likely to be rejected by their peers. On the basis of our findings that primary and secondary psychopaths describe high levels of anger, Lee-Evans and I suggested that these patients might also be characterized by biased expectations of malevolent intent in others (Blackburn and Lee-Evans, 1985). However, principles of complementarity suggest that interpersonal styles distinguished along the dominance–submission axis are supported by opposite expectations, i.e. dominant people should expect others to be submissive. It would therefore be anticipated that primary and secondary psychopaths would have different patterns of expectations.

To test this hypothesis, we have used a simple measure of social expectations. This asks patients to indicate how often they expect other people to avoid them, criticize them, behave in a hostile way, be sympathetic, and so on, the selection of the 32 items being guided by the interpersonal circle. There are three factors in the data which reflect expectations that others are likely to be challenging (argue, wind you up, be sarcastic), attentive (friendly, sincere, confide), and yielding (do things your way, be fearful, admit you are right). There are significant differences ($P < 0.001$) between the four SHAPS groups on these factors (Table 7.2). Secondary psychopaths expect others to challenge them and not to be friendly or attentive. Primary psychopaths, in contrast, do not expect others to be challenging, but expect attentive interactions, and also expect others to be more yielding, in line with the principles of complementarity. Controlled and withdrawn patients do not expect challenge or attention. The data appear encouraging for the theory.

The interpersonal model has clear implications for treatment. To the extent that aggressive offenders create the conditions for violent acts by an interpersonal style which is supported by distorted expectations, the target for change is the individual's dysfunctional belief system. This is the goal of cognitive therapies developed by Ellis (1977) and Beck and Freeman (1990), but several North American therapists, notably Kiesler (1983) and Safran (1990), are currently exploring procedures guided explicitly by interpersonal theory. Dif-

Table 7.2   Standard scores of four patient clusters on social expectations factors

	Expectations of others		
	Challenging	Attentive	Yielding
Primary psychopath	−0.206	0.721	0.311
Secondary psychopath	0.861	−0.088	0.079
Controlled	−0.477	−0.186	−0·278
Inhibited	−0.108	−0.175	−0.039

ferentiating personality disorders within aggressive offenders may help to structure the therapeutic conditions necessary to change their maladaptive styles of interaction.

REFERENCES

Achenbach T. M., Edelbrock C. S. (1978). The classification of child psychopathology: a review and analysis. *Psychological Bulletin*: **85**: 1275–1301.

American Psychiatric Association (1987). *Diagnostic and Statistical Manual of Mental Disorders*, 3rd edn (revised). Washington, DC: American Psychiatric Association.

Beck A. T., Freeman A. (1990). *Cognitive Therapy of Personality Disorders*. New York: Guilford.

Blackburn R. (1968). Personality in relation to extreme aggression in psychiatric offenders. *British Journal of Psychiatry*; **114**: 821–8.

Blackburn R. (1971). Personality types among abnormal homicides. *British Journal of Criminology*; **11**: 14–31.

Blackburn R. (1975). An empirical classification of psychopathic personality. *British Journal of Psychiatry*; **127**: 456–60.

Blackburn R. (1982a). *The Special Hospitals Assessment of Personality and Socialisation*. Unpublished manuscript, Park Lane Hospital, Liverpool.

Blackburn R. (1982b). On the relevance of the concept of the psychopath. In: *Issues in Criminological and Legal Psychology*, no. 2 (Black D. A., ed.). Leicester: British Psychological Society.

Blackburn R. (1984). The person and dangerousness. In *Psychology and Law*. (Müller D. J., Blackman D. E., Chapman A. J., eds). Chichester: Wiley.

Blackburn R. (1986). Patterns of personality deviation among violent offenders: replication and extension of an empirical taxonomy. *British Journal of Criminology*: **26**: 254–69.

Blackburn R. (1988). On moral judgements and personality disorders: the myth of the psychopathic personality revisited. *British Journal of Psychiatry*; **153**: 505–12.

Blackburn R., Lee-Evans J. M. (1985). Reactions of primary and secondary psychopaths to anger evoking situations. *British Journal of Clinical Psychology*; **24**: 93–100.

Blackburn R., Maybury C. (1985). Identifying the psychopath: the relation of Cleckley's criteria to the interpersonal domain. *Personality and Individual Differences*; **6**: 375–86.

Block R. (1977). *Violent Crime*. Lexington, MA: Lexington Books.

Carson R. C. (1979). Personality and exchange in developing relationships. In: *Social Exchange in Developing Relationships* (Burgess R. L., Huston T. L., eds). New York: Academic Press.

Caspi A., Bem D. J., Elder G. H. (1989). Continuities and consequences of interactional styles across the life course. *Journal of Personality*; **57**: 375–406.

Cleckley H. (1976). *The Mask of Sanity*, 6th edn. St Louis: Mosby.

Dodge K. A. (1986). A social-information processing model of social competence in children. In *Minnesota Symposium on Child Psychology*. (M. Perlmutter, ed.). Hillsdale, N. J: Erlbaum.

Ellis A. (1977). The basic clinical theory of rational–emotive therapy. In *Handbook of Rational–Emotive Therapy*, (Ellis A., Erieger R., eds). New York: Springer.

Gordon R. A. (1977). A critique of the evaluation of Patuxent Institution, with particular attention to the issues of dangerousness and recidivism. *Bulletin of the American Academy of Psychiatry and the Law*; **5**: 210–55.

Hare R. D. (1985). A comparison of procedures for the assessment of psychopathy. *Journal of Consulting and Clinical Psychology*; **53**: 7–16.

Hare R. D., McPherson L. M. (1984). Violent and aggressive behaviour by criminal psychopaths. *International Journal of Law and Psychiatry*; **7**: 35–50.

Harpur T. J., Hare R. D., Hakstian A. R. (1989). Two-factor conceptualisation of psychopathy: construct validity and assessment implications. *Psychological Assessment: A Journal of Consulting and Clinical Psychology*; **1**: 6–17.

Heilbrun A. B., Heilbrun M. R. (1985). Psychopathy and dangerousness: comparison, integration, and extension of two psychopathic typologies. *British Journal of Clinical Psychology*; **24**: 181–95.

Henderson M. (1982). An empirical classification of convicted violent offenders. *British Journal of Criminology*; **22**: 1–20.

Home Office Department of Health and Social Security (1975). *Report of the Committee on Abnormal Offenders*. London: HMSO.

Huesmann L. R., Eron L. D., Lefkowitz M. M., Walder L. O. (1984). Stability of aggression over time and generations. *Developmental Psychology*; **20**: 1120–34.

Jones E. E. (1986). Interpreting interpersonal behavior: the effects of expectancies. *Science*; **234**: 41–6.

Kiesler D. J. (1983). The 1982 interpersonal circle: a taxonomy for complementarity in human transactions. *Psychological Review*; **90**: 185–214.

Leary T. (1957). *Interpersonal Diagnosis of Personality*. New York: Ronald Press.

McCord W. M., McCord J. (1964). *The Psychopath: An Essay on The Criminal Mind*. New York: Van Nostrand.

McGurk B. J. (1978). Personality types among normal homicides. *British Journal of Criminology*; **18**: 146–61.

McGurk B. J., McGurk R. E. (1979). Personality types among prisoners and prison officers. *British Journal of Criminology*; **19**: 31–49.

Megargee E. I. (1966). Undercontrolled and overcontrolled personality types in extreme antisocial aggression. *Psychological Monographs*. **80**: no. 611.

Millon T. (1981). *Disorders of Personality: DSM-III, Axis II*. New York: Wiley.

Millon T. (1983). *Millon Clinical Multiaxial Inventory*, 3rd ed. Minneapolis: Interpretive Scoring Systems.

Patterson G. R. (1982). *Coercive Family Process*. Eugene, OR: Castalia.

Pichot P. (1978). Psychopathic behaviour: a historical overview. In *Psychopathic Behaviour: Approaches to Research* (Hare R. D., Schalling D., eds). Chichester: Wiley.

Quay H. C. (1987). Patterns of delinquent behavior. In *Handbook of Juvenile Delinquency* (Quay H. C., ed.). New York: Wiley.

Safran J. D. (1990). Toward a refinement of cognitive therapy in light of interpersonal theory. *Clinical Psychology Review*; **10**: 85–107.

Schneider K. (1950). *Psychopathic Personalities*, 9th ed. London: Cassell.

Sullivan H. S. (1953). *The Interpersonal Theory of Psychiatry*. New York: Norton.

Tedeschi J. T. (1983). Social influence theory and aggression. In *Aggression: Theoretical and Empirical Reviews*, Vol. 1. (Geen R. G., Donnerstein E. I., eds). New York: Academic Press.

Widiger T. A., Frances A. (1985). The DSM-III personality disorders: perspectives from psychology. *Archives of General Psychiatry*; **42**: 615–23.

Wiggins J. S. (1982). Circumplex models of interpersonal behaviour in clinical psychology. In Kendall P. C., Butcher J. N., (eds). *Handbook of Research Methods in Clinical Psychology*, New York: Wiley.

Wiggins J. S., Pincus A. L. (1989). Conceptions of personality disorders and dimensions of personality. *Psychological Assessment: A Journal of Consulting and Clinical Psychology*; **1**: 305–16.

Zillmann D. (1979). *Hostility and Aggression*. Hillsdale, NJ: Erlbaum.

8 Violence and psychosis

SIMON WESSELY

INTRODUCTION

It is well-known that some mentally ill people are capable of extreme violence. However, how often mental illness and violence occur together, and for what reasons, remains a surprisingly controversial subject. It has been argued that the mentally ill are less violent, as violent, or more violent than the rest of us, and evidence can be found to support all three propositions (Taylor, 1982).

Before proceeding further, it is important to define the area of interest. Mental illness is a term that cannot be precisely defined, and is, indeed, explicitly undefined in the Mental Health Acts. Fortunately, this paper covers a rather narrower field, that of psychosis. This is perhaps a less precise term than we might care to admit, but nevertheless, the major psychoses can at least be diagnosed with sufficient reliability to permit comparisons between studies. The rest of this chapter will be restricted to psychosis in general, and usually the schizophrenic psychoses in particular.

Considerable differences exist in the perception of the risk posed by the mentally ill. Monahan (1992) has highlighted the differences between the public perception of the dangerous lunatic, and the professional consensus of the lack of dangerousness of the mentally ill. Many have remarked on the tendency of the media to emphasize the links between mental illness and violence. A recent example was a series of dramatic stories concerning the murderous exploits of a Texas mental hospital patient. In a series of stories attracting such headlines as 'Ex mental patient tells police he's killed 100 women', few journalists pointed out that the person in question had been hospitalized for 23 years before the current offences (Shain and Phillips, 1991). Given this preoccupation, it is perhaps both surprising and gratifying that it is still only a minority, albeit a substantial one, of the British public that believes that the mentally ill are likely to be violent (Appleby and Wessely, 1988).

In contrast to the public perception, the professional consensus usually holds that the mentally ill are no more likely to be violent than the rest of us. This view, which for a considerable period of time was held by perhaps the majority of those professionals and academics

Table 8.1 Influence of prior arrest record on subsequent offending

Author	Odds ratios	95% confidence interval
Payne *et al.* (1974)*	11.1	4.8–25.8
Durbin *et al.* (1977)	9.0	3.0–27.5
Steadman *et al.* (1978)	13.0	9.0–18.8
Soskowsky (1980)	4.0	2.4–6.6
Shore *et al.* (1989)*	3.6	2.0–6.2

*Schizophrenic only.
From Wessely and Taylor (1991).

writing on this subject, states that crime and/or violence committed by the mentally ill is associated with the same factors that determine crime or violence in the non-mentally ill, namely low social class, poverty, being male, alcohol and so on. Any reported increase in violent behaviour in samples of the mentally ill was assumed to be the result of an excess of one or more of these variables – i.e. confounding. Pamela Taylor and I have labelled this the criminological view (Wessely and Taylor, 1991). This position does have a substantial amount of evidence in its favour. I shall look at just some of the evidence, which is reviewed in greater detail elsewhere (Monahan and Steadman, 1983; Wessely and Taylor, 1991).

There is no doubt that many of the variables implicated in 'normal' offending are also important in determining the risk of offending in the mentally abnormal. It is beyond dispute that once any offending career begins, one of the best predictors of subsequent offending is previous offending (West and Farrington, 1973). Exactly the same can be found with respect to offending and psychosis. One of the strongest associations of reoffending by the mentally ill is the existence of previous offending behaviour (Walker and McCabe, 1973; Steadman *et al.*, 1978; Gibbens and Robertson, 1983). Several studies give sufficient data to enable calculation of the effect of a prior criminal record on subsequent offending. This is achieved by use of the odds ratio, which indicates the magnitude of any increase in the risk of subsequent offending associated with possessing a preadmission arrest record (Table 8.1). The strength of the association is clear.

There is also evidence that the greater the number of previous convictions, the greater the probability of reconviction – a dose–response curve (Steadman *et al.*, 1978; Klassen and O'Connor, 1988). This relationship is of considerable importance; for example, the work of Steadman and colleagues in the USA has demonstrated that one reason for the apparent increase in the risk of criminal behaviour by patients discharged from state mental institutions that has occurred over the last 30 years (see Rabkin, 1979) is a change in the input to the mental health system. They have shown that the proportion of patients possessing a prior arrest record has increased over time. In 1947 15% of men released from mental hospitals had a prior arrest record, but by 1968 this had risen to 32%. The change in the rate of criminality in mental patients is thus explained by confounding, since prior offending is strongly associated with subsequent offending, and now is also associated with mental hospital admission.

Further support for the criminological position comes from the Baxstrom studies (Steadman and Keveles, 1972). These serendipitous investigations began when the state of New York was forced abruptly to discharge 967 patients detained because of continuing alleged dangerousness. From a series of follow-up studies Cocozza and Steadman (1974) developed variables that predicted those who offended again, and these were previous violent convictions, juvenile convictions, number of previous offences, severity of initial offence and being under 50. It will be clear that these are similar to those variables identified in 'normal' criminals.

The work of Guze and his colleagues is also frequently cited in support of the lack of relationship between psychosis and violence. After a series of cross-sectional and follow-up studies on convicted criminals they concluded that 'sociopathy, alcoholism and drug addiction were the only psychiatric disorders found more frequently among the index subjects [felons] than in the general population' (Guze *et al.*, 1969). They reached the same conclusions after studies of the criminal histories of patients in mental hospitals (Guze *et al.*, 1974).

Thus Monahan and Steadman (1983) concluded: 'There is no consistent evidence that the true prevalence rate of criminal behaviour among former mental patients exceeds the true prevalence rate of criminal behaviour among the general population matched for demographic factors and prior criminal history'.

THE ROLE OF SELECTION BIAS

Such conclusions as outlined above are frequently cited, but are they true, and if so, how generalizable are they? A crucial question concerns sample. For example, how relevant are studies of the psychiatric health of prisoners? It is easy to believe that the prisons are filling up with psychiatric patients. However, this is far from the case, and in fact the filter preventing those with major mental illness, or at least psychosis, from joining the sentenced population is partially effective, if extremely inefficient (Gunn *et al.*, 1991). Although this is a desirable objective from the perspective of public policy and humane care, it does create some epidemiological problems. We are, of course, relieved that the police dislike prosecuting, the courts convicting, and the prisons housing the mentally ill, but should thus be cautious about drawing general conclusions from any official statistics of offending, or indeed studies of mental abnormalities among those with criminal labels, i.e. prisoners. Guze's studies may thus only mean that the filter system operated by the local criminal justice system was reasonably effective.

Thus studies of sentenced prisoners are subject to a powerful selection bias. One American study found that released psychiatric patients who became violent in the community were twice as likely to be returned to hospital as arrested (Klassen and O'Connor, 1988), and similar trends have been noted in the UK (MacKay and Wight, 1984). An earlier study reported that although 18% of those newly admitted to a psychiatric hospital had been violent before admission, only 1% were arrested (Lagos *et al.*, 1977). The Northwick Park studies of first-episode schizophrenia (Johnstone *et al.*, 1986) found that 94 (37%) had been violent in the previous month. Fifty-five (22%) had police contact between the onset of illness and admission (MacMillan and Johnson, 1987), but only 23 had been dealt with by the courts. Of these, 12 received orders under Section 60 of the 1959 Mental Health Act, and thus should not have acquired a criminal record, leaving only 11 with a formal conviction.

This filtering begins at an early stage. Robertson (1988) found that schizophrenic offenders were more likely to be arrested at the scene of the crime, to give themselves up, or to be arrested by uniformed officers, all suggesting they are easier to detect than their non-psychotic criminal counterparts. This has been rather uncharitably labelled the 'turkey' effect. Teplin (1985) claims the police are more likely to arrest disordered rather than non-disordered offenders, although these conclusions are not universally accepted.

The conclusion is that the majority of violent or criminal acts committed by those with psychosis goes unrecorded. This 'information bias' is not random and, like all selection biases, introduces a systematic bias to all studies that are not population-based.

FURTHER PROBLEMS

There are also a number of other methodological problems in the literature on violence and psychosis. Just as once one has been labelled as mentally ill, much further antisocial behaviour is dealt with within the medical system, a similar but reverse process operates once one has acquired a criminal label (Landau, 1981). Another substantial problem is that of confounding – a factor which is associated with both being psychotic and also offending. One example is that of alcohol or drug abuse. Schizophrenia can be associated with both drug and alcohol abuse, known in the current jargon as comorbidity.

Many studies recognize this and now routinely adjust, using a variety of complex, and often overcomplex, statistical techniques. Other factors that are routinely controlled for include low social class, unemployment, ethnic background and so on. However, new advances in the epidemiology of schizophrenia have cast doubt on such procedures, since social class, urban birth and ethnicity may also be risk factors for psychosis. Similarly, increased understanding of the neurodevelopmental basis of schizophrenia (Murray *et al.*, 1988) reminds us that premorbid features such as petty criminality and antisocial behaviour may be intimately linked with the disease process. For all these reasons unthinking adjustment may hide the effect of interest. Farrington has frequently warned that it may be statistically inappropriate to attempt to control for variables that are intimately related to each other – the problem of multicolinearity (Farrington, 1988). Overzealous attempts to adjust for all known associations of criminal and/or violent behaviour may hide associations of interest. These and other methodological problems are addressed in more detail elsewhere (see Rabkin, 1979; Farrington, 1988; Wessely and Taylor, 1991).

THE PSYCHIATRIC VIEW

If there is a substantial literature in favour of the criminological position, there is also a smaller literature stating the opposite – that there is a definite association between psychosis and violence. Pamela Taylor and I have labelled this the psychiatric view (Wessely and Taylor, 1991). First, there exists a substantial literature on the relationship between diagnosis and violence, of which some supports an association between violence and psychosis. For example, Tardiff and colleagues have found an association between schizophrenia and violent behaviour, either before or during hospital admission (Tardiff and Sweillam, 1980, 1982) but, interestingly, not in psychiatric outpatients (Tardiff and Koenigsberg, 1985), again highlighting the problem of selection bias that prevents generalization from hospital inpatient studies.

High rates of violent behaviour before admission to hospital are confirmed by two studies already cited, one from the USA (Lagos *et al.*, 1977), the other from the UK (Johnstone *et al.*, 1986). Indeed, Levine (1970) reported that a local attorney judged that the behaviour of 70% of the admissions to a US state hospital had violated the law. Numerous studies attest to the unacceptably high rates of violence in psychiatric facilities, many of which find schizophrenics to be over-represented among the violent sample (Pearson *et al.*, 1986; Karson and Bigelow, 1987). Violent behaviour occurring in the context of acute hospitalization often is accompanied by 'positive' symptoms of psychosis, and decreases after adequate medication (Yesavage, 1984; Volavka and Krakowski, 1989). The issues posed by such behaviour are addressed in Chapter 9.

These and other studies suggest that not only is violence both prior and during admission common, it is also particularly associated with diagnoses of schizophrenia. What is the picture in the criminal justice setting?

We have seen how Guze and colleagues concluded from studies of convicted prisoners that schizophrenia occurred no more often in such samples than would be expected by chance. A recent UK survey also confirmed that psychosis remained unusual in sentenced prisoners (Gunn *et al.*, 1991). However, this may be misleading. The impression that the courts do indeed act as a reasonably effective filter, at least as far as psychosis is concerned, led Taylor to begin a series of studies of remanded prisoners at Brixton jail, a sample that is by definition pretrial (Taylor and Gunn, 1984). Here a different picture emerged. Of those remanded, 9% showed symptoms of psychosis, the majority of schizophrenia. In particular, those with schizophrenia were substantially over-represented among those charged with homicide (11%). This last figure is of particular concern, since homicide is the crime with the greatest clear-up rate, and for which offenders are almost invariably remanded in custody. Those charged with homicide are probably a representative sample of all those charged with murder, and the figure of 11% may not be subject to substantial bias. A similar figure for schizophrenic murderers was reported from California (Wilcox, 1985), whilst the figures provided by Hafner and Boker (1982) suggest that 6.8% of the male killers in West Germany were schizophrenic.

Mentally ill offenders differ demographically from their mentally normal counterparts. Surveys of mentally abnormal offenders show them to be older, and to have begun their offending careers later. Gibbens and Robertson (1983) have demonstrated that patients detained in English mental hospitals under the criminal provisions of the Mental Health Act began their offending later than normal. The mean age of first conviction of the male mentally ill patients was 27 (compared to 19 for the personality-disordered patients), and was 33 for the females (Robertson, unpublished data). In a Danish study of psychiatric referrals of those accused of murder, psychotic defendants were older than non-psychotic non-psychotic defendants (Gottlieb *et al.*, 1987), whilst there was an 8-year difference between the mean age of the mentally disordered and non-disordered offenders in a large West German survey (Hafner and Boker, 1982). A Canadian study of police arrests found that the only variable separating those identified by the police as mentally ill from those seen as 'normal' was that the former were older (Arboleda-Florez and Holley, 1988).

However, just as the literature supporting the criminological position has limitations, the opposite psychiatric position can also not be accepted uncritically. Many of the studies that conclude that no association exists between violence and psychosis contain serious flaws. Many studies that show how many violent incidents in psychiatric hospitals are perpetrated by those with schizophrenia do not give the proportion of schizophrenics in the hospital. Hospital-based studies have the flaw that violence and disturbed behaviour is perhaps the single most important reason for hospital admission, particularly in the current climate favouring community care. Thus all hospital samples are biased towards the disturbed and violent. Nevertheless, even in a community survey of 364 patients with schizophrenia in Southampton, 49% had shown harmful behaviour during a single month (Gibbons *et al.*, 1984).

THE SECOND GENERATION OF STUDIES

It appears that arguments both for and against a relationship between violence and psychosis may be based on inadequate data. However, in recent years researchers became more aware of these limitations, and a new generation of studies is starting to appear. These new studies conform to one of two types: cohort studies ('criminal careers') and population-based studies. I shall provide one example of each to illustrate how such research challenges the conventional wisdom outlined at the beginning of this chapter. Lindquist and Allebeck (1990) published the criminal careers of a cohort of 644 schizophrenics discharged from Stockholm mental hospitals in 1971 and still alive in 1985. The sample was based on a case register, and thus contained all the schizophrenics from that area discharged during a single year. The analysis was by indirect standardization, using the age- and sex-specific Swedish crime rates to compare observed and expected number of offences. Looking at all offending, there were no more convictions than expected in the male schizophrenics, but there was a substantial increase in risk across the sexes. Although standardized criteria were not used, it is, however, likely that the sample corresponded to what we would also label schizophrenia. However, although based on a case register, by using only hospital discharges important potential biases remain. For example, schizophrenics with either single mild illnesses, or perhaps strong social networks, may never have been admitted to hospital. As they may represent a group at low risk of offending such a selection bias may have important effects. The use of national statistics can also be questioned. A controlled study of the criminal careers of schizophrenics in Camberwell is nearing completion, and may answer some of these outstanding questions. It is already clear that the principal findings of Lindquist and Allebeck will be replicated in this comprehensive sample.

Table 8.2 Prevalence of violence during the past year in ECA sample, by diagnosis

Diagnosis	% Violent
No diagnosis	2.1
Schizophrenia	12.7
Major depression	11.7
Mania or bipolar	11.0
Alcohol abuse/dependence	24.6
Drug abuse/dependence	34.7

From Swanson *et al.* (1990), with permission.

Lindquist and Allebeck reported an important population-based longitudinal study of crime and schizophrenia. A different perspective comes from a new cross-sectional community study of violence and schizophrenia. This arose from the Epidemiologic Catchment Area (ECA) Program, the most complex and expensive piece of psychiatric epidemiology ever undertaken, involving direct interviews of a representative stratified sample of the population of the USA. One of the aims of the study was to determine the prevalence of antisocial personality disorder. Five questions were therefore included about violent behaviour, such as hitting a partner, being in fights and using a weapon. A secondary analysis of these data was published by Swanson and colleagues (1990). The questions chosen are, of course, crude. However, the results presented by Swanson and colleagues conformed to the known demographic correlations of violence, suggesting at least some validity. As one might expect, they confirmed the strong relationship with substance abuse. However, not only was there evidence of a substantial interaction between psychosis and substance abuse and the risk of violence, they also showed an independent and robust association between violence and all the major psychoses (Table 8.2).

A second community study confirms this. One of the doyens of psychiatric epidemiology, Link *et al.* (1992) conducted a population-based study in New York using the psychiatric epidemiology research interview. Link and his colleagues analysed some of the results, and compared the rates of arrest and self-reported violence between community controls and other samples of former psychiatric patients. The patient group were always more violent than the community controls. This difference persisted even when a vast number of adjustments, for example, sex, class, alcohol, ethnicity, social support and so on, were made, but was eliminated when adjusted for current psychotic symptomatology. After that there were no differences between cases and controls. It appears that the excess risk of violence in the cases was explained by their current psychotic experiences.

VIOLENCE AND PSYCHOSIS: POSSIBLE MECHANISMS

We, and others, concluded that there is now considerable evidence for a relationship between psychosis and violence (Wessely and Taylor, 1991; Monahan, 1992), although, as others have noted, it may not be a strong one (Walker, 1987; see below). If there is such an association, what are the possible mechanisms?

Clearly, as the sociological literature demonstrates, a substantial part of the link will be via joint risk factors, such as social deprivation, neurological impairment etc. However, the evidence reviewed above suggests that at least part of the association is mediated by the experience of mental illness itself.

Some indirect evidence in support of this comes from other sources. For a long time the term paranoid schizophrenia was reserved for a subtype of psychosis characterized by a predominantly delusional presentation. Less attention is now given to such classic subtypes of schizophrenia, because of lack of convincing evidence of substantial genetic, prognostic or treatment differences between them. However, of relevance to the current discussion is the trend for an association with paranoid schizophrenia, especially during the period shortly before or after admission to hospital (Krakowski *et al.*, 1986; Taylor *et al.*, 1992).

Even less attention is paid to the old category of paranoia, now resurfacing as delusional disorder, but evidence is again accumulating that this – fortunately unusual – condition conveys a particular risk of violent behaviour. Other unusual but potentially dangerous delusional syndromes include morbid jealousy, erotomania and the misidentification syndromes (Taylor *et al.*, 1992).

Further detail comes from Taylor's studies of remand prisoners at Brixton Prison (Taylor and Gunn, 1984; Taylor, 1985). She used direct interviews shortly after remand, and independent of the legal process, thus making them less liable to bias than the usual court report. Overall, only 9 of the 121 were sympton-free when they offended. Turning to the role of delusions, 23 of the 121 psychotic offenders were judged to have definite, and a further 29 to have probable, delusional motivation (Taylor, 1985). When the group was divided according to delusional or non-delusional motivation, those whose offences were judged to be the result of delusions were older, had higher scores on a standard measure of psychopathology, and had shown more serious violence. Such findings are not in keeping with the view that 'illness related crimes are infrequent' (Guze, 1976), but instead confirm the findings of a number of older, less systematic studies of the motives of mentally abnormal offenders in high-security hospitals (Gibbens, 1958, Lanzkron, 1963). Nevertheless, one must emphasize that although those offenders judged to have delusional motivations had committed more serious offences, the typical schizophrenic remanded in custody is usually accused of offences such as minor assaults against the police, criminal damage or rather sad thefts such as stealing milk from doorsteps (Coid, 1988).

Why might delusions be associated with violence? Clearly, there are occasions when the content of the delusion specifies the nature of the violent offence, for example, when a paranoid individual turns on his or her alleged persecutors. However, somewhat surprisingly, neither Taylor (1985) nor Hafner and Boker (1982) found a significant association between persecutory delusions and violent behaviour in their samples of violent men. Instead, both concluded that passivity delusions were more associated with risk. Hafner and Boker reported that both delusions of physical influence and bodily hallucinations were associated with an increased risk of violence, and concluded that 'when a systematic delusion of persecution is accompanied by the experience of danger or threats to life, then this apparently constitutes a real risk of violence by schizophrenic offenders'. It remains unclear as to whether the delusion is an elaboration of a primary perceptual abnormality, or whether the abnormal perception provides confirmation of the correctness of a prior delusional intuition, but it is plausible to assume that specific risk results when the erroneous explanation incorporates another person.

Hafner and Boker noted a further factor – the violent offenders did not withdraw from social relationships, unlike their non-violent controls. Similarly, in the Brixton Prison studies reviewed above there was an association between severe delusional violence and the presence of a partner. The relationship between intimacy and psychotic violence, and its links to the expressed emotion literature, remains an area worthy of study, but there is sufficient to suggest that distancing, both physical and emotional, may be a protective response by many with chronic psychosis.

We have argued that among the phenomenological features of schizophrenia, delusions are those most associated with violent behaviour (Taylor et al., 1992). Of course, psychosis in general, and schizophrenia in particular, has many other characteristics that can be associated with violence. These include other distorted thought processes, hallucinations, disordered emotions such as anger, profound anxiety and so on. These are discussed in greater detail elsewhere (Arieti, 1974; Tidmarsh, 1990). The role of personality and violence is beyond the scope of this chapter, but the often deleterious influence of schizophrenia on personality must not be forgotten – an observation that casts doubt on the often tedious dissection of the relative contributions of illness and personality ('mad or bad') that can dominate medicolegal argument.

DURATION AND GENERALIZABILITY

Delusional violence does not occur early in the course of a psychotic illness – in the West German study of all mentally abnormal offenders only 16% had been ill for less than a year at the time of the offence, and 55% had been ill for at least 5 years (Hafner and Boker, 1982). Mowat (1966) found that the mean duration of delusional jealousy prior to killing was 4.5 years. However, Planansky and Johnston (1977), reporting a general hospital sample, found that the majority of the violent men did so during their first illness episode.

Why the discrepancy? Once again this may be related to sample differences. Aitken (1984) recorded 41 assaults on an acute admission ward. Of these only 5 appeared to be determined by delusions, the rest resulting from the circumstances surrounding compulsory admission, such as requests to leave the ward, or arguments over medication. This is in contrast to the studies of offences leading to admission to a high-security hospital, in which delusions play a far more important role.

Both the studies of Taylor and those from West Germany were of a violent sample. How generalizable are these findings? Delusions remain the commonest symptoms of psychosis. However, relatively little attention has been paid to how frequently deluded patients act upon their abnormal beliefs. Most textbooks state this is a rare occurrence (see Wessely *et al.* in press). However, we recently studied the frequency of such behaviour in a sample of subjects with delusions and psychosis admitted to the Maudsley Hospital, and found that the prevalence of acting on delusions, either by self-report or noticed by a relative, was far from low. Over half had either probably or definitely acted in accordance with at least one delusional belief in the month before they came into hospital. Thus delusional behaviour is far more common than previously suspected. However, we were unable to find a significant association between delusional behaviour and violence, and most delusional behaviour was not by itself of an antisocial nature.

CONCLUSIONS

Can one synthesize the above evidence? Accepting that any generalization is both simplistic and imperfect, the literature suggests that violence occurring early in a psychotic illness is often the result of acute behavioural disturbance manifested in a variety of ways. Such violence is also frequently situational, and directed at those attempting to control the subject, such as the police and ward staff. However, severe violence, that may be of homicidal intensity, may have different characteristics. It occurs later in the illness. It may be the result of chronic delusions, especially when these incorporate someone with whom the subject is in close and regular contact.

Many will disagree with this conclusion, and it is still possible to use the literature on crime, violence and psychosis to make whatever point one wished concerning the relationship, or the lack of relationship, between these variables. Some of these opposing viewpoints are the consequence of the tendency to draw firm conclusions from a frequently methodologically suspect literature. However, it must also be conceded that both apparently opposite conclusions may be valid. Criminologists and sociologists, who are rarely clinicians, tend to concentrate on larger population samples, and to make extensive use of criminological statistics. Psychiatrists, on the other hand, are less interested in the experiences of populations and cohorts, are less statistically sophisticated, but are more interested in the practical problems of violence on their wards or in their clinics. They are often more concerned on the individual level with perhaps only small numbers of disturbed patients. Thus the broad criminological literature tends to report crime, the narrower psychiatric literature violence. These are two very different constructs, and the opposing conclusions perhaps reflect these perspectives.

THE PUBLIC HEALTH PERSPECTIVE

Even if violence and psychosis are associated, how important is this? The data provided by Swanson *et al.* (1990) permit one further calculation. The relative risk of violence associated with schizophrenia was about 4, a substantial excess. However, because the study is population-based, it is also possible to calculate the population-attributable risk, which is 3%. One way for understanding this figure is to say that if schizophrenia were abolished, the amount of violent behaviour in the community would decrease by only 3%.

Thus one concludes that most psychotic patients are neither criminal nor violent. Most criminals are not psychotic. The general public has little to fear from those with psychosis. However, little does not mean nothing, and there appears to be a consistent relationship between psychosis and offending behaviour. This relationship is most marked in those with schizophrenia of both long duration and a predominatly delusional presentation.

One should also not conclude that these issues are only of relevance to forensic psychiatry – in the meticulous series of Chestnut Lodge follow-up studies (McGlashan, 1986), out of a vast number of potential predictor variables, the presence of psychotic assaultiveness was one of the three robust associations of poor outcome.

What else does the literature tell us? I have purposefully avoided discussing issues of treatment and public policy, since these will be covered in detail elsewhere. However, the literature on violence, crime and psychosis does give one important lead. It seems well-established that the majority of serious offences committed by those with schizophrenia occur not just in those with long illness histories, but who have also drifted out of any medical care or supervision (Walker and McCabe, 1973; Hafner and Boker, 1982; Monahan, 1988). It is logical to assume that the single most effective public health intervention would be to improve the standard and range of aftercare.

REFERENCES

Aitken G. (1984). Assaults on staff in a locked ward: prediction and consequences. *Medicine, Science and the Law*, **24**: 199–207.

Appleby L., Wessely S. (1988). Public attitudes to mental illness: the influence of the Hungerford massacre. *Medicine, Science and the Law*; **28**: 291–5.

Arboleda-Florez J., Holley H. (1988). Criminalisation of the mentally ill: part II. Initial detention. *Canadian Journal of Psychiatry*; **33**: 87–95.

Arieti S. (1974). *The Interpretation of Schizophrenia*. New York: Basic Books.

Cocozza J., Steadman H. (1974) Some refinements in the measurement and prediction of dangerous behaviour. *American Journal of Psychiatry*; **131**: 1012–14.

Coid J. (1988). Mentally abnormal prisoners on remand: I – Rejected or accepted by the NHS? *British Medical Journal*; **296**: 1779–82.

Durbin J., Pasewark R., Albers, D. (1977). Criminality and mental illness: a study of arrest rates in a rural state. *American Journal of Psychiatry*; **143**: 80–3.

Farrington D. (1988). Studying changes within individuals: the causes of offending. In: *Studies of Psychosocial Risk: The Power of Longitudinal Data* (Rutter M., ed.) Cambridge: Cambridge University Press.

Gibbens T. (1958). Sane and insane homicide. *Journal of Criminal Law, Criminology and Police Science*; **49**: 110–15.

Gibbens T., Robertson G. (1983). A survey of the criminal careers of hospital order patients. *British Journal of Psychiatry*; **143**: 362–9.

Gibbons J., Horn S., Powell J., Gibbons J. (1984). Schizophrenic patients and their families: a survey in a psychiatric service based on a DGH unit. *British Journal of Psychiatry*; **144**: 70–7.

Gottlieb P., Gabrielsen G., Kramp P. (1987). Psychotic homicides in Copenhagen from 1959–1983. *Acta Psychologica Scandinavica*; **76**: 285–92.

Gunn J., Maden T., Swinton M. (1991). Treatment needs of prisoners with psychiatric disorders. *British Medical Journal*; **303**: 338–41.

Guze S.B. (1976). *Criminality and Psychiatric Disorders*. London: Oxford University Press.

Guze S., Goodwin D., Crane J. (1969). Criminality and psychiatric disorders. *Archives of General Psychiatry*; **20**: 583–91.

Guze S., Woodruff R., Clayton P. (1974). Psychiatric disorders and criminality. *Journal of the American Medical Association*; **227**: 641–2.

Hafner H., Boker W. (1982). *Crimes of Violence by Mentally Abnormal Offenders: A Psychiatric and Epidemiological Study* (translated by H. Marshall). Cambridge: Cambridge University Press.

Johnstone E., Crow T., Johnson A., MacMillan J. (1988). The Northwick Park study of first episodes of schizophrenia. 1: Presentation of the illness and problems relating to admission. *British Journal of Psychiatry*; **149**: 51–6.

Karson C., Bigelow L. (1987). Violent behaviour in schizophrenic inpatients. *Journal of Nervous Mental Diseases*; **175**; 161–4.

Klassen D. O'Connor W. (1988). Crime, inpatient admission and violence among male mental patients. *International Journal Law and Psychiatry*; **11**: 305–12.

Krakowski M., Volavka J., Brizer D. (1986). Psychopathology and violence: a review of the literature. *Comprehensive Psychiatry*; **27**: 131–48.

Lagos J. Perlmutter K. Saexinger H. (1977). Fear of the mentally ill: empirical support for the common man's response. *American Journal of Psychiatry*; **134**: 1134–7.

Landau S. (1981). Juveniles and the police. *British Journal of Criminology*; **21**: 27–46.

Lanzkron J. (1963). Murder and insanity: a survey. *American Journal of Psychiatry*; **119**: 754–8.

Levine D. (1970). Criminal behaviour and mental institutionalisation. *Journal of Clinical Psychology*; **26**: 279–84.

Lindquist P, Allebeck P. (1990). Schizophrenia and crime: a longitudinal follow-up of 644 schizophrenics in Stockholm. *British Journal of Psychiatry*; **157**: 345–50.

Link B., Andrews H., Cullen F. (1992). The violent and illegal behaviour of mental patients reconsidered. *American Sociological Review*; **57**: 275–92.

McGlashan T. (1986). The prediction of outcome in chronic schizophrenia: IV. The Chestnut Lodge follow-up study. *Archives of General Psychiatry*; **43**: 167–76.

Mackay R., Wight R. (1984). Schizophrenia and anti-social (criminal) behaviour–some responses from suffers and relatives. *Medicine, Science and Law*; **24**: 192–8.

MacMillan J., Johnson A. (1987). Contact with the police in early schizophrenia: its nature, frequency and relevance to the outcome of treatment. *Medicine Science and the Law*; **27**: 191–200.

Monahan J. (1988). Risk assessment of violence among the mentally disordered: generating useful knowledge. *International Journal of Law and Psychiatry*; **11**: 249–57.

Monahan J. (1992). Mental disorder and violent behaviour: attitudes and evidence. *American Psychologist*; **47**; 511–21.

Monahan J., Steadman H. (1983). Crime and mental illness: an epidemiological approach. In: *Crime and Justice, vol. 4* Morris N., Tonry M. eds), pp. 145–89. Chicago: University of Chicago Press.

Mowat R. (1966). *Morbid Jealousy*. London: Tavistock.

Mulvey E., Blumstein A., Cohen J. (1986). Reframing the research question of mental patient criminality. *International Journal of Law Psychology*; **9**: 57–65.

Murray R., Lewis S., Owen M., Forster A. (1988). The neurodevelopmental origins of dementia praecox. In: *Schizophrenia: The Major Issues* (Bebbington P., McGuffin P. eds) pp. 90–107. London: William Heinemann.

Payne C., McCabe S., Walker N. (1974). Predicting offender patients' reconvictions. *British Journal of Psychiatry*; **125**: 60–4.

Pearson M., Wilmot E., Padi M. (1986). A study of violent behaviour among inpatients in a psychiatric hospital. *British Journal of Psychiatry*; **149**: 232–5.

Planansky K., Johnston R. (1977) Homicidal aggression in schizophrenic men. *Acta Psychiatrica Scandinavica*; **55**: 65–73.

Rabkin J. (1979). Criminal behaviour of discharged mental patients: a critical appraisal of the research. *Psychological Bulletin*; **86**: 1–27.

Robertson G. (1988). Arrest patterns among mentally disordered offenders. *British Journal of Psychiatry*; **153**: 313–16.

Shain R. Phillips J. (1991). The stigma of mental illness: labelling and stereotyping in the news. In: *Risky Business: Communicating Issues of Science, Risk, and Public Policy.* (Wilkins L., Patterson P., eds), pp. 61–74. New York. Greenwood Press.

Shore D., Filson R., Johnston W. et al. (1989). Murder and assault arrests of white house cases: Clinical and demographic correlates of violence subsequent to civil commitment. *American Journal of Psychiatry*; **146**: 645–51.

Sosowsky L. (1980). Explaining the increased arrest rate among mental patients: a cautionary note. *American Journal of Psychiatry*; **137**: 1602–5.

Steadman H., Cocozza J., Melick M. (1978). Explaining the increased arrest rate among mental patients: the changing clientele of state hospitals. *American Journal of Psychiatry*; **135**: 816–20.

Steadman H. Keveles G. (1972). The community adjustment and criminal activity of the Baxstrom patients 1966–1970. *American Journal of Psychiatry*; **129**: 304–10.

Swanson J., Holzer C., Ganju V., Jono R. (1990). Violence and psychiatric disorder in the community: evidence from the epidemiologic catchment area surveys. *Hospital Community Psychiatry*; **41**: 761–70.

Tardiff K. Koenigsberg H. (1985). Assaultive behaviour among psychiatric outpatients. *American Journal of Psychiatry*; **142**: 960–3.

Tardiff K. Sweillam A. (1980). Assault, suicide and mental illness. *Archives of General Psychiatry*; **37**: 164–9.

Tardiff K., Sweillam A. (1982). Assaultive behaviour among chronic inpatients. *American Journal of Psychiatry*; **139**: 212–15.

Taylor P. (1982). Schizophrenia and violence. In: *Abnormal Offenders, Deliquency, and the Criminal Justice System* (Gunn J. Farrington D. eds), pp. 269–84. Chichester: Wiley.

Taylor P. (1985). Motives for offending amongst violent and psychotic men. *British Journal of Psychiatry*; **147**: 491–8.

Taylor P., Gunn J. (1984). Violence and psychosis 1 – risk of violence among psychotic men. *British Medical Journal*; **288**: 1945–9.

Taylor P. Mullen P., Wessely S. (1993). Psychosis, violence and crime. In: *Forensic Psychiatry: Clinical, Ethical and Legal Issues* (Gunn J., Taylor P.J., eds). London: Heinemann, in press.

Teplin L. (1985). The criminality of the mentally Ill: a dangerous misconception. *American Journal of Psychiatry*; **142**: 593–9.

Tidmarsh D. (1990). Schizophrenia and crime. In: *Principles and Practice of*

Forensic Psychiatry (Bluglass R. Bowden P., eds). Edinburgh: Churchill Livingstone.

Volavka J. Krakowski M. (1989). Schizophrenia and violence. *Psychological Medicine*; **19**: 559–62.

Walker N. (1987). *Crime and Criminology: A Critical Introduction*. Oxford: Oxford University Press.

Walker N. McCabe S. (1973). *Crime and Insanity in England*: vol. 2. Edinburgh: Edinburgh University Press.

Wessely S., Buchanan A., Reed A., et al. The prevalence of delusional behaviour. *British Journal of Psychiatry*, in press.

Wessely S. Taylor P. (1991). Madness and crime: criminology versus psychiatry. *Criminal Behaviour and Mental Health*; **1**: 193–228.

West D, Farrington D. (1973). *Who Becomes Delinquent?* London, Heinemann.

Wilcox D. (1985). The relationship of mental illness to homicide. *American Journal of Forensic Psychology*; **6**: 3–15.

Yesavage J. (1984). Correlates of dangerous behaviour by schizophrenics in hospital. *Journal of Psychiatric Research*; **18**: 225–31.

9 *The psychiatric management of violence*

TONY MADEN

The psychiatrist is concerned with only a small fraction of all violence in society, that associated with mental disorder. This includes actual or potential violence directed towards others, the self or property. The 'management of violence' is convenient shorthand but in reality the psychiatrist manages patients suffering from psychiatric disorders associated with violence. This is not a trivial matter of terminology; one theme of the following account is that correct management of the psychiatric disorder goes a long way towards avoiding violent incidents.

The management of violence is discussed in three locations – within hospitals, in the community and in prison. This review of the area is very selective and will focus on some of the broader issues arising, moving from a consideration of the individual patient, through a discussion of practice on individual wards, to end with a look at the management of the whole institution. This account will be particularly concerned with the problems which can arise at various levels when violence is managed in psychiatric hospitals. After describing the management of violence in this setting, I will then make brief reference to the problems which arise from attempts to manage the potentially violent patient in a changing system of psychiatric care. The decreasing use of institutions must mean a change in ways of managing violence. The potentially violent patient living at home presents a new set of problems, as does the patient in prison.

MANAGEMENT OF VIOLENCE IN HOSPITALS

There is now a large volume of work on this subject. It is estimated that about one in 10 patients will assault staff. The emphasis of a lot of the work in this area is on describing the factors that lead to violence and attempting to avoid them.

The risk of violence by inpatients is increased by being young and male, having a psychosis or organic brain syndrome, drug or alcohol abuse, compulsory detention and history of previous violence. These findings will surprise few people and are rather limited in their perspective. A recent *British Medical Journal* editorial entitled 'Managing violence in psychiatric hospitals' (Schipperheijd and Dunn, 1991) ran through these factors and responses to them. There was some critical correspondence in reply, suggesting that the authors had neglected institutional factors such as the provision of alarm bells in interview rooms and the design of buildings to allow adequate surveillance. It is insufficient to describe good practice; staff also need a working environment that allows and encourages its implementation. Hospital management is discussed in more detail below.

The following account of responses to violence in hospital is not a comprehensive review but will draw attention to some broader issues raised by work in this area. Responses to the potentially violent patient can be considered under five headings:

1. Nursing care.
2. Medication.
3. Seclusion.
4. Psychotherapy.
5. Psychological approaches.

Nursing care

This includes a broad range of interpersonal skills, from the anticipation of possible flashpoints, through to control and restraint techniques. A visit to the special hospitals demonstrates that some of the most violent patients can be managed in a peaceful and safe atmosphere, almost entirely because of the high standards of nursing care.

A discussion of nursing must also include the environment in which patients are cared for and the demands placed upon them. Some violence can be understood as a reaction to stresses or demands with which a patient is unable to cope and it is important to tailor the environment to match the patient, rather than attempt to force all patients into a particular regime, in the name of rehabilitation.

Medication

Medication may be aimed at treating a specific mental illness or at reducing aggression. In general, the adequate treatment of a mental illness reduces the chances of violence by the patient. There is increasing interest in the use of medication to control aggressive behaviour (see Chapter 10).

Seclusion

Seclusion can be defined as 'supervised denial of the company of other people within a closed environment at any time of the day or night'. It is a form of *restraint*, the enforced control of patients' ability to behave in ways that threaten or cause harm to themselves, others or property. Restraint may be manual, mechanical, situational or pharmacological; seclusion is one form of situational restraint. With the emergence of 'moral treatment' in the early 19th century, seclusion came to be preferred to the use of mechanical restraints.

Its use has always been controversial. As early as 1868, the commissioners in lunacy criticized the excessive seclusion of the more violent patients in Broadmoor (this was only 5 years after the opening of the hospital). The use of seclusion has legal and clinical aspects.

Legal aspects

The guiding legal principles in seclusion are those of common law, based around the concept of reasonableness, which has two components:

1. The force used should not exceed that required to achieve the desired object.
2. The reaction must be in proportion to the harm threatened.

Common law would not justify any element of retaliation, revenge, punishment or prolonged confinement to prevent harm. In practice, the patient subjected to seclusion finds it unpleasant and may well see it as a form of punishment.

Clinical aspects

There is a continuing debate on the value of seclusion. On one side, it is argued that more effective drugs and a more liberal policy in hospitals mean that seclusion is as outdated as the use of mechanical restraints. The counterargument is that some form of restraint is necessary in certain circumstances and diminishing the use of one form of restraint can only be achieved by increasing reliance on other methods. If hospitals abandon all methods of restraint, the fear is that they will also abandon violent patients, adopting the simple expedient of refusing to admit them. Patients may then find themselves in inappropriately high security or in prison.

The evidence is limited. Little research has been done, probably because this is a rather embarrassing topic for psychiatry. The Mental Health Act Commission in 1984 surveyed 42 psychiatric hospitals and found that 35 had a seclusion policy whereas seven operated without the use of seclusion, i.e. one in six hospitals manages without seclusion.

A study in Newcastle (Thompson, 1986) looked at the use of seclusion between 1981 and 1984, finding that the number of patients secluded fell during this time, from 33 per 1000 admissions in 1981 to

26 per 1000 in 1984. Seclusion was not used frequently but in some cases it was a response to threats of violence, rather than actual violence, or a response to self-harm. It was argued that the decline was mainly due to changing staff attitudes, in particular the adoption of other responses to threatened violence and to self-harm.

Another study (Kingdon and Bakewell, 1988) described a district psychiatric service in Bassetlaw which had adopted a non-seclusion policy. Patients who would have been secluded were given a high level of nursing supervision. They found that 1.2/1000 admissions per annum could not be coped with in this environment. They also went to some trouble to show that they were not rejecting patients during the study period.

One message emerging from work of this type is that seclusion depends to a large extent on staff attitudes, staffing levels and the availability of other methods of control. Anecdotally, recent changes in procedure at a secure hospital resulted in a fall in the use of seclusion, by dramatically increasing the documentation required. Seclusion became too much trouble, increasing the incentives to find alternative methods of managing actual or potential violence. Similarly, an intensive care ward for mentally handicapped women was able to reduce dramatically the use of seclusion by introducing male staff, who were better able to make use of manual restraint when attacked. The barrier to this action in the past had been the attitude of staff, who were reluctant to accept integration. There has been little research on the effects of staff gender on ward behaviour but it may be that introducing female staff on to all-male wards brings about beneficial changes in the ward culture and leads to lower levels of violence. Definitive evidence is lacking but it is now policy within the special hospitals to increase the number of wards with integrated staff.

The problems associated with the use of seclusion must be balanced against the hazards of other methods of dealing with violence. High doses of neuroleptic medication (which may be described in some circumstances as pharmacological restraint) have a range of side-effects, some of which may be fatal in occasional cases.

Present empirical evidence does not support the case for abandoning the use of seclusion. However, the onus is on psychiatry to carry out more self-critical studies of practice in this area. The suggestion is that seclusion has been used in the past as a routine response which is convenient for the institution, if uncomfortable for the patient. The challenge is to define precisely its role in the management of violence and to evaluate alternative strategies.

Hospitals now have rigid guidelines for the seclusion of patients. In contrast, prisons have far fewer safeguards for the inmate, whatever the nature of his or her psychiatric disorder. An important consideration is that the price of giving up seclusion may be that hospitals are more reluctant to admit the mentally disordered offender.

Psychotherapy

In concentrating on the management of violent incidents it is easy to forget that the main purpose of a hospital is to provide treatment. Hospitals such as the Henderson, offering treatment in a therapeutic community setting, can help people who are violent towards themselves or others to regain control over their impulses. Grendon prison has a similar function within a prison setting. Psychotherapy receives much criticism on the grounds that its efficacy has not been established. In the case of HMP Grendon, short- (Gunn *et al.*, 1978) and long-term studies (Gunn and Robertson, 1982) have shown a decrease in neurotic symptoms and violent incidents but have failed to show any effect on reconviction rates. The latter criterion is a harsh one, given that recidivism is so unresponsive to interventions of all types. It is also inappropriate; many of Grendon's patients are professional criminals (Genders and Player, 1989) and it is unrealistic to expect psychiatric intervention to guide them towards a change of career. Grendon offers a form of treatment that could usefully be extended within the health service, where treatment of this type is very restricted. It serves as a useful illustration of a powerful therapeutic intervention which lowers the rate of violent incidents without use of restraints, by encouraging self-control.

Psychological techniques

Group psychotherapy can also be seen as a psychological technique in the management of violence but is usually kept separate, perhaps because of its association with psychoanalysis, whilst psychology would rather stress its scientific origins. The distinction is artificial but the present text adheres to this convention.

A broad range of techniques may be useful, including token economies, social skills training, relapse prevention and anger management. The names and theoretical perspectives vary but they share common principles and two general approaches can be distinguished – the operant control of aggression and cognitive-behavioural approaches. They are described in more detail in Chapter 12 but are mentioned here as an introduction to problems which can arise in any institution dealing with potentially violent individuals.

Operant control of aggression

The aim is to alter the consequences of behaviour when it is considered that they are reinforcing undesirable acts. In its simplest form, this may amount to ignoring behaviour when it is felt that attention is reinforcing aggression. There may also be differential reinforcement of more desirable behaviours that are incompatible with aggression.

Application of these methods depends on a skilled analysis of behaviour and its reinforcements. It also raises practical and ethical problems. Some aggressive behaviour is difficult, if not impossible, to ignore, limiting the technique to verbal or threatened aggression in many cases.

Ethically, there is a fine line between an effective system and abuse of power. The regime may be seen as punishment which, quite apart from the ethical objection, has notoriously unpredictable effects on behaviour. Staff may find the techniques very attractive, as they can be dramatically effective. If there is an escalation of violent behaviour or threats, a difficult patient can soon find him- or herself subject to intolerable and indefensible restrictions. A good example would be the recent 'pindown' controversy, over a behavioural regime for dealing with difficult adolescents in a children's home. Leaving aside individual staff failings, this was in part a well-intentioned attempt to control difficult behaviour, implemented by untrained staff in an unsupervised manner. This regime was rightly condemned but it is possible to see elements of it in many behavioural regimes for managing violence. It serves as a reminder of the need for training, supervision and outside scrutiny in any institution using such techniques.

A further example is the use of planned time out from positive reinforcement. This is meant to differ from seclusion, which is an emergency procedure; it is easy for this distinction to be lost in practice and the crucial issue is monitoring of standards of practice. Particular techniques may be less important than the management, in the broadest sense, of the institutions in which they are applied.

Cognitive-behavioural modification

As the name suggests, the approach is eclectic; cognition and behaviour together encompass a considerable part of life. Novaco's approach to anger regulation by cognitive mediation is a useful illustration; treatment aims to modify the way in which information is processed, resulting in a change in behaviour.

The approach is attractive and, as a theoretical explanation of behaviour, can be applied in many situations; a recent paper by Novaco and Welsh (1989) uses the Kent State killings and the attempted assassinations of President Reagan and the Pope as examples. Its practical applications remain to be delineated and it is an area where an expansion of research is to be expected in the near future.

WIDER ISSUES: THE MANAGEMENT OF INSTITUTIONS

Over and above the question of responses to actual or potential violence, there is the issue of managing the context in which practical techniques are applied. The management of violence can be looked at in a technical way but it has powerful emotional and moral connotations, which cannot be ignored within any institution which attempts to treat violent patients.

A useful introduction is to consider what happens when things go wrong in psychiatric hospitals. John Martin, a sociologist, gives an excellent account of this subject in his book *Hospitals in Trouble* (Martin, 1984), which is concerned with enquiries into psychiatric hospitals. Violent patients can easily become the victims of abuse by staff. One example in his study is the characterization of patients' behaviour as 'bad' rather than 'ill'; violent behaviour is particularly likely to be regarded in this way. Staff come to distinguish two forms of challenging behaviour; 'illness' deserves care, 'badness' deserves punishment. Informal punishments come to be justified as a way of teaching the patient to cooperate.

Martin also emphasizes the context of some abuses. One of the consultants speaking to the South Ockenden Hospital enquiry in 1974 described his reactions on coming to the hospital's locked ward, where most abuses took place:

> about a dozen patients were regularly violent and [the violence]. . . occurred every day. Very often it was against members of staff. . .I was surprised when I first came how this was accepted by the staff as being just part of their job and something which really could not be altered and there was no hope of altering it (Martin, 1984, p. 103).

This account conveys a powerful sense of an intolerable working environment and demoralized staff. The problem is taken beyond that of individual wrong-doing, important though this may be in its own right.

A number of general points emerge from Martin's work. The first is that abuses are likely to occur in any environment where violent patients are managed, particularly if they are cared for on a long-term basis. The priority is to take steps to prevent this, with an emphasis on staff recruitment, training and supervision. It is also essential to reduce professional isolation; outside scrutiny is a powerful corrective to problems of this type and a protection for both patients and staff.

These are management issues. The problem of the violent patient in hospital becomes the problem of managing an institution. Adequate management of the institution is a prerequisite for the effective use of any techniques for managing the violent patient.

Having considered the problem of violence in hospitals, the following sections consider issues arising when the violent patient is managed in other settings, namely the community and the prison.

MANAGEMENT OF THE VIOLENT PATIENT IN THE COMMUNITY

The guiding principle is correct management of the psychiatric disorder, with adequate supervision. This necessitates a multidisciplinary approach, involving nursing, social services, psychology and probation in addition to psychiatry.

Forensic psychiatrists often consider the question of the prediction of dangerousness. This may be a less important issue in managing most patients than is the need to ensure adequate aftercare of discharged patients. In general, violence in psychotic patients is correlated with their psychosis; treatment of the psychosis reduces the risk of violence.

Management in the community is more complicated than the management of violence in hospitals. The outpatient has access to many possible precipitants of violence, such as alcohol, which are less readily available to the inpatient. The patient also has access to a different range of victims, in most cases members of his or her family. These problems are not discussed in detail here but I would like to draw attention to the difficulty of ensuring adequate standards of care in these circumstances.

Most external reviews of the quality of psychiatric care, whether they are reports by the Hospital Advisory Service or the activities of the Mental Health Act Commission, are concerned with inpatient care. There is much less scrutiny of outpatient care. It is easy for the outpatient to be out of sight and out of mind. The prison survey carried out by the Department of Forensic Psychiatry at the Institute of Psychiatry (Gunn *et al.*, 1991a) revealed some examples of failures of psychiatric care. Generally, these were failures of outpatient supervision, even when treatment had been made a condition of a previous probation order. Failure to attend for an outpatient appointment may elicit no response other than a letter offering a further appointment. In one case, this was the only response to a relapsing schizophrenic patient, despite several letters from the probation officer to the consultant expressing concern about the patient's threatening behaviour.

The new guidelines of the Royal College of Psychiatrists (1989) may go some way towards solving these problems but it remains to be seen how well they can be enforced. One concern is that much of the responsibility of caring for the patient in the community falls on the patient's family and a frequent complaint from families is a lack of support in dealing with aggressive behaviour. Any meeting of the National Schizophrenia Fellowship will produce stories of having to call the police to deal with a relative, when the hospital has been less than helpful. This is unpleasant for all concerned and one aim of psychiatric management must be to minimize police involvement whenever possible. Domestic violence has always been a neglected area and this may be where the violent outpatient causes most problems and receives least attention from services.

The police also serve as a means of admission to hospital for patients on Section 136. Research in this area (Fahy *et al.*, 1987) does not support allegations that the police abuse their powers and confirms that people brought to hospital are usually judged to be ill when seen by a psychiatrist. The real concern must be about the quality of psychiatric services if excessive numbers of patients are entering treatment in this unsatisfactory way, particularly if ethnic minorities are over-represented among those detained under Section 136.

THE MANAGEMENT OF VIOLENCE IN PRISON

It could be argued that this falls outside the scope of this chapter. In fact, some violent, mentally disordered offenders receive their treatment primarily within prison. Prison also provides a context for the foregoing account; violent patients who are not managed in hospital or in the community, for whatever reason, are likely to find themselves in prison.

Managing psychiatric disorder in prison raises questions about the conflict between medical and disciplinary aims. These are illustrated by the use of medication, seclusion and psychotherapy in relation to the violent mentally disordered prisoner.

Medication

The concern about the use of medication in prison is that it is overused to deal with legitimate protest against the prison regime. The 'liquid cosh' is often mentioned in newspapers but there is little evidence for it in present-day prisons in England and Wales. The Mental Health Act does not apply in prisons so medication cannot be given to a prisoner who does not want it, except in an emergency under the provisions of common law. During the prison survey (Gunn *et al.*, 1991b), we found that it was a common myth among inmates that difficult people were 'drugged up'. The only inmates in the sample on large doses of medication were suffering from a psychotic illness and had consented. A more likely problem is that of undermedication, as it is not possible to provide adequate treatment for a small minority of seriously mentally disordered prisoners.

Prisons do not rely extensively on medication but use other

techniques to control violence–mostly disciplinary or institutional measures.

Seclusion

This is also known in prison as the use of 'unfurnished accommodation', referred to by most people as the 'strip cell'. This may be used without some of the safeguards which apply to the use of seclusion in psychiatric hospitals. If there is a question of mental disorder being present, a doctor is required to sanction the use of unfurnished accommodation and state that the inmate is fit for such confinement. The doctor's role here is a difficult one, with a possible conflict between the best interests of the patient and the priorities of the institution.

This is most controversial in the case of violence against the self. The Prison Department's Circular Instruction 20/89 sets out a four-pronged strategy for dealing with self-harm, emphasizing:

1. Identification of risk.
2. Provision of help and support.
3. Reduction of opportunity.
4. Staff awareness and training.

Common practice following self-harm, in the prisons visited during our survey of sentenced inmates, appeared to be a brief psychiatric assessment and transfer to a strip cell with regular observation by staff. Of the four components, priority was given to reducing or even eliminating the physical opportunity for self-harm and the practical consequence of this was that the inmate was placed in unfurnished accommodation.

There are several problems with this approach. First, the number of prison suicides suggests that it is not effective. Second, prisons blur the uses of seclusion and deprivation of privileges. Many inmates associate the strip cell with punishment. Third, it bears little resemblance to the management of self-harm in most of the health service. The Howard League is pressing for the use of strip cells to be banned in managing self-harm. There is room for a review of medical practice in this area, which could focus on the feasibility of using a ward within the prison hospital for the management of actual or threatened self-harm.

Finally, a mention for *psychotherapy* and *psychological techniques* within prison. It is probably easier for a violent patient to get group psychotherapy in prison, at Grendon or the Wormwood Scrubs annexe, than it is for a patient within the National Health Service. Similarly, prison psychologists do a lot of useful work on anger management and similar techniques. A further specialist facility consists of the special units for prisoners who present serious control problems. These units do not have a medical orientation but a recent survey (Coid *et al.*, 1991) of the unit at HMP Parkhurst showed that all of the inmates suffered from psychiatric disorders.

CONCLUSION: THE BOUNDARIES OF PSYCHIATRY

The prisons have accumulated a degree of expertise in managing violent patients that is not easily found within the National Health Service, except in the special hospitals. Many prisoners who receive treatment in prison fall into the diagnostic categories of personality disorder or sexual disorder and treatment provision outside the prisons is very limited. This raises the question of the boundaries of psychiatry's intervention in mental disorders which are associated with violence. It is not clear why treatments for certain types of problem should be provided only or largely within prison. On the other hand, many of these patients fit uneasily into a psychiatric service designed mainly for patients suffering from schizophrenia. Within the health service, the diagnosis of personality disorder may be used as a reason for rejecting patients (Lewis and Appleby, 1988).

The rejection of the violent patient can be understood in terms of two common feelings elicited in the professional. One is fear of the patient's violence and its possible consequences; the second is helplessness, a concern that the patient is untreatable and incapable of change. A possible response to this problem is the 'violence clinic' (Tennent and Wood, 1990). The patient is seen by appointment only in a structured outpatient setting, using a multidisciplinary team that can draw on a variety of social, medical and psychological interventions. In addition to pooling expertise, team members provide mutual support in dealing with difficult behaviours.

The violence clinic is almost unknown in this country and its efficacy must be regarded as untested. Hopefully, empirical studies will be carried out in the near future. Meanwhile, the concept appears to have advantages as a positive alternative to the 'therapeutic nihilism' (Lewis, 1974) that has often characterized psychiatry's response to the violent patient.

REFERENCES

Coid J., Robertson G., and Gunn J. (1991). A psychiatric study of inmates in Parkhurst Special Unit. In: *Managing Difficult Prisoners: The Parkhurst Special Unit* (Walmsley R., ed.). pp. 75–80. Home Office Research Study 122. London: HMSO.

Commissioners in Lunacy (1868). *Report on Broadmoor Criminal Lunatic Asylum.* London: House of Commons.

Fahy T. A., Bermingham D., Dunn J. (1987). Police admissions to psychiatric hospitals: a challenge to community psychiatry? *Medicine, Science and the Law*; **27**: 263–8.

Genders E., Player E. (1989). *Grendon: A Study of a Therapeutic Community within the Prison System*. Oxford: University of Oxford Centre for Criminological Research.

Gunn J., Robertson G. (1982). An evaluation of Grendon prison. In: *Abnormal Offenders, Delinquency and the Criminal Justice System*. (Gunn J., Farrington D. P., eds). Chichester: Wiley.

Gunn J., Robertson G., Dell S., Way C. (1978). *Psychiatric Aspects of Imprisonment*. London: Academic Press.

Gunn J., Maden T., Swinton M. (1991a). *Mentally Disordered Prisoners*. London: Home Office.

Gunn J. Maden A., Swinton M. (1991b). Treatment needs of prisoners with psychiatric disorders. *British Medical Journal*; **303**: 338–41.

Kingdon D. G., Bakewell E. W. (1988). Aggressive behaviour: evaluation of a non-seclusion policy of a district psychiatric service. *British Journal of Psychiatry*; **153**: 631–4.

Lewis A. (1974). Psychopathic personality: a most elusive category. *Psychological Medicine*; **4**: 133–40.

Lewis G., Appleby L. (1988). Personality disorder: the patients psychiatrists dislike. *British Journal of Psychiatry*; **153**: 44–9.

Martin J. P. (1984). *Hospitals in Trouble*. Oxford: Blackwell.

Novaco R. W., Welsh W. N. (1989). Anger disturbances: cognitive mediation and clinical prescriptions. In: *Clinical Approaches to Violence* (Howells K., Hollin C. R., eds). Chichester: Wiley.

Royal College of Psychiatrists (1989). *Working Party Report on Good Practice in Discharge and Aftercare Procedures for Patients Discharged from Inpatient Psychiatric Treatment*. London: Royal College of Psychiatrists.

Schipperheijd J. A., Dunn F. J. (1991). Managing violence in psychiatric hospitals. *British Medical Journal*; **303**: 71–2.

Tennent G., Wood R. (1990). The management of violence. In: *Principles and Practice of Forensic Psychiatry* (Bluglass R., Bowden P., eds), pp. 653–68. London: Churchill Livingstone.

Thompson P. (1986). The use of seclusion in the Newcastle area. *British Journal of Psychiatry*; **149**: 471–4.

10 Prospects for antiaggressive drugs

ALYSON J. BOND

INTRODUCTION

Pathological aggression is usually described as a potential for committing acts of aggression without what is normally thought of as provocation. The controlling system is disturbed and the individual has low tolerance so that aggression is more likely to occur. The sequence of an aggressive response is illustrated schematically in Figure 10.1. The individual perceives some form of provocation to which he or she responds with a negative emotion. This emotion may be anxiety or anger, depending on numerous modifying influences, both internal and external. Internal influences involve personality, self-perception, gender and age. External influences are present in the form of social and cultural factors as well as the prevailing circumstances at the time. This emotion, which may be experienced only fleetingly and may be triggered by cognitions or bodily symptoms (Berkowitz, 1989), may then lead to a behavioural response. In the case of anxiety this results in escape (flight) or paralysis (freezing) or submissive behaviour to reduce the threat. In the case of anger, the individual acts out aggressively either physically towards a person or object, or verbally.

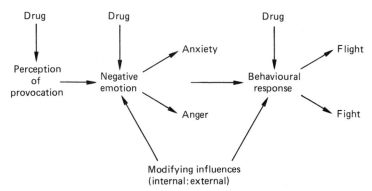

Fig. 10.1 *The sequence of an aggressive response.*

The behavioural response chosen is also subject to numerous modifying influences, e.g. the higher the intelligence the wider the range of responses available, and the better the socialization the more likely a conciliatory response to reduce the threat. A history of physical abuse may increase the likelihood of an aggressive response (Pollock *et al.*, 1990). These responses are also dependent on the nature of the provocation itself in normal aggression although the element of interpretation or perception is also important (Sutton, 1991). However, in pathological aggression, the perceptual threshold may be lowered and a much wider range of stimuli are thus seen as potentially threatening or provocative (Egdell, 1980). This is most likely in certain groups. Violent offenders may engage in violence for passionate or lucrative reasons. In psychiatric patients the behaviour may be secondary to the illness, as in paranoid schizophrenia or temporal lobe epilepsy or part of a syndrome as in intermittent explosive disorder, attention deficit disorder and borderline as well as impulsive and antisocial personality disorder.

Brain damage both from brain injury and disease may lead to impaired impulse control, unpredictable violence and rage responses. An elevated frequency of less severe brain damage, possibly due to prenatal or perinatal factors, has been found in violent delinquent and adult offenders (Mednick *et al.*, 1988). This may in part account for violence in the mentally handicapped or those with learning disabilities who often have episodes of aggression against a background of behavioural disorders. Modification of aggressive behaviour may take many forms, including social and behavioural interventions, and the clinician looks toward experimental aggression research with the hope of learning about more rational treatment options. Whatever the underlying cause, a wealth of pharmacological treatments has been tried and drugs are commonly used to attempt to reduce such behaviour in the clinic. However, none is specifically licensed for this indication and few have been examined in well-controlled, double-blind trials and even where they have, questions such as optimal length of treatment or comparisons with other potential pharmacotherapies have often not been addressed. The main findings with each major drug group used will be reviewed briefly as other more inclusive reviews exist (Miczek, 1987; Eichelman, 1988; Sheard, 1984, 1988).

CURRENT THERAPIES

Antipsychotics

The antipsychotics are the most used group of compounds. They are the treatment of preference in controlling aggression in schizophrenia

(Yudofsky *et al.*, 1987). Many compounds have been used and their efficacy in controlling rather than treating aggressive behaviour was established in many early studies in the 1960s and 1970s (Itil and Wadud, 1975). A review some years ago suggested that chlorpromazine and trifluopromazine were the most effective of the phenothiazines (Levanthal and Brodie, 1981). Of the other groups, haloperidol is often used unless a depot formulation is required, when flupenthixol decanoate has been shown to be effective. New compounds have also been tried with some degree of success (Tuason, 1986). The rationale behind use of these drugs to control aggression is often pragmatic, weighing risks against side-effects, rather than comparing efficacy. It seems that thioridazine, chlorpromazine and haloperidol are all commonly used in the USA and UK (Wressell *et al.*, 1990; Yudofsky *et al.*, 1990) but it is difficult to establish differences between compounds as they have rarely been compared in controlled trials with properly matched samples. Where antipsychotics have not been effective in significantly reducing aggressive behaviour, other drugs have been added and these include beta-blockers, carbamazepine and tryptophan. These studies will be discussed under the other drug headings.

Antipsychotics are also used to control acute episodes of disturbed behaviour whatever the pathology. This is termed rapid tranquillization and is primarily a sedative effect (Pilowsky *et al.*, 1992). Although most studies have focused on the use of antipsychotics to control aggressive behaviour in schizophrenia, their efficacy in this respect has also been shown in other disorders. It is interesting that antipsychotics, including thiothixene and haloperidol, have proved helpful in treating impulsiveness and aggressive outbursts in borderline and impulsive and antisocial personality disorder in low doses, where no obvious tranquillization is present (Goldberg *et al.*, 1986; Soloff *et al.*, 1986; Tyrer and Seivewright, 1988). In one crossover study trifluoperazine hydrochloride (7.8 mg/day) improved the clinical state of patients with borderline personality disorder and prominent behavioural dyscontrol (Cowdry and Gardner, 1988). In another placebo-controlled study (Montgomery, 1987), the depot neuroleptic fluphenthixol 20 mg per month reduced repeated suicide attempts in a group of patients with borderline or histrionic personality disorder.

Antipsychotics are also widely used in patients with learning disabilities and apart from early studies, two more recent studies have shown improvements. One (Gualtieri and Schroeder, 1989) used low-dose (2–8 mg) fluphenazine and found a decrease in both self-injury and aggression. The other found that pipothiazine palmitate (a depot phenothiazine) reduced aggression (Lynch *et al.*, 1985). Some antipsychotics have also been evaluated in patients with organic brain disease but the improvement in symptoms such as hostility and uncooperativeness is usually only modest (Coccaro *et al.*, 1990). Antipsychotics must be used with caution in epilepsy or related conditions as they lower the seizure threshold.

Benzodiazepines

Benzodiazepines have been much used in the past in the control of aggressive behaviour and there are studies in many groups of patients demonstrating their efficacy (Bond and Lader, 1979). Recently the use of benzodiazepines has been advocated in the control of acute behavioural disturbance (Mendoza *et al.*, 1987). This has met with some well-founded criticism (Graham, 1988) but benzodiazepines are often used in conjunction with antipsychotics in rapid tranquillization (Salzman, 1988). The antiaggressive efficacy of benzodiazepines apart from sedation has never been established and recently evidence has been accruing of their proaggressive properties. There have been reports of rage reactions from early marketing days but it was always considered to be a paradoxical response and associated with high doses in predisposed individuals. However, it has been suggested that it may be much more common than hitherto realized and may represent an under-reported general rise in irritability, sometimes leading to uncontrolled aggressive outbursts (DiMascio *et al.*, 1969). A review by Dietch and Jennings (1988) estimated that less than 1% of patients treated with benzodiazepines experienced aggressive dyscontrol but a review of the use of clonazepam in seizure disorders found an incidence of irritability and hostility of 15% (Browne, 1978). This may have been because most of the patients were children and whereas a phenomenon may be called self-assertion in anxious adults, it is differently labelled as aggression by parents. Two factors seem to be important in the reported incidence noted here. Firstly, provocation may be necessary to produce such reactions, which parents may provide unintentionally by trying to discipline their children. Secondly, in adults any adverse reactions are assessed by the patient's own report and so maybe we should be interviewing relatives of patients to ask about changes in behaviour or mood, not the patients themselves; benzodiazepines, like alcohol, may impair judgement or awareness.

Animal studies have shown both anti- and proaggressive actions for benzodiazepines. It has been suggested that these drugs merely strengthen the current or prevailing behavioural tendency (Dantzer, 1977) but this does not explain why people supposedly behave out of character and may do the same when rechallenged despite the apparent prevailing mood at the time (Regestein and Reich, 1985). Mos and Olivier (1987) conclude from a review of the proaggressive effects of benzodiazepines, mainly in animals, that benzodiazepines enhance aggression when basal levels are low to moderate. This may be true of studies in anxious or neurotic patients and in laboratory models used in normal subjects (Gardos *et al.*, 1968; Salzman *et al.*, 1974; Wilkinson, 1985; Bond and Lader, 1988) but does not apply when they are used to treat aggressive behaviour *per se*. Two or three recent reports have detailed the incidence of hostility following a newer high-potency benzodiazepine, alprazolam, in different patient groups. In one study, 8 out of 80 patients treated with this benzodiazepine displayed extreme anger or hostile behaviour (Rosenbaum *et al.*, 1984). The initial hostility occurred within the first week in all patients and after a single dose in two. Discontinuing the drug led to a disappearance of symptoms within a few hours. Three patients were rechallenged and 2 of the 3 became hostile. The authors conclude that alprazolam-induced hostility is an early and idiosyncratic effect and may be more likely in patients with well-suppressed chronic anger and resentment. In patients with borderline personality disorder where basal levels of aggression are high, alprazolam has also been found to make such symptoms worse. The incidence of episodes of serious dyscontrol after alprazolam (58%) was much higher than after placebo (8%) in these disturbed patients (Gardner and Cowdry, 1985) and it was difficult to predict the occurrences. This does not accord with suggestions from the animal literature and the fact that incidents could occur at any time in the 6-week treatment period does not support the notion that it is an initial effect. It should be noted here that triazolam, a high-potency benzodiazepine hypnotic, has recently been withdrawn from the UK market because of problems with adverse reactions, including disinhibition and aggression (*Drug and Therapeutics Bulletin*, 1991). Considering this evidence, it would seem advisable to avoid benzodiazepines in the treatment of aggression but this may be premature as there appear to be differences among compounds and oxazepam, which has not been shown to increase aggressive behaviour in normal subjects (Gardos *et al.*, 1968; Bond and Lader, 1988), has been recommended as a specific antihostility tranquillizer (Salzman *et al.*, 1975). It has also been shown to be more effective than placebo or chlordiazepoxide in patients with a history of hostile outbursts associated with anxiety (Lion, 1979).

Lithium

In psychiatric patients, most evidence for the efficacy of lithium in the control of aggressive behaviour comes from case studies and uncontrolled reports but a consistent improvement over previous treatments, e.g. the use of phenothiazines or benzodiazepines, has been shown, clearly suggesting superiority over previous drug therapy (Shader *et al.*, 1974). There is convincing evidence for the efficacy of lithium in both explosive and aggressive personality disorder and in violent prisoners with mixed diagnoses. A series of studies in the USA showed a reduction in violent incidents and serious assaults without a dulling of affect (Sheard, 1971; 1975; Sheard *et al.*, 1976). Although two of these studies were carried out single-blind, patients and the staff who rated their behaviour were blind to treatment, which varied from 4 to 12 weeks. A longer study (mean length of treatment 9.9 months) was conducted in 27 chronically aggressive prisoners of mixed diagnoses (Tupin *et al.*, 1973) and both a reduction in the average number of disciplinary actions for violent behaviour and an improvement in security classification were found. Despite this seemingly favourable evidence, lithium does not appear to have been studied much in patients with antisocial or borderline personality disorder. This could be because of potential side-effects but it has been suggested that when administered every second day, lithium maintains efficacy with much reduced side-effects (Mellerup and Plenge, 1990). One preliminary report found favourable effects for lithium in borderline personality disorder (Links *et al.*, 1989) and the improvement relative to both desipramine and placebo was on impulsivity, not depression.

Various trials with lithium have been conducted in children who display aggressive behaviour for a variety of reasons. It has been shown to be effective in conduct disorder without impairing cognition (Platt *et al.*, 1984). This is an extremely important consideration in the treatment of children and one well-constructed study (Campbell *et al.*, 1984) found it compared favourably with haloperidol in these patients. The staff felt that lithium reduced explosiveness and therefore aided self-control whereas haloperidol only made the children more manageable by slowing them down.

There is also evidence from retrospective studies that lithium may be useful in patients with learning disabilities. In one study (Luchins and Dojka, 1989), computerized pharmacy records were examined to screen for lithium treatment of at least 3 months' duration. Eleven patients were identified for whom lithium had been used to treat both self-injury and aggression. In 10 of these it had been added to antipsychotic medication but a significant decrease in the frequency of both behaviours was found during lithium treatment. Another study (Spreat *et al.*, 1989) looked at 38 patients for whom baseline rates of aggression were available 4 months prior to lithium treatment. Again 70% of the patients were also receiving antipsychotics but impulsive aggressive behaviour, in particular hyperactivity and violent or destructive behaviour, showed a decrease after the institution of lithium. Some authors have suggested that hyperactivity is in fact the mediating variable in predicting lithium-responsiveness amongst those with developmental disabilities (Sovner and Hurley, 1981; Tyrer *et al.*, 1984) but it may in fact be impulsivity as in other disorders. The use of lithium in patients with temporal lobe epilepsy or interictal aggressive behaviour is controversial as one study has shown a deterioration in these patients (Jus *et al.*, 1973).

Beta-blockers

Numerous case reports and open studies have shown high-dose beta-adrenergic antagonists to be effective in controlling aggression in patients in whom other medication (antipsychotics, benzodiazepines, antidepressants, anticonvulsants) has failed (Elliott, 1977; Yudofsky *et al.*, 1981; Greendyke *et al.*, 1984). This has particularly been shown for patients with organic brain disease or injury and there have been two well-controlled, double-blind studies by the same group. In the first (Greendyke *et al.*, 1986), propranolol (520 mg/day sustained release) was shown to be effective in the management of violent behaviour associated with organic brain disease but side-effects of hypotension and bradycardia meant that careful patient monitoring was necessary. In the second study, pindolol, a partial agonist, was used in a similar but more severely symptomatic group of patients who had all proved refractory to other pharmacological treatments. The optimal dose of 40–60 mg/day was found to have a faster onset of action than propranolol and minimal side-effects (Greendyke and Kanter, 1986). Propranolol has also been reported to reduce aggressive and self-injurious behaviour in children and adolescents with organic brain dysfunction (Williams *et al.*, 1982) and in patients with learning disabilities and autism (Ratey *et al.*, 1987; Luchins and Dojka, 1989). Ratey *et al.* (1986) found a much lower dose of propranolol (40–240 mg/day) to be effective in an open trial of patients with severe learning disabilities. They state that the duration of treatment is important and that often dosage is increased prematurely because a rapid result is required. However the majority of their patients were on other concurrent medications.

It has been speculated that the beta-blockers may have a bimodal action, first in the periphery and second in the central nervous system and this is supported by work showing nadolol, a peripherally acting beta-blocker, to be as effective as propranolol (Polakoff *et al.*, 1986) when added to mesoridazine. A report of two case studies (Kastner *et al.*, 1990) showed that administration of metoprolol (200–250 mg/day) allowed other drugs (thioridazine and alprazolam respectively) to be withdrawn and clinical improvement was maintained for 1–2 year follow-ups. A recent review of studies using beta-blockers in people with learning disabilities cautioned that the impressive response rate was based solely on case reports and open clinical trials (Ruedrich *et al.*, 1990).

In schizophrenia, beta-blockers have been added to maintenance antipsychotic treatment and where this has been done systematically, there has been some evidence of improvement (Sorgi *et al.*, 1986). Although a more recent study with adjunctive nadolol (80–120 mg/day) showed only a trend towards decreased aggression (Alpert *et al.*, 1990), the authors rightly point out that any consistent trend when a drug is added double-blind to a behavioural programme is important in a severely disturbed group of patients. However, beta-blockers can elevate the levels of some antipsychotics and so caution with this combination is advocated (Hanssen *et al.*, 1980; Silver *et al.*, 1986). There is some preliminary work to show that propranolol can be useful in intermittent explosive disorder (426 mg/day) although patients preferred carbamazepine and tolerated it better (Mattes *et al.*, 1984). A case can therefore be made for trying beta-blockers in treatment-resistant assaultive patients, especially those with accompanying organic brain disease or injury. A useful practical guide to the treatment of these patients is given by Yudofsky *et al.* (1990), in which they point out that the antiaggressive effects of various non-sedative compounds may have a delayed onset of 4–8 weeks.

Anticonvulsants

Electrical disturbances in the brain have been implicated as a cause of episodic human violent behaviour but anticonvulsants, e.g. phenytoin, have had mixed results in the control of such aggressive behaviour over and above the control of epilepsy. Some open trials have been favourable but controlled trials have not always replicated these results, leading to a conclusion of the probable inefficacy of most anticonvulsants in controlling aggressive behaviour in adults (Eichelman, 1987) or children (Conners *et al.*, 1971). However, carbamazepine, which has been found to have mood-stabilizing and antimanic properties in addition to its anticonvulsant action, has shown efficacy in managing aggressive behaviour in various patient groups. In an open study comparing propranolol with carbamazepine, carbamazepine was found to be effective in controlling the aggressive outbursts of patients with intermittent explosive disorder (Mattes *et al.*, 1984). Although patients improved with both drugs, more patients were able to tolerate carbamazepine (20 versus 9). A later report suggested that propranolol was more effective in patients with attention deficit disorder (Mattes, 1990). A controlled trial (Gardner and Cowdry, 1986) which found carbamazepine to be superior to placebo for symptoms of behavioural dyscontrol in patients with borderline personality disorder blindly substituted phenytoin to patients, who had developed skin rashes to carbamazepine, without effect. In this double-blind crossover trial which compared four active medications (alprazolam, carbamazepine, trifluoperazine hydrochloride and tranylcypromine sulphate) and placebo (Cowdry and Gardner, 1988), carbamazepine (average dose 820 mg/day) was the only drug to produce dramatic and significant improvement in the behavioural dyscontrol associated with borderline personality disorder. This was independent of effects on mood.

Carbamazepine has also been added to antipsychotic treatment in schizophrenics. In a double-blind 15-week crossover study of carba-mazepine (200 mg t.i.d.) and placebo, all 11 patients showed some improvement and 5 were markedly clinically better (Neppe, 1983). In fact 10 of the 11 continued on carbamazepine, allowing the dose of antipsychotic to be subsequently reduced. Another retrospective study showed a reduction in recorded aggressive episodes post-carbamazepine treatment (Luchins, 1984) and there are many other open and single-case studies confirming improvement in symptoms such as aggression and hostility. There is no evidence, however, that carbamazepine is effective in schizophrenics not exhibiting symptoms of dyscontrol. In fact it may produce deterioration because of a lowering of serum levels of antipsychotics (Kidron *et al.*, 1985). It has therefore been suggested that the rationale for adjunctive carbamaze-pine treatment in non-responsive psychosis should be the presence of target symptomatology such as hostility or affective lability (Neppe, 1988, 1990). A number of case reports describe positive effects in organic brain disorders (Elphick, 1989; Gleason and Schneider, 1990) but this was not confirmed in a double-blind study of patients with severe dementia (Chambers *et al.*, 1982). As only 3 of the 19 patients showed any evidence of physical aggression, it is difficult to make a definitive conclusion for this review. However, 87% of patients showed signs of restlessness which was not improved, whereas Reid *et al.* (1981) found that overactivity was improved in a double-blind trial of carbamazepine and placebo in patients with severe mental handi-cap. Carbamazepine has also been found to improve symptoms of poor impulse control and violence in other disorders, e.g. post-traumatic stress disorder (Wolf *et al.*, 1988) but surprisingly, there are no research reports of carbamazepine being added to the treatment regimen of epileptics who are still violent when their seizures have been clinically controlled with other anticonvulsants. A review of the use of carbamazepine in psychiatry concluded that it could be useful in the control of overactive, irritable and aggressive symptoms whatever the diagnosis and recommended its use on this basis in symptom control (Elphick, 1989). However, too few controlled trials have as yet been completed.

Stimulants and antidepressants

Methylphenidate, dextroamphetamine and pemoline have all shown some efficacy in the treatment of attention-deficit disorder in children and adolescents (Miczek, 1987) and there is some evidence that this effect is also shown in adults who still exhibit symptoms of minimal brain dysfunction. Hyperactivity and poor concentration usually improve with age but where aggressive behaviour is part of the syndrome, it may worsen. Stimulants have limited therapeutic indica-tions as abuse of stimulants and high-dose intoxication can lead to extreme aggression (Ellinwood, 1971), although this is often second-ary to a psychotic paranoid state. Although tricyclic antidepressants generally are not effective in the control of aggression, there is some limited evidence, from open trials, of the efficacy of monoamine oxidase inhibitors in attention-deficit disorder and borderline per-sonality disorder and as newer selective and reversible inhibitors such as moclobemide are developed, they should be tested.

Summary of drugs currently used

The drugs which are currently used have been developed to treat psychiatric, neurological or medical conditions and not aggressive behaviour *per se* and therefore any beneficial effects on symptoms of aggression are secondary. The antipsychotics are still the standard treatment for controlling aggressive behaviour across diagnoses but they have the disadvantage of serious side-effects such as tardive dyskinesia which make it important to consider alternatives. There is a growing body of evidence that two mood-stabilizing drugs used in the treatment of manic-depressive psychosis, lithium and carbamaze-pine, may have independent effects in controlling aggression and impulsiveness. They seem to be particularly helpful in patients who are unable but wish to control their own aggressive impulses but individuals who indulge their aggressiveness tend to deny the benefits even though they may respond (Cloninger, 1987). There is some recent evidence that beta-blockers are particularly useful in treating symptoms of aggression and rage associated with brain damage and can be added to antipsychotics to improve such symptoms in schizo-phrenia. However, it has been suggested that the efficacy of adjunctive beta-blockers is due in part to their modulation of neuroleptic-induced akathisia (Ratey *et al.*, 1985). Stimulants have only a limited role in the treatment of aggression associated with minimal brain dysfunction. The evidence for benzodiazepines is much more contro-versial and they are contraindicated in personality disorder. It is perhaps with this group of drugs that the distinction between thera-peutic and drugs of abuse becomes most blurred. Although they may be of benefit to some patients, there are no reliable predictive indices and so their use in the control of aggression should be limited to the acute phase during which sedation may be necessary while other longer-term treatment is instituted.

Although several of these drug groups have been shown to be effective in various types of aggression, if we ask to what extent they act specifically, it is doubtful if we yet have a specific antiaggressive compound. Currently used drugs probably exert a non-specific effect on all three components of the aggressive response (Fig. 10.1), whereas what we are looking for is a drug to act on the first component to increase the perceptual threshold.

THE ROLE OF SEROTONIN IN AGGRESSIVE BEHAVIOUR

There has been a lot of recent work on the monoamine neurotransmitter, serotonin (5HT). It has been termed the neurotransmitter most closely associated with mood (Montgomery and Fineberg, 1989) and there is a lot of evidence accruing that it has an inhibitory role in aggressive and impulsive behaviour. This evidence comes from two major sources: cerebrospinal fluid (CSF) analysis and hormonal responses. Studies of CSF analysis have been conducted both post-mortem from the brains of suicide victims (Traskman *et al.*, 1981; Asberg *et al.*, 1984;) and antemortem from people who have recently attempted suicide (Virkkunen *et al.*, 1989a) or an impulsive act, e.g. homicide or arson (Linnoila *et al.*, 1989; Virkkunen *et al.*, 1989b), or with a history of both aggressive behaviour and suicide attempts (Brown *et al.*, 1979, 1982).

This work is reviewed in more detail in Chapter 5, but the results consistently show a relationship between low levels of 5HT in the brain and impulsive acts. This is based on the measurement of 5-hydroxyindolacetic acid (5-HIAA: the main metabolite of 5HT), low levels of which are associated with inadequate impulse control (van Praag, 1991). One study has also been conducted in normal volunteers (Roy *et al.*, 1988). A negative correlation was found between 5-HIAA concentration in CSF and scores on the 'urge to act out hostility' subscale of the hostility and direction of hostility questionnaire (Foulds, 1965). The other method of studying 5HT in the brain has been by examining a hormone response (prolactin) to a challenge with a 5HT probe, e.g. with fenfluramine hydrochloride. Fenfluramine increases neurotransmission by increasing 5HT release which results in the release of prolactin.

Patients with various disorders such as borderline personality disorder, a history of suicide attempts or episodic alcohol abuse exhibited reduced prolactin responses to fenfluramine challenge compared with normal controls (Siever *et al.*, 1987; Coccaro *et al.*, 1989). Another study measured the prolactin response to a challenge with m-chlorophenylpiperazine (m-CPP) in men with antisocial personality disorder with substance abuse compared with healthy controls (Moss *et al.*, 1990). They found that assaultive aggression, resentment and irritability were associated with a diminished prolactin response to m-CPP. This work therefore confirms the correlation between reduced indices of 5HT function and irritable, impulsive aggression. The way forward in treatment therefore would seem to be in manipulating levels of serotonin.

The association between a deficiency in 5HT and impulsive aggression does not mean necessarily that the abnormality is causal in the behaviour but it should lead us systematically to evaluate the effects of serotonergic compounds. There are several types of serotonergic

Table 10.1   Specific serotonergic compounds

Receptor	Action	Drug
$5HT_{1A}$	Partial agonist	Buspirone Gepirone Ipsapirone Flesinoxam
$5HT_1$	Agonist	Eltoprazine Fluprazine
5HT	Reuptake inhibitor	Fluoxetine Fluvoxamine Sertraline Paroxetine

compound in existence (precursors, releasers, agonists, antagonists and reuptake inhibitors) and recently multiple receptor subtypes have been identified along with agents that act selectively at them.

Serotonergic effects of current compounds

Although none of the currently used compounds are specific to 5HT, many of them do have effects on the system which Coccaro (1989) has postulated may account for their beneficial effects on aggression. Tryptophan, a precursor for 5HT, has been shown to have some effects when added to maintenance antipsychotic treatment in schizophrenics convicted of violent crime or who have exhibited episodes of threatening aggression (Morand *et al.*, 1983). In another study, it showed an indirect effect by decreasing the need for p.r.n. injectable medication in aggressive psychiatric inpatients (Volavka *et al.*, 1990). Both lithium and carbamazepine enhance 5HT activity. Propranolol has antagonist properties at $5HT_{1A}$ and $5HT_{1B}$ receptors and although the efficacy of the antipsychotics would seem to be due to their antidopaminergic and sedative effects, they have been shown to block $5HT_2$ receptors (Glennon, 1990). However much more specific serotonergic compounds now exist, of which the agonists and uptake inhibitors (Table 10.1) will be detailed below.

Serotonin agonists

The prototype $5HT_{1A}$ agonist, buspirone, has been marketed for the treatment of anxiety in the post-benzodiazepine era but there is evidence that the later compounds, gepirone, ipsapirone and flesinoxam, are more specific in their action on 5HT without the additional dopaminergic effects of buspirone. These drugs have also been shown to have some antidepressant effect and may in fact have mood-stabilizing qualities in neurotic disorders. Animal work has pointed to the importance of the $5HT_{1A}$ and $5HT_{1B}$ receptor subtypes in the modulation of aggressive behaviour and a class of drugs which act specifically on the $5HT_1$ receptor (Sijbesma *et al.*, 1990), named the Serenics – eltoprazine and fluprazine – have been developed for their putative antiaggressive effects (Rasmussen *et al.*, 1990). These are the first drugs to be specifically developed to treat aggressive behaviour and we await the results of clinical trials. However the $5HT_{1B}$ receptor has not been identified in the human brain (Hoyer *et al.*, 1986) and other animal work has suggested that two serotonin classes of receptor may be differentially involved in the modulation of aggression: stimulation of an inhibitory $5HT_1$ receptor and blockade of the $5HT_2$ receptor (Lindgren and Kantak, 1987), producing antiaggressive effects. As there is interaction between these two receptors, antagonism of $5HT_2$ may enhance the function of $5HT_1$ (Montgomery and Fineberg, 1989), still implying a major role for the $5HT_1$ receptor in aggression. However, Montgomery and Fineberg (1989) have cautioned of the weakness of the link between animal models and psychiatric illness itself and we should bear in mind that all significant developments in psychopharmacology to date have happened by chance (Healy, 1991) so establishing the clinical efficacy of the serenics would represent a major advance.

The only 5HT receptor agonist yet to be tested formally in aggression is buspirone. There was a suggestion of a reduction in irritability from the original anxiety studies (Glitz and Pohl, 1991) and a series of case reports in people with developmental disabilities showed a decrease in aggression and self-injury (Ratey *et al.*, 1989). This has been confirmed in one double-blind study of aggression and anxiety in 6 patients with mild to moderate learning disabilities (Ratey *et al.*, 1991). These patients showed decreased aggressive and self-injurious behaviour after buspirone (up to 45 mg). The authors also noted a decrease in anxiety and agitation with no effect on cognitive performance. This latter may be an advantage which can be exploited with buspirone as it may mean that it can be used in conjunction with psychological therapies such as behaviour modification without impairing learning. Other case studies have shown buspirone to decrease aggressive, hostile and threatening behaviour in patients with brain damage (Colenda, 1988; Tiller, 1988; Levine, 1988) and one case report showed a dramatic improvement in impulsivity, anger and irritability in a patient with adult attention-deficit disorder (Balon, 1990). In an open-label crossover study of 4 autistic children, buspirone showed variable effects but it was superior to both fenfluramine and methylphenidate (Realmuto *et al.*, 1989). In an interesting case study comparing buspirone alone or in combination with a serotonin-enhancing diet (Gedye, 1991), it was found that both aggressive outbursts and self-injurious behaviour were improved by buspirone but greater efficacy was shown by the combination. There is thus some evidence accruing for a beneficial effect with buspirone but any interpretation is complicated by its effects on dopamine.

Serotonin reuptake inhibitors

The serotonin reuptake inhibitors, which increase central 5HT indirectly (by blocking reuptake and altering the availability of 5HT to one or other receptor) have been marketed as antidepressants but have had most success in treating obsessive–compulsive disorder which may itself be linked to impaired impulse control. It has been suggested that they work by inducing a state of indifference to intrusive thoughts (Healy, 1990) and so it is also possible that they will increase the perceptual threshold to potential sources of provocation and thereby reduce the likelihood of an impulsive aggressive response. Taken together with the work associating lowered central nervous system levels of 5HT and impulsive aggression, serotonergic compounds may be exerting a normalizing effect on a pre-existing deficiency (Fig. 10.2). Although it has been suggested that the serotonin reuptake inhibitors are effective on symptoms of impulsivity and irritability associated with panic and anxiety, there have been no systematic studies of their use to treat aggressive behaviour. Currently work is being conducted into the use of fluoxetine in borderline personality disorder (Coccaro, personal communication) and of paroxetine in symptoms of irritable aggression (Morton and Bond, unpublished work). An open trial of adjunctive fluoxetine in 8 patients with severe learning disabilities (Markowitz, 1990) did show an improvement in self-injurious behaviour when fluoxetine was added to antipsychotic medication. There is evidence of a hostile attributional bias in children and adolescents displaying high levels of reactive aggression (Dodge and Coie, 1987; Dodge *et al.*, 1990). They are more likely to attribute blame to others and thus to see any aversive act as provocation leading to anger and acting out. It would therefore be interesting to see if this attributional bias could be modified pharmacologically with either a 5HT agonist or reuptake inhibitor.

EVALUATION OF POTENTIAL ANTIAGGRESSIVE DRUGS

Although many studies have been cited in this chapter, the quality of drug trials in the study of aggressive behaviour is generally poor. There are some clinical guidelines for treatment (Yudofsky *et al.*, 1990), but very few studies comparing two or more putative antiaggressive compounds. The original work showing promising results

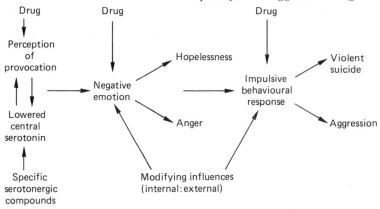

Fig. 10.2 *The effects of current drugs and the potential effects of serotonergic factors and manipulations on the aggressive response.*

with lithium has not been extended. It is therefore important to bear in mind certain elements in design (Table 10.2), apart from the obvious placebo and double-blind conditions. It is essential, as in any disorder, to describe the problem and to use classification criteria. However, in aggression, it is not necessarily diagnosis which is required but rather definition of symptom complexes. Furthermore it is important to use proper measures of evaluation. In outpatients, subjective reports should be supplemented by reports from relatives and in more severe inpatients, observer ratings are invaluable. Simple observer ratings do exist (Yudofsky *et al.*, 1986) but a well-constructed, fuller scale is described in this volume (Chapter 12). The design of the trial is important. Although crossover trials have advantages over attempting to match patient groups, often the length of active treatment is insufficient. Newer compounds have a delayed onset and may exert a more specific action not related to sedation which takes some weeks to show an effect. Neppe (1990) makes this point in relation to carbamazepine but it equally applies to more specific serotonergic compounds.

Finally, whenever drug treatment is considered, the therapeutic

Table 10.2 Elements necessary to establish the efficacy of a potential antiaggressive drug

1. Comparison of two putative antiaggressive compounds
2. Classification of the problem – symptom complexes, target behaviour
3. Proper measures of evaluation
4. Design: independent groups, crossover, single case
5. Compatibility with psychological treatment?

alliance and circumstances of treatment must be addressed, as has been made crystal clear by recent experiences with benzodiazepines. This means a drug which is non-sedative and does not impair skills-based learning is more readily compatible with psychological treatment. The drug may be given while other methods of behavioural management or anger control (Novaco, 1977) are instituted and then later withdrawn. This does not preclude that a few patients may need much longer – if not lifetime – treatment if they are unable or unwilling to learn new strategies. Although this is a contentious issue (Gunderson, 1986), many patients are already on antipsychotics or benzodiazepines long-term as a method of behavioural control, often without evidence of lasting efficacy and accompanied by potentially serious side-effects (Linaker, 1990; Wressell *et al.*, 1990). These elements may seem stringent for potential experimenters. However, trials do not have to be carried out in large groups. This is difficult in rare conditions and one of the reasons for so many case reports. Single case designs using strict criteria and randomization have been used in psychology for some time (Kazdin, 1982) and could be useful in psychopharmacology (Guyatt *et al.*, 1986).

IMPORTANCE OF SEROTINERGIC COMPOUNDS: CONCLUSIONS

Currently available evidence points to a major inhibitory role of 5HT in impulsive and aggressive behaviour. It is therefore important to evaluate both non-specific enhancers of 5HT, e.g. lithium, carbamazepine, and more specific newer compounds like agonists, e.g. buspirone, eltoprazine and reuptake inhibitors, e.g. fluoxetine, paroxetine, for their inhibitory effects on the various types of aggressive behaviour seen in the clinic. It is also important to remember that manipulation of one neurotransmitter system often leads to secondary alterations in other systems and so the alterations in one or several systems might have contributed to the observed effect. In particular, it appears that there is substantial overlap between the 5HT and dopaminergic systems. Low levels of homovanillic acid (HVA), a metabolite of dopamine, are also associated with suicidal acts (Montgomery, 1987; Traskman *et al.*, 1981) and levels of homovanillic acid and 5HIAA in the CSF are highly correlated. Antidopaminergic drugs are the currently preferred method of treating aggressive behaviour and other drugs are generally only used when they fail. Buspirone, although exerting its principal effects on 5HT, also has effects on dopamine and it may be that reuptake inhibitors are also indirectly neuroleptic (Healy, 1991). However, there may be a rationale for the use of drugs which are either principally dopaminergic or serotonergic. Cloninger (1987) suggests that instrumental or predatory aggression is exacerbated by dopamine and should therefore respond to drugs that act by blocking dopamine receptors, whereas reactive, affective aggression is inhibited by 5HT. It is this dimension of disinhibited, impulsive aggression directed at the self and/or others which is associated with observed indices of lowered central 5HT activity which should respond to specific serotonergic compounds. The effects of serotonergic compounds in other disorders, e.g. anxiety, obsessive–compulsive disorder, are not based on sedation and are not seen acutely. It is likely then that any antiaggressive effects will only be seen after several weeks' treatment and other more sedative drugs may be necessary in the interim. These compounds are, however, relatively safe alternatives with few side-effects and if their efficacy can be demonstrated, they may fast become the treatment of choice in the control of irritable, impulsive aggression.

REFERENCES

Alpert M., Allan E.R., Citrome L., Laury G., Sison C., Sudilovsky A. (1990). A double-blind, placebo-controlled study of adjunctive nadolol in the management of violent psychiatric patients. *Psychopharmacology Bulletin*; **26**: 367–71.

Asberg M., Bertilsson L., Martensson B., Scalia-Tomba G.P., Thoren P., Traskman L. (1984). CSF monoamine metabolites in melancholia. *Acta Psychiatrica Scandinavica*; **69**: 201–19

Balon R. (1990). Buspirone for attention deficit hyperactivity disorders. *Journal of Clinical Psychopharmacology*; **10**: 77.

Berkowitz L. (1989). The frustration-aggression hypothesis: an examination and reformulation. *Psychological Bulletin*; **106**: 59–73.

Bond A.J., Lader M.H. (1979). Benzodiazepines and aggression. In: *Psychopharmacology of Aggression* (Sandler M., ed.), pp. 173–82. New York: Raven Press.

Bond A., Lader M. (1988). Differential effects of oxazepman and lorazepam on aggressive responding. *Psychopharmacology*; **95**: 369–73.

Brown G.L., Goodwin F.K., Ballenger J.C., Goyer P.F., Major L.F. (1979). Aggression in humans correlates with cerebrospinal fluid amine metabolites. *Psychiatry Research*; **1**: 131–9.

Brown G.L., Ebert M.H., Goyer P.F. *et al.* (1982). Aggression, suicide and serotonin: relationship to CSF amine metabolites. *American Journal of Psychiatry*; **139**: 741–6.

Browne T.R. (1978). Clonazepam. *New England Journal of Medicine*; **299**: 812–16.

Campbell M., Small A.M., Green W.H., *et al.* (1984). Behavioral efficacy of haloperidol and lithium carbonate. *Archives of General Psychiatry*; **4**: 650–6.

Chambers C.A., Bain J., Rosbottom R. *et al.* (1982). Carbamazepine in senile dementia and overactivity: a placebo controlled double blind trial. *IRCS Medical Science*; **10**: 505–6.

Cloninger C.R. (1987). Pharmacological approaches to the treatment of antisocial behavior. In: *The Causes of Crime: New Biological Approaches* Sarnoff A., Mednick S.A., Moffit T.E., Stack S.A., eds). Cambridge: Cambridge University Press.

Coccaro E.F. (1989). Central serotonin and impulsive aggression. *British Journal of Psychiatry*; **155** (suppl. 8): 52–62.

Coccaro E.F., Siever L.J., Klar H.M. *et al.* (1989). Serotonergic studies in patients with affective and personality disorders. *Archives of General Psychiatry*; **46**: 587–99.

Coccaro E.F., Kramer E., Zemishlany Z. *et al.* (1990). Pharmacologic treatment of noncognitive behavioral disturbances in elderly demented patients. *American Journal of Psychiatry*; **147**: 1640–5.

Colenda C.C. (1988). Buspirone in treatment of agitated demented patient. *Lancet*; **I**: 1169

Conners C.K., Kramer R., Rothschild G.H., Schwartz L., Stone A. (1971). Treatment of young delinquent boys with diphenylhydantoin sodium and methylphenidate. *Archives of General Psychiatry*; **24**: 156–60.

Cowdry R.W., Gardner D.L. (1988). Pharmacotherapy of borderline personality disorder: alprazolam, carbamazepine, trifluoperazine and tranylcypromine. *Archives of General Psychiatry*; **45**: 111–19.

Dantzer R. (1977). Behavioral effects of benzodiazepines: a review. *Biobehavioural Reviews*; **1**: 71–86.

Dietch J.T., Jennings R.K. (1988). Aggressive dyscontrol in patients treated with benzodiazepines. *Journal of Clinical Psychiatry*; **49**: 184–8.

DiMascio A., Shader R.I., Harmatz J. (1969). Psychotropic drugs and induced hostility. *Psychosomatics*; **10**: 46–7.

Dodge K.A., Coie J.D. (1987). Social-information-processing factors in reactive and proactive aggression in children's peer groups. *Journal of Personality and Social Psychology*; **53**: 1146–58.

Dodge K.A., Price J.M., Bachorowski J.-A., Newman J.P. (1990). Hostile attributional biases in severely aggressive adolescents. *Journal of Abnormal Psychology*; **99**: 385–92.

Drug and Therapeutics Bulletin (1991). The sudden withdrawal of triazolam – reasons and consequences. *Drug and Therapeutics Bulletin*; **29**: 89–90.

Egdell H. (1980). Problem personalities – recognition and management. *Medicine*; **35**: 1789–93.

Eichelman B. (1987). Neurochemical and psychopharmacologic aspects of aggressive behaviour. In: *Psychopharmacology: The Third Generation of Progress* (Meltzer H.Y., ed.), pp. 697–704. New York: Raven Press.

Eichelman B. (1988). Toward a rational pharmacotherapy for aggressive and violent behaviour. *Hospital and Community Psychiatry*; **39**: 31–9.

Ellinwood E.H. (1971). Assault and homicide associated with amphetamine abuse. *American Journal of Psychiatry*; **127**: 90–5.

Elliott F.A. (1977). Propranolol for the control of belligerent behavior following acute brain damage. *Annals of Neurology*; **1**: 489–91.

Elphick M. (1989). Clinical issues in the use of carbamazepine in psychiatry: a review. *Psychological Medicine*: **19**: 591–604.

Foulds G. (1965). *Personality and Personal Illness*. London: Tavistock.

Gardner D.L., Cowdry R.W. (1985). Alprazolam-induced dyscontrol in borderline personality disorder. *American Journal of Psychiatry*; **142**: 98–100.

Gardner D.L., Cowdry R.W. (1986). Positive effects of carbamazepine on behavioral dyscontrol in borderline personality disorder. *American Journal of Psychiatry*; **143**: 519–22.

Gardos G., DiMascio A., Salzman C., Shader R.I. (1968). Differential actions of chlordiazepoxide and oxazepam in hostility. *Archives of General Psychiatry*; **18**: 758–60.

Gedye A. (1991). Buspirone alone or with serotonergic diet reduced aggression in a developmentally disabled adult. *Biological Psychiatry*; **30**: 88–91

Gleason R.P., Schneider L.S. (1990). Carbamazepine treatment of agitation in Alzheimer's outpatients refractory to neuroleptics. *Journal of Clinical Psychiatry*; **51**: 115–18.

Glennon R.A. (1990). Serotonin receptors: clinical implications. *Neuroscience and Biobehavioural Reviews*; **14**: 35–47.

Glitz D.A., Pohl R. (1991). 5-HT$_{1A}$ partial agonists. What is their future? *Drugs*; **41**: 11–18.

Goldberg S.C., Shulz S.C., Shulz P.N., Resnick R.J., Haymer R.M., Friedelro R.O. (1986). Borderline and schizotypal personality disorders treated with low dose of thiothixene versus placebo. *Archives of General Psychiatry*; **43**: 580–6.

Graham M.A. (1988). Misuse of midazolam. *Journal of Clinical Psychiatry*; **49**: 244.

Greendyke R.M., Kanter D.R. (1986). Therapeutic effects of pindolol on behavioral disturbances associated with organic brain disease: a double-blind study. *Journal of Clinical Psychiatry*; **47**: 423–6.

Greendyke R.M., Schuster D.B., Wooton J.A. (1984). Propranolol in the treatment of patients with organic brain disease. *Journal of Clinical Psychopharmacology*; **4**: 282–5.

Greendyke R.M., Kanter D.R., Schuster D.B., Verstreate S., Wooton J. (1986). Propranolol treatment of assaultive patients with organic brain disease. A double-blind crossover, placebo-controlled study. *Journal of Nervous and Mental Disease*; **174**: 290–4.

Gualtieri C.T, Schroeder S.R. (1989). Pharmacotherapy for self-injurious behavior: preliminary tests of the D1 hypothesis. *Psychopharmacology Bulletin*; **25**: 364–1.

Gunderson J.G. (1986). Pharmacotherapy for patients with borderline disorders. *Archives of General Psychiatry*; **43**: 690–700.

Guyatt G., Sackett D., Taylor W., Chong J., Roberts R., Pugsley S. (1986). Determining optimal therapy – randomized trials in individual patients. *New England Journal of Medicine*; **314**: 889–92.

Hanssen T., Heyden T., Sundberg I., Alfredsson G., Nybäck H., Wetterberg L. (1980). Propranolol in schizophrenia: clinical, metabolic and pharmacological findings. *Archives of General Psychiatry*; **37**: 685–90.

Healy D. (1990). The psychopharmacological era: notes towards a history. *Journal of Psychopharmacology*; **4**: 152–67.

Healy D. (1991). The marketing of 5-hydroxytryptamine: depression or anxiety. *British Journal of Psychiatry*; **158**: 737–42.

Hoyer D., Pazos A., Probst A., Palacios J.M. (1986). Serotonin receptors in human brain. I. Characterization and autoradiographic localisation of 5HT$_{1A}$ recognition sites. Apparent absence of 5HT$_{1B}$ sites. *Brain Research*; **376**: 85–96.

Itil T.M., Wadud A. (1975). Treatment of human aggression with major tranquilizers, antidepressants and newer psychotropic drugs. *Journal of Nervous and Mental Diseases*; **160**: 83–99.

Jus A., Villeneuve J.A., Gautier J. (1973). Some remarks on the influence of lithium carbonate on patients with temporal lobe epilepsy. *International Journal of Clinical Pharmacology Therapy and Toxicology*; **7**: 67–74.

Kastner T., Burlingham K., Friedman F.L. (1990). Metoprolol for aggressive behaviour in persons with mental retardation. *American Family Physician*; **42**: 1585–8.

Kazdin A.E. (1982). *Single-case Research Designs: Methods for Clinical and Applied Settings*. New York: Oxford University Press.

Kidron R., Averbuch I., Klein E., Belmaker R.H. (1985). Carbamazepine-induced reduction of blood levels of haloperidol in chronic schizophrenia. *Biological Psychiatry*; **20**: 219–22.

Levanthal B.L., Brodie H.K.H. (1981). The pharmacology of violence. In: *Biobehavioral Aspects of Aggression* (Hamburg D. A., Trudeau M.B., eds), pp. 85–106. New York: Liss.

Levine A.M. (1988). Buspirone and agitation in head injury. *Brain Injury*; **2**: 165–87.

Linaker O.M. (1990). Frequency of determinants for psychotropic drug use in an institution for the mentally retarded. *British Journal of Psychiatry*; **156**: 525–30.

Lindgren T., Kantak K.M. (1987). Effects of serotonin receptor agonists and antagonists on offensive aggression in mice. *Aggressive Behaviour*; **13**: 87–96.

Links P.S., Boiago I., Steiner M. (1989). Usefulness of lithium for borderline patients. *Biological Psychiatry*; **25**: 84A–9A.

Linnoila M., De Jong J., Virkkunen M. (1989). Family history of alcoholism in violent offenders and impulsive fire setters. *Archives of General Psychiatry*; **46**: 613–16.

Lion J.R. (1979). Benzodiazepines in the treatment of aggressive patients. *Journal of Clinical Psychiatry*; **40**: 70–1.

Luchins D. (1984). Carbamazepine in violent nonepileptic schizophrenics. *Psychopharmacology Bulletin*; **20**: 569–71.

Luchins D.J., Dojka D. (1989). Lithium and propranolol in aggression and self-injurious behavior in the mentally retarded. *Psychopharmacology Bulletin*; **25**: 372–5.

Lynch D.M., Eliatamby C.L.S., Anderson A.A. (1985). Pipothiazine palmitate in the management of aggressive mentally handicapped patients. *British Journal of Psychiatry*; **146**: 525–9.

Markowitz P.I. (1990). Fluoxetine treatment of self-injurious behaviour in mentally retarded patients. *Journal of Clinical Psychopharmacology*; **10**: 299–300.

Mattes J.A. (1990). Comparative effectiveness of carbamazepine and propranolol for rage attacks. *Journal of Neuropsychiatry*; **2**: 159–64.

Mattes J.A., Rosenberg J., Maya D. (1984). Carbamazepine versus propranolol in patients with uncontrolled rage outbursts. *Psychopharmacology Bulletin*; **20**: 98–106.

Mednick S.A., Brennan P., Kandel E. (1988). Predisposition to violence. *Aggressive Behaviour*; **14**: 25–33.

Mellerup E.T., Plenge P. (1990). The side effects of lithium. *Biological Psychiatry*; **28**: 464–6.

Mendoza R., Djenderedjian A.H., Adams J., Ananth J. (1987). Midazolam in acute psychotic patients with hyperarousal. *Journal of Clinical Psychiatry*; **48**: 291–2.

Miczek K.A. (1987). The psychopharmacology of aggression. In: *Handbook of Psychopharmacology*, vol. 19. *New Directions in Behavioral Pharmacology* (Iversen L.L., Iversen S.D., Snyder S.H., eds), pp. 183–328. New York: Plenum Press.

Montgomery S.A. (1987). The psychopharmacology of borderline personality disorders. *Acta Psychiatrica Belgica*; **87**: 260–6.

Montgomery S.A., Fineberg N. (1989). Is there a relationship between serotonin receptor subtypes and selectivity of response in specific psychiatric illnesses? *British Journal of Psychiatry*; **155** (suppl. 8): 63–70.

Morand C., Young S.N., Ervin F.R. (1983). Clinical response of aggressive schizophrenics to oral tryptophan. *Biological Psychiatry*; **18**: 575–8.

Mos J., Olivier B. (1987). Pro-aggressive actions of benzodiazepines. In: *Ethopharmacology of Agonistic Behaviour in Animals and Humans* Olivier B., Mos J., Brain P.F., eds), pp. 187–206. Dordrecht: Martinus Nijhoff.

Moss H.B., Yao J.K., Panzak G.L. (1990). Serotonergic responsivity and behavioral dimensions in antisocial personality disorder with substance abuse. *Biological Psychiatry*; **28**: 325–38.

Neppe V.M. (1983). Carbamazepine as adjunctive treatment in nonepileptic chronic inpatients with EEG temporal lobe abnormalities. *Journal of Clinical Psychiatry*; **44**: 326–31.

Neppe V.M. (1988). Carbamazepine in nonresponsive psychosis. *Journal of Clinical Psychiatry*; **49** (suppl. 4): 22–8.

Neppe V.M. (1990). Carbamazepine in the non-affective psychotic and in non-psychotic dyscontrol. *International Clinical Psychopharmacology*; **5** (suppl. 1): 43–54.

Novaco R.W. (1977). A stress inoculation approach to anger management in the training of law enforcement officers. *American Journal of Community Psychology*; **45**: 600–8.

Pilowsky L.S. Ring H., Shine P., Batlersby M., Lader M. (1992). Rapid tranquillisation – a survey of emergency prescribing in a general psychiatric hospital. *British Journal of Psychiatry*; **160**: 831–5.

Platt J.E., Campbell M., Green W.H., Grega D.M. (1984). Cognitive effects of lithium carbonate and haloperidol in treatment-resistant aggressive children. *Archives of General Psychiatry*; **41**: 657–62.

Polakoff S.A., Sorgi P.J., Ratey J.J. (1986). The treatment of impulsive and aggressive behaviour with nadolol. *Journal of Clinical Psychopharmacology*; **6**: 125–6.

Pollock V.E., Briere J., Schneider L., Knop J., Mednick S.A., Goodwin D.W. (1990). Childhood antecedents of antisocial behaviour: Parental alcoholism and physical abusiveness. *American Journal of Psychiatry*; **147**: 1290–3.

Rasmussen D.I., Olivier B., Raghoebar M., Mos J. (1990). Possible clinical applications of serenics and some implications of their preclinical profile for their clinical use in psychiatric disorders. *Drug Metabolism and Drug Interactions*; **8**: 159–86.

Ratey J., Sorgi P., Polakoff S. (1985). Nadolol as a treatment for akathisia. *American Journal of Psychiatry*; **142**: 640–1.

Ratey J.J., Mikkelsen E.J., Bushnell Smith G. *et al.* (1986). β-blockers in the severely and profoundly mentally retarded. *Journal of Clinical Psychopharmacology*; **6**: 103–7.

Ratey J.J., Mikkelsen E., Sorgi P. *et al.*, (1987). Autism: the treatment of aggressive behaviors. *Journal of Clinical Psychopharmacology*; **7**: 35–41.

Ratey J.J., Sovner R., Mikkelsen E., Chmielinski H.E. (1989). Buspirone therapy for maladaptive behavior and anxiety in developmentally disabled persons. *Journal of Clinical Psychiatry*; **50**: 382–4.

Ratey J., Sovner R., Parks A., Rogentine K. (1991). Buspirone treatment of aggression and anxiety in mentally retarded patients: a multiple-baseline, placebo lead-in study. *Journal of Clinical Psychiatry*; **52**: 159–62.

Realmuto G.M., August G.J., Garfinkel B.D. (1989). Clinical effect of buspirone in autistic children. *Journal of Clinical Psychopharmacology*; **9**: 122–5.

Regestein Q.R., Reich P. (1985). Agitation observed during treatment with newer hypnotic drugs. *Journal of Clinical Psychiatry*; **46**: 280–3.

Reid A.H., Naylor C.J., Kay D.S. (1981). A double-blind, placebo-controlled crossover trial of carbamazepine in overactive, severely mentally handicapped patients. *Psychological Medicine*; **11**: 109–13.

Rosenbaum J.F., Woods S.W., Groves J.E., Klerman G.L. (1984). Emergence of hostility during alprazolam treatment. *American Journal of Psychiatry*; **141**: 792–3.

Roy A., Adinoff B., Linnoila M. (1988). Acting out hostility in normal volunteers: negative correlation with levels of 5HIAA in cerebrospinal fluid. *Psychiatry Research*; **24**: 187–94.

Ruedrich S.L., Grush L., Wilson J. (1990). Beta adrenergic blocking medications for aggressive or self-injurious mentally retarded persons. *American Journal on Mental Retardation*; **95**: 110–19.

Salzman C. (1988). Use of benzodiazepines to control disruptive behavior in inpatients. *Journal of Clinical Psychiatry*; **49** (suppl.): 13–15.

Salzman C., Kochansky G.E., Shader R.I., Porrino L.J., Harmatz J.S., Swett C.P. (1974). Chlordiazepoxide-induced hostility in a small group setting. *Archives of General Psychiatry*; **31**: 401–5.

Salzman C., Kochansky G.E., Shader R.I., Harmhatz J.S., Ogletree A.M. (1975). Is oxazepam associated with hostility? *Disorders of the Nervous System*; **36**: 30–2.

Shader R.I., Jackson A.H., Dodes L.M. (1974). The antiaggressive effects of lithium in man. *Psychopharmacologia*; **40**: 17–24.

Sheard M.H. (1971). Effects of lithium in human aggression. *Nature*; **230**: 113–14.

Sheard M.H. (1975). Lithium in the treatment of aggression. *Journal of Nervous and Mental Disease*; **160**: 108–18.

Sheard M.H. (1984). Clinical pharmacology of aggressive behavior. *Clinical Neuropharmacology*; **7**: 173–83.

Sheard M.H. (1988). Clinical pharmacology of aggressive behaviour: a review. *Clinical Neuropharmacology*; **11**: 483–92.

Sheard M.H., Marini J.L., Bridges C.I., Wagner E. (1976). The effect of lithium in impulsive aggressive behavior in man. *American Journal of Psychiatry*; **133**: 1409–13.

Siever L.J. Coccaro E.F., Zemishlany Z. *et al.* (1987). Psychobiology of personality disorders: pharmacologic implications. *Psychopharmacology Bulletin*; **23**: 333–6.

Sijbesma H., Schipper J., De Kloet E.R. (1990). Eltoprazine, a drug which reduces aggressive behavior, binds selectively to 5-HT₁ receptor sites in the rat brain: an autoradiographic study. *European Journal of Pharmacology*; **177**: 55–66.

Silver J.M., Yudofsky S.C., Kogan M., Katz B.L. (1986). Elevation of thioridazine plasma levels by propranolol. *American Journal of Psychiatry*; **143**: 1290–2.

Soloff P.H., George A., Nathan R.S., Schulz P.M., Ulrich R.F., Perel J.M. (1986). Progress in pharmacotherapy of borderline disorders: a double blind study of amytriptyline, haloperidol and placebo. *Archives of General Psychiatry*; **43**: 691–7.

Sorgi P.J., Ratey J.J., Polakoff S. (1986). β-adrenergic blockers for the control of aggressive behavior in patients with chronic schizophrenia. *American Journal of Psychiatry*; **143**: 775–6.

Sovner R., Hurley A. (1981). The management of chronic behaviour disorders in mentally retarded adults with lithium carbonate. *Journal of Nervous and Mental Disease*; **169**: 191–5.

Spreat S., Behar D., Reneski B., Miazzo P. (1989). Lithium carbonate for aggression in mentally retarded persons. *Comprehensive Psychiatry*; **30**: 505–11.

Sutton C. (1991). Safety and threat. Neglected concepts in psychology. *Psychologist*; **14**: 459–61.

Tiller J.G. (1988). Short-term buspirone treatment in disinhibition with dementia. *Lancet*; **1**: 1169.

Traskman L., Asberg M., Bertilsson L., Sjostrand L. (1981). Monoamine metabolites in CSF and suicidal behavior. *Archives of General Psychiatry*; **38**: 631–6.

Tuason V.B. (1986). A comparison of parenteral loxapine and haloperidol in hostile and aggressive acutely schizophrenic patients. *Journal of Clinical Psychiatry*; **47**: 126–9.

Tupin J.P., Smith D.B., Clanon T.L., Kim L.I., Nugent A., Groupe A. (1973). The long-term use of lithium in aggressive prisoners. *Comprehensive Psychiatry*; **14**: 311–17.

Tyrer P., Seivewright N. (1988). Pharmacological treatment of personality disorders. *Clinical Neuropharmacology*; **11**: 493–9.

Tyrer S.P., Walsh A., Edwards D.E., Berney T.P., Stephens D.A. (1984). Factors associated with a good response to lithium in aggressive mentally handicapped subjects. *Progress in Neuro-psychopharmacology and Biological Psychiatry*; **8**: 751–5.

van Praag H.M. (1991). Serotonergic dysfunction and aggression control. *Psychological Medicine*; **21**: 15–19.

Virkkunen M., De Jong J., Bartko J., Linnoila M. (1989a). Psychobiological concomitants of history of suicide attempts among violent offenders and impulsive fire setters. *Archives of General Psychiatry*; **46**: 604–6.

Virkkunen M., De Jong J., Bartko J., Goodwin F.K., Linnoila M. (1989b).

Relationship of psychobiological variables to recidivism in violent offenders and impulsive fire setters. *Archives of General Psychiatry*; **46**: 600–3.

Volavka J., Crowner M., Brizer D., Convit A., van Praag H., Suckow R. (1990). Tryptophan treatment of aggressive psychiatric inpatients. *Biological Psychiatry*; **28**: 728–32.

Wilkinson C.J. (1985). Effects of diazepam (Valium) and trait anxiety on human physical aggression and emotional state. *Journal of Behavioural Medicine*; **8**: 101–14.

Williams D.T., Mehl R., Yudofsky S., Adams D., Roseman B. (1982). The effect of propranolol on uncontrolled rage outbursts in children and adolescents with organic brain dysfunction. *Journal of the American Academy of Child Psychiatry*; **21**: 129–35.

Wolf M.E., Alavi A., Mosnaim A.D. (1988). Post-traumatic stress disorder in Vietnam veterans. Clinical and EEG findings; possible therapeutic effects of carbamazepine. *Biological Psychiatry*; **23**: 642–4.

Wressell S.E., Tyrer S.P., Berney T.P. (1990). Reduction in antipsychotic drug dosage in mentally handicapped patients. A hospital study. *British Journal of Psychiatry*; **157**: 101–6.

Yudofsky S., Williams D., Gorman J. (1981). Propranolol in the treatment of rage and violent behavior in patients with chronic brain syndrome. *American Journal of Psychiatry*; **138**: 218–20.

Yudofsky S.C., Silver J.M., Jackson W., Endicott J., Williams D. (1986). The overt aggression scale: an operationalised rating scale for verbal and physical aggression. *American Journal of Psychiatry*; **143**: 35–9.

Yudofsky S.C., Silver J.M., Schneider S.E. (1987). Pharmacologic treatment of aggression. *Psychiatric Annals*; **17**: 397–407.

Yudofsky S.C., Silver J.M., Hales R.E. (1990). Pharmacologic management of aggression in the elderly. *Journal of Clinical Psychiatry*; **51** (suppl. 10): 22–8.

11 *The treatment of challenging behaviour in people with learning difficulties*

GLYNIS MURPHY

Historically, the study of learning difficulties has been marked by disputes over terminology. The terms 'idiocy' and 'subnormality' of the 1950s now sound profoundly insulting. The terms which replaced these, 'mental deficiency' and 'mental retardation' also seem pejorative now. In the UK, the current preferred term is no longer 'mental handicap' but, rather, 'learning difficulties' and this is preferred by People First, an organization for people with such disabilities.

Disputes have also arisen about the best terms for undesirable behaviour. 'Maladaptive behaviour', 'problem behaviour', 'behaviour disorder', 'difficult behaviour' all appear in the clinical and research literature and all have been criticized recently because the terms imply that the client is the seat of the problem (and thus that it is only the client who needs treatment). The current preferred alternative, which is intended to emphasize the role of services, is 'challenging behaviour' and Emerson *et al.* (1988) have defined this as:

> behaviour of such intensity, frequency or duration that the physical safety of the person or others is likely to be placed in serious jeopardy, or behaviour which is likely to seriously limit or delay access to and use of ordinary community facilities.

In the 1980s, the South East Thames Regional Health Authority in the UK set up several specialist services for people with learning difficulties to support those with special needs, as one of the largest hospitals in the UK (Darenth Park Hospital in Dartford) was going to close in 1987. Two of these services, the Special Development Team (SDT; Emerson *et al.*, 1987, 1988) and the Mental Impairment Evaluation and Treatment Service (MIETS; Murphy and Clare, 1991; Murphy *et al.*, 1991) were designed to support clients with challenging behaviour. Both services found that aggressive behaviour was by far the most common challenge to services, amongst the clients referred, even though the SDT served people with severe/profound learning difficulties and MIETS served people with mild learning difficulties, so

Table 11.1   The five most common challenging behaviours at referral to two regional services for people with learning difficulties

SDT (n = 31)		MIETS (n = 19)	
Physical assault	85%	Physical assault	58%
Damage to environment	52%	Arson	21%
Self-injury	26%	Sexual offences	16%
Severe non-compliance	16%	Self-injury	5%
Faecal smearing	16%	Theft	5%

SDT = Special Development Team; MIETS = Mental Impairment Evaluation and Treatment Service.

that the other referral problems to the two services were somewhat different (Table 11.1).

This review will concentrate on aggressive behaviour. Many of the treatment issues are very similar for different challenging behaviours (see, for example, Holland and Murphy, 1990; Oliver and Head, 1990).

DEFINITIONS

Aggression has been defined as 'behaviour directed towards causing, or threatening to cause physical injury to others' (Klama, 1988). Green (1990) gives a more extensive definition:

1.   Aggression consists of the delivery of noxious stimuli by one organism to another.
2.   The noxious stimuli are delivered with the intent to harm the victim.
3.   The aggressor expects that the noxious stimuli will have their intended effect.

Both of these definitions include the notion of intent. People with learning difficulties frequently develop no spoken language and some may have little or no understanding of language either. Aggressive behaviour has therefore been defined more in terms of topography than by intent in learning difficulties (Day *et al.*, 1991) and two kinds of aggression are recognized: hostile aggression and instrumental aggression. Green (1990) defines hostile (or affective or angry) aggression as being 'accompanied by strong negative emotional states'. He asserts that this type of aggression has as 'its main goal. . .injury or harm to the provocateur' and that 'it is accompanied by distinctive patterns of activity in the central and autonomic nervous system'. Instrumental aggression, in contrast, he notes, 'is not associated with anger. The primary goal is not injury or harm to the victim but some other desired end' (Green, 1990).

This distinction between instrumental and hostile aggression is difficult to apply in people with learning difficulties. It is often impossible to determine for someone with severe learning disabilities whether or not they are angry and whether or not their goal at any point in time is to injure or harm someone. Consequently, most aggressive behaviour amongst people with severe learning difficulties (without language) has been assumed to be instrumental aggression; aggression amongst less disabled people has recently been assumed to be hostile aggression. In both cases, these assumptions may be incorrect at times.

PREVALENCE

Recent total population surveys of people in touch with services for those with learning difficulties estimate that between 11 and 18% are physically aggressive to others (Jacobson, 1982; Harris, 1992). The prevalence of challenging behaviour in general and aggression in particular is thought to be higher amongst people with learning difficulties than amongst other populations. There are numerous possible reasons for this and some of the treatment techniques discussed below are linked to particular views of the causes of this raised prevalence. It is possible, for example, that brain damage or dysfunction leads directly to challenging behaviour as well as to learning difficulties. Direct links of this kind certainly appear to exist for some disorders, such as for Lesch–Nyhan syndrome (with self-injury) and Prader–Willi syndrome (with overeating). However, for most challenging behaviour there is little evidence of such direct links and it is likely that social and environmental factors are more important (Murphy, 1992a).

Much aggressive behaviour arises out of social interactions and people with learning difficulties tend to have poor social skills, particularly if they are autistic, with necessarily poorer negotiating skills because of their language lag (Clements, 1987). Equally, people with learning difficulties are thought to be less skilled at self-control (Whitman, 1990), so that they may be more likely to act aggressively when angry. They suffer a raised incidence of psychiatric disorders and this has also been suggested as a possible cause of the increased rates of challenging behaviour by some, though the confusion over definitions, terminology and reliable diagnosis makes this a difficult hypothesis to disprove. Finally, those in the normalization movement have proposed that 'deviant' behaviour results from the poor quality of life and the low value of social roles assigned to people with learning difficulties (Wolfensberger, 1980, 1983), though some maintain that this is an ideological rather than a scientific position.

INSTRUMENTAL AGGRESSION AND OPERANT TREATMENT

Initially, the psychological treatment of aggression amongst people with learning difficulties relied on an operant model of aggression, which was assumed to be instrumental in origin. In the 1960s and 1970s the presumption was that the consequences of a person's aggressive behaviour must be positively or negatively reinforcing, in the operant sense, leading to an increased likelihood of similar responding in the future. In assessment and treatment, relatively little attention was paid to the antecedent term (A) in the $A \rightarrow B \rightarrow C$ model (where B = behaviour) and there was usually a concentrated effort to remove or modify C, the consequences. Often, the treatment reports involved either single cases or very small numbers of extremely aggressive clients.

Many early studies relied on the application of aversive consequences to suppress the aggressive behaviour. In some cases the aversive stimulus employed was time out from positive reinforcement. Hamilton *et al.* (1967), for example, demonstrated that it was possible to employ exclusionary time to reduce the aggressive, self-injurious and destructive behaviour of 5 severely disabled women resident on an 'overcrowded and understaffed' ward of a state hospital in the USA. Little mention was made of positive reinforcement procedures and it was tacitly assumed that the function of the challenging behaviours was to gain staff attention. This may have been the case, given the poor staffing levels, and it appeared to be certainly true for the 18-year-old profoundly disabled woman who Vukelich and Hake (1971) treated by time out, with additional attention. Other studies employed more punitive methods: Risley (1968) employed contingent electric shock to reduce the aggressive and dangerous climbing behaviour of a 6-year-old autistic girl (extinction and time out procedures having already failed to eliminate the challenging behaviours) and Birnbauer (1968) also used contingent electric shock to eliminate the aggressive biting of a 14-year-old profoundly disabled boy.

These early studies frequently reported on the treatment of severely aggressive, extremely disabled young people, who were often living in deprived hospital conditions. There is considerable evidence that challenging behaviour leads to hospitalization, rather than vice versa but there is also now a general acceptance that hospital settings provide very impoverished environments and rarely assist in skill-building. The studies above would be heavily criticized now on three main counts:

1.   that they did not adopt a constructional approach;
2.   that insufficient attention was paid to the analysis of the naturally occurring antecedents and consequences (i.e. that there was an inadequate functional analysis); and
3.   that aversive stimuli were too readily applied.

The constructional approach to the treatment of challenging behaviours (Cullen and Partridge, 1981; Donnellan *et al.*, 1988) requires the therapist to consider what the client *should* have been doing *instead* of the aggressive (or other) behaviour. Treatment then focuses on building that alternative behaviour, using positive reinforcement techniques such as differential reinforcement of other behaviour (DRO) or differential reinforcement of incompatible behaviour (DRI). Examples of treatment studies where such an approach was used for reducing severe aggression are rare although occasional early studies made a clear attempt to attend to the positive aspects of treatment, in combination with aversive stimuli (Vukelich and Hake, 1971).

Mace *et al.* (1983), however, eliminated the tantrums and aggression (hitting scratching and head-butting) of an adolescent boy with severe learning difficulties by positively reinforcing behaviours incompatible with the challenging behaviours and by teaching positive compliance (i.e. without providing any direct consequences to the aggression and tantrums). At 8-month follow-up, no challenging behaviours were reported and the client had been able to move to a community-based setting, out of the institution where the treatment had been carried out.

The rapid resorting to aversive stimuli seen in early treatment studies is now considered to constitute unacceptable practice. Some therapists believe that aversive stimuli should never be considered (Guess *et al.*, 1987; Donnellan and LaVigna, 1991), some that certain kinds of aversive stimuli should always be rejected (Horner, 1990; Murphy, 1992b) and the remainder believe that aversive stimuli should occasionally be employed but only when positive programming has been properly tried (and shown to have failed) and the client's right to effective treatment is otherwise endangered (Mulick, 1990; Linscheid *et al.*, 1990).

There is general agreement that the early reliance on aversive stimuli may well have stemmed partly from inadequate functional analyses, as Carr *et al.* (1991) have proposed. Essentially, it is possible for aggressive behaviour to develop a variety of operant functions in a person's life, regardless of how and why the behaviour begins. It may occur under conditions of low levels of staff attention, may be unwittingly reinforced when followed by the provision of staff attention and hence develop an attention-gaining function (e.g. Vukelich and Hake, 1971). Alternatively, it may occur under conditions of high demand or on presentation of tasks, be negatively reinforced when followed by the removal of the tasks or demands and hence develop a demand escape or demand avoidance function (Carr *et al.*, 1980). It is also possible, particularly for people with sensory deficits and/or those living under conditions of sensory deprivation, that the behaviour may be positively reinforced by sensory stimuli which ensue (such as the cries of the victim and shouts of staff members) so that the behaviour develops a sensory stimulation function. In addition, the behaviour may appear when the person is relatively deprived of food or drink, may be positively reinforced when followed by provision of food or drink and thus develops the function of obtaining tangible reinforcers.

Until the early 1980s, there were relatively few adequate techniques for determining the function of a person's challenging behaviour and frequently functional analysis received scant attention in treatment studies. The reliance on aversive stimuli to suppress behaviour can be seen as an inevitable consequence of this, since the provision of certain forms of treatment (such as 'extinction' by removal of staff attention) would have been successful in reducing challenging behaviour with one function (e.g. an attention-gaining function) but would have worsened the same behaviour if it had a different function (e.g. escaping tasks). The therapist may then have turned in desperation to aversive stimuli, saying that she or he had tried other methods but to no avail.

Since the early 1980s, however, the technology for examining the function of challenging behaviour in people who lack speech (and cannot therefore tell anyone about their feelings and motivations) has advanced considerably (Durand and Crimmins, 1988; Oliver, 1991). In Iwata *et al.*'s (1982) seminal paper, a set of analogue conditions were proposed. These were brief sessions intended to mimic natural conditions in a person's life (e.g. provision of demands, deprivation of attention, provision of attention, deprivation of sensory stimuli and provision of sensory stimuli) and in which rates of challenging behaviour could be observed, so that conclusions could be drawn about the function of a behaviour. As an example of this approach, Slifer *et al.* (1986) analysed a profoundly disabled 13-year-old boy's aggression using analogue conditions and concluded that the function of his aggression was to escape from demands. The behavioural treatment phase involved positively reinforcing compliance with requests, provision of guided assistance with requests (to reduce task difficulty, which is known to be an important factor in demand avoidance) and termination of demands only when *no* aggression was occurring. This proved extremely successful: aggression was reduced from about 70 to about 5 responses per hour with staff and compliance increased from about 38 to 63% with staff and with similar changes with the boy's family. Neuroleptic medication, which had been used in an attempt to reduce the aggressive behaviour, was gradually withdrawn and the boy was discharged from hospital, with follow-up 12 weeks later showing good short-term maintenance.

It is also possible to view challenging behaviours as having a communicative function (Carr and Durand, 1985). In the above example, it could be said that initially the boy's aggression had the function of 'telling' staff and parents that he did not wish to do something. Similarly, for the person Vukelich and Hake (1971) treated, it could be said that the aggressive behaviour functioned as a request for staff attention. Clearly aggressive behaviour could also appear to act as a request for something tangible or for something to do. Thus the challenging behaviours of many children and adults with severe or profound learning difficulties could be considered to have the effect of a communicative act. The behaviour is not likely always to be accompanied by evidence of intent, so that it must be considered to be perlocutionary rather than illocutionary or locutionary behaviour (Day *et al.*, 1986). Nevertheless, viewing the behaviour as communicative has heuristic value since it turns the therapist's attention to the possibility of reducing the challenging behaviour by teaching an acceptable communicative response (functional communication training).

Precisely this approach was adopted by Carr and Durand (1985) in working with autistic children in a classroom setting. A functional analysis, using analogue conditions, indicated that some of the children's challenging behaviour had an escape function and appeared when the tasks set were too hard for them; others showed challenging behaviour only when there were relatively low levels of teacher attention. Without providing direct consequences of any kind to the aggressive and/or self-injurious behaviour, Carr and Durand taught the children either to request help ('Help me' or 'I don't understand') or to ask for staff praise ('Am I doing good work?'). The results demonstrated the effectiveness of providing communication training linked to the function of the child's behaviour, as their challenging behaviour reduced while their use of the appropriate phrase increased (but it did not reduce when the phrase taught did not match the function of the aggression or self-injury).

Since this study, a number of others have confirmed the short- and long-term effectiveness of functional communication training for a variety of challenging behaviours with more disabled children and adults, including those with sensory impairments (Durand and Kishi, 1987; Wacker *et al.*, 1990; Durand and Carr, 1991). Considerable ingenuity has been evident in assisting the clients to make communicative responses despite their being severely or profoundly disabled and non-speaking. Wacker *et al.* (1990), for example, taught one young woman to press a switch on a tape recorder (with a continuous tape) on which was recorded a communicative message ('I am bored, give me something to do') while Durand and Kishi (1987) taught their clients to give tokens to the staff at appropriate times, the communicative message being written on the token.

HOSTILE AGGRESSION

In the 1930s Dollard and colleagues proposed that all human aggression was the result of frustration (Dollard *et al.*, 1939). It is now thought that although Dollard was wrong to include instrumental aggression, much hostile aggression is indeed triggered by frustration. Berkowitz (1988), however, suggested that frustrations only produced aggressive behaviour 'to the extent that they are aversive and give rise to negative affect'. He proposed that aversive events which give rise to negative affect, might lead to a variety of behavioural responses (such as fight and flight) as well as to cognitions (expectations, attributions, etc.). Aversive stimuli known to produce anger and aggression include physical pain, physical discomfort (such as results from viewing disgusting scenes) and stimuli associated with previous strong negative affect (Berkowitz, 1988) as well as the well-recognized stimuli arising in social interactions (such as insults, perceived inequity and hostility).

In the clinical field, most treatment for hostile aggression has been based on anger management training, developed nearly 20 years ago by Novaco (1975, 1978). Novaco's model of anger (Fig. 11.1) was similar to Berkowitz's and proposed that aversive external events (insults, assaults, inequity) produced cognitions (appraisals, expectations, private speech) and may lead to anger. Anger in turn could produce physically aggressive behaviour but might also result in verbal abuse, withdrawal, passive resistance or escape. In anger control training, the client was taught to recognize external triggering events, to monitor their cognitions (and to control them), to monitor and control their level of arousal (anger) and to choose a behavioural response, rather than to act impulsively. The technique has been used successfully with a wide range of people with anger control difficulties (Goldstein and Keller, 1987), including adolescents (Feindler and Ecton, 1986), violent offenders (Alves, 1985), child-abusing parents (Nomellini and Katz, 1983) and policemen (Novaco, 1977).

The recognition that some of the aggressive behaviour shown by people with learning difficulties might be hostile rather than instrumental (and hence that anger control rather than operant techniques might be the treatment of choice) is relatively recent. Benson (1986), for example, described a 12-session programme designed for people with mild learning difficulties, based on the Novaco model. In the initial sessions, clients were taught to monitor their mood as far as possible and to identify external triggering events for their anger. In

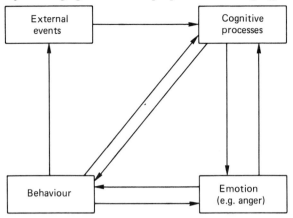

Fig. 11.1 *Navaco's model of hostile aggression.*

the next stage, they learnt to recognize and differentiate emotional states (such as anger, sadness, fear) and to recognize early signs of anger.

Relaxation training followed, in order for clients to learn one way of controlling their levels of arousal and, once mastered, relaxation was practised in role play of anger-arousing situations. Self-instructional training was provided, to teach clients coping statements (such as 'I can handle this') as opposed to trouble statements (such as 'Who does he think he is?' 'He's got it in for me'). These were also practised in role play. Finally, problem-solving was taught, based on the Meichenbaum (1985) four-step process (What is my problem? What is my plan? Am I using my plan? How am I doing?).

A number of single-case reports and small group studies exist which suggest that anger control training methods are successful for people with mild learning difficulties, including for those who have offended (Cole *et al.*, 1985; Holland and Murphy, 1990; Murphy and Clare, 1991) and some studies suggest that self-monitoring in the form of anger diaries, like that in Figure 11.2, is a particularly crucial part of the process. Few larger studies exist, apart from that by Benson's own group (Benson *et al.*, 1986), which compared the separate effects of relaxation, self-instruction and problem-solving training separately with combined anger management for 54 people with mild or moderate learning difficulties. Measures were taken of self-reported anger, supervisors' ratings and behaviour in a role play test (voice tone, voice loudness and gesture) and findings suggested that the package was effective in reducing anger and aggression. Benson and colleagues were unable to detect any between-group differences, however, so that it was unclear which aspect of the training (relaxation training, self-instruction, problem-solving) was the effective component.

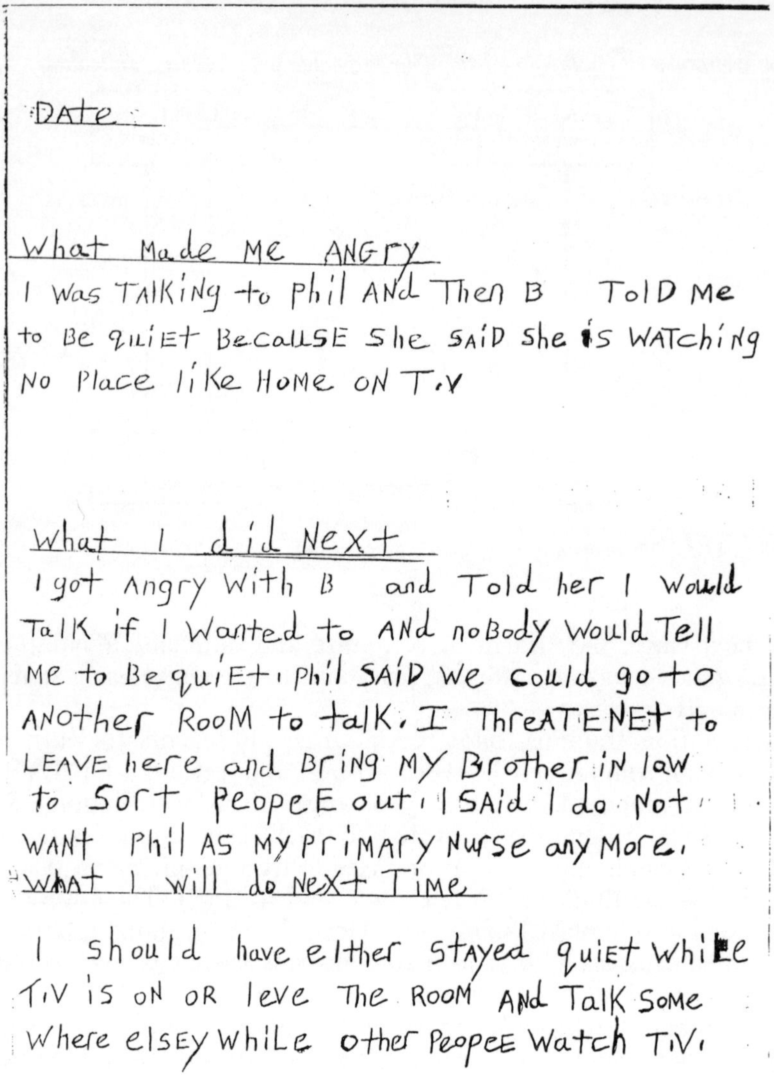

Date:

What Made ME ANGry
I Was TAlKiNg to Phil ANd Then B ToID Me
to Be quiEt BecaUSE She SAiD she is WATching
No Place liKe HoME oN T.V

What I did Next
I got Angry With B and Told her I Would
Talk if I Wanted to ANd noBody Would Tell
Me to BequiEt. Phil SAiD We could go to
ANOther RooM to talK. I ThreATENEt to
LEAVE here and BriNg MY Brother iN law
to Sort PeopeE out. I SAid I do Not
WANt Phil AS MY PriMAry Nurse any More.
What I will do Next Time

I Should have eIther StAyed quiet While
TiV is oN oR leve The RooM ANd TalK Some
Where elSEy whiLe other PeopeE Watch TiV.

Fig. 11.2 *An extract from the anger diary of a young man with mild learning difficulties and violent behaviour.*

THE FUTURE

The psychological treatment of aggressive (and other challenging) behaviour in people with learning difficulties thus began with a somewhat simplistic operant model and often involved the manipulation of consequences of behaviour, frequently employing aversive stimuli. The behavioural treatment of instrumental aggression has recently become less punitive with the appearance of better techniques of functional analysis and the major advance of functional communication training. Anger management training has also appeared for people who appear to be engaging in hostile aggression and, although

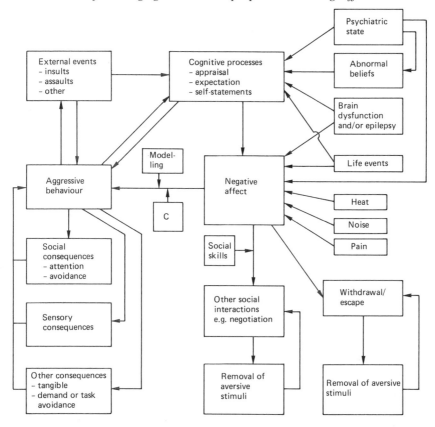

Fig. 11.3 *A proposed model for aggressive behaviour in people with learning difficulties. C = cultural beliefs.*

this form of training is based on a more complex model of aggression than is functional communication training, the two techniques share a basic 'skills deficit' view of aggressive behaviour. So far, there have been few suggestions as to how to decide whether anger control training is more appropriate than operant treatment (e.g. functional communication training) for any individual client, though Black *et al.* (1988) have commented on the important role of client motivation in anger control training.

Until now, little attention has been paid by clinical psychologists to theories of aggression for people with learning difficulties. Relatively few reviewers attempt to provide a general model to assist the clinician in understanding a particular client's aggressive behaviour and in formulating an overall approach (except for Gardner and Moffat, 1990). In particular, many treatment programmes designed for individuals still imply that the client is the seat of the problem and both the skills deficits models referred to above can be criticised for this, even though both take some account of the environment. A more complete model is proposed in Figure 11.3. The model combines what is known about the physical environment (e.g. heat, noise) with aspects of the psychological environment for people with learning difficulties, and combines the Novaco model of hostile aggression with the operant model of instrumental aggression, since these are not mutually exclusive. Ways in which other factors are known to influence aggressive behaviour in this population (psychiatric state, life events) are also proposed. The task for the future is to test out such a model and to develop a better understanding of how all the aspects of the physical and social environment and the physiological and cognitive characteristics of the individual fit together, in order to be better able to help people with learning difficulties live in the community as valued individuals.

REFERENCES

Alves E. A. (1985). The control of anger in the mentally abnormal offender. In *Current Issues in Clinical Psychology*: (Karas E., ed.). New York: Plenum Press.

Benson B. A. (1986). Anger management training. *Psychiatric Aspects of Mental Retardation Review*; **5**: 51–5.

Benson B. A., Rice C. J., Miranti S. V. (1986). Effects of anger management training with mentally retarded adults in group treatment. *Journal of Consulting and Clinical Psychology*; **54**: 728–9.

Berkowitz L. (1988). Frustrations, appraisals and aversively stimulated aggression. *Aggressive Behaviour*; **14**: 3–11.

Birnbauer J. S. (1968). Generalisation of punishment effects – a case study. *Journal of Applied Behaviour Analysis*; **1**: 201–11.

Black L., Cullen C., Dickens P., Turnbull J. (1988). Anger control. *British Journal of Hospital Medicine*; **22**: 325–9.

Carr E. G., Durand V. M. (1985). The social communicative basis of severe behaviour problems in children. In *Theoretical Issues in Behaviour Therapy*: (Reiss S., Bootzin R., eds). New York: Academic Press.

Carr E. G., Newson C. D., Binkoff J. A. *et al.* (1980). Escape as a factor in the aggressive behaviour of two retarded children. *Journal of Applied Behaviour Analysis*; **13**: 101–17.

Carr E. G., Robinson S., Palumbro L. W. (1991). The wrong issue: aversive versus non-aversive treatment; the right issue: functional versus non-functional treatment. In *Aversive and Non-aversive Treatment: The Great Debate in Developmental Disabilities*: (Repp A., Singh N., eds). DeKalb, IL: Sycamore Press.

Clements J. (1987). *Severe Learning Disabilities and Psychological Handicap.* London: John Wiley.

Cole C. L., Gardner W. I., Karan O. C. (1985). Self-management training of mentally retarded adults presenting severe conduct difficulties. *Applied Research in Mental Retardation*; **6**: 337–47.

Cullen C., Partridge K. (1981). The constructional approach: a way of using different data. *Apex: Journal of the British Institute of Mental Handicap*; **8**: 135–6.

Day R. M., Johnson W. L., Schusler N. G. (1986). Determining the communicative properties of self-injury: research, assessment and treatment implications. *Advances in Learning and Behavioural Disabilities*; **5**: 117–39.

Day R. M., Rea J. A., Zwabl M. A., Johnson W. L. (1991). Treatment of aggression among persons experiencing severely handicapping conditions. *Advances in Mental Retardation and Developmental Disabilities*; **4**: 93–120.

Dollard J., Doob L. W., Miller N. E., Mowrer O. H., Sears R. R. (1939). *Frustration and Aggression*. New Haven: Yale University Press.

Donnellan A. M., LaVigna G. W. (1991). Myths about punishment. In: *Aversive and Non-aversive Treatment: the Great Debate in Developmental Disabilities*. (Repp A., Singh N., eds). DeKalb, IL: Sycamore Press.

Donnellan A. M., LaVigna G. W., Negri-Shoultz N., Fassbender L. L. (1988). *Progress without Punishments*. New York: Teachers College Press.

Durand V. M., Carr E. (1991). Functional communication training to reduce challenging behaviour: maintenance and application in new settings. *Journal of Applied Behaviour Analysis*; **24**: 251–64.

Durand V. M., Crimmins D. B. (1988). Identifying the variables maintaining self-injurious behaviour. *Journal of Autism and Developmental Disorders*; **18**: 99–117.

Durand V. M., Kishi G. (1987). Reducing severe behaviour problems among persons with dual sensory impairments: an evaluation of a technical assistance model. *Journal of the Association for Persons with Severe Handicaps*; **12**: 2–10.

Emerson E., Toogood A., Mansell J. *et al.* (1987). Challenging behaviour and community services. I. Introduction and overview. *Mental Handicap*; **15**: 166–8.

Emerson E., Cummings R., Barrett S., Hughes H., McCool C., Toogood A. (1988). Challenging behaviour and community services II. Who are the people who challenge services? *Mental Handicap*; **16**: 16–19.

Feindler E. L., Ecton R. B. (1986). *Adolescent Anger Control: Cognitive Behavioural Techniques*. New York: Pergamon.

Gardner W. I., Moffat C. W. (1990). Aggressive behaviour: definition, assessment, treatment. *International Review of Psychiatry*; **2**: 91–100.

Goldstein A. P., Keller H. (1987). *Aggressive Behaviour: Assessment and Intervention*. New York: Pergamon Press.

Green R. G. (1990). *Human Aggression*. Milton Keynes: Open University Press.

Guess D., Helmstetter E., Turnbull R. R. III, Knowlton S. (1987). *The Use of Aversive Procedures with Persons who are Disabled: An Historical View and Critical Analysis*. Seattle: The Association for Persons with Severe Handicaps.

Hamilton J., Stephens L., Allen P. (1967). Controlling aggressive and destructive behaviour in severely retarded institutionalised residents. *American Journal of Mental Deficiency*; **71**: 852–6.

Harris P. (1992). The nature and extent of aggressive behaviour amongst people with learning difficulties (mental handicap) in a single health district. *Journal of Mental Deficiency Research*; (in press).

Holland A., Murphy G. (1990). Behavioural and psychiatric disorder in adults with mild learning difficulties. *International Review of Psychiatry*; **2**: 117–36.

Horner R. (1990). Ideology, technology and typical community settings; use of severe stimuli. *American Journal of Mental Retardation*; **95**: 166–8.

Iwata B. A., Dorsey M. F., Slifer K. J., Bauman K. E., Richman G. S. (1982). Towards a functional analysis of self-injury. *Analysis and Intervention in Developmental Disabilities*; **2**: 3–20.

Jacobson J. W. (1982). Problem behaviour and psychiatric impairment within a developmentally disabled population I: behaviour frequency. *Applied Research in Mental Retardation*; **3**: 121–39.

Klama J. (1988). *Aggression: Conflict in Animals and Humans Reconsidered.* Harlow, Essex: Longman Scientific and Technical.

Linscheid R. R., Iwata B. R., Ricketts R. W., Williams D. E., Griffin J. C. (1990). Clinical evaluation of the SIBIS. *Journal of Applied Behaviour Analysis*; **23**: 53–78.

Mace F. C., Kratochwill T. R., Fiello R. A. (1983). Positive treatment of aggressive behaviour in a mentally retarded adult: a case study. *Behaviour Therapy*; **14**: 689–96.

Meichenbaum D. (1985). *Stress Inoculation Training.* New York: Pergamon Press.

Mulick J. A. (1990). The ideology and science of punishment in mental retardation. *American Journal on Mental Retardation*; **95**: 142–56.

Murphy G. (1992a). Understanding challenging behaviour. In *Residential and Vocational Services for People with Severe Learning Difficulty and Challenging Behaviour.* (Emerson E., McGill P., Mansell J., eds). London: Chapman & Hall (in press).

Murphy G. (1992b). The use of aversive stimuli in treatment: technical, philosophical and ideological issues. *Journal of Mental Deficiency Research*; (in press).

Murphy G., Clare I. C. H. (1991). MIETS: a service option for people with mild mental handicaps and challenging behaviour or psychiatric problems – 2. Assessment, treatment and outcome for service users and service effectiveness. *Mental Handicap Research*; **4**: 180–206.

Murphy G., Holland A., Fowler P., Reep J. (1991). MIETS: a service option for people with mild mental handicaps and challenging behaviour or psychiatric problems – 1. Philosophy, service and service users. *Mental Handicap Research*; **4**: 41–66.

Nomellini S., Katz R. (1983). Effects of anger control training on abusive parents. *Cognitive Therapy and Research*; **7**: 57–68.

Novaco R. W. (1975). *Anger Control: The Development and Evaluation of an Experimental Treatment.* Lexington: D. C. Health.

Novaco R. W. (1977). A stress inoculation approach to anger management in the training of law enforcement officers. *Journal of Community*; **5**: 327–46.

Novaco R. W. (1978). Anger and coping with stress. In: *Cognitive Behaviour Therapy* (Foreyt J. P., Rathjen D. P., eds). New York: Penguin.

Oliver C. (1991). The application of analogue methodology to the functional analysis of challenging behaviour. In: *The Challenge of Severe Mental Handicap: A Behaviour Analytic Approach* (Remington B., ed.). Chichester: John Wiley.

Oliver C., Head D. (1990). Self-injurious behaviour in people with learning difficulties: determinants and interventions. *International Review of Psychiatry*; **2**: 101–16.

Risley T. (1968). The effects and side effects of punishing the autistic behaviours of a deviant child. *Journal of Applied Behaviour Analysis*; **1**: 21–34.

Slifer K. R., Ivancic M. T., Parrish J. M., Page T. J., Burgio L. D. (1986). Assessment and treatment of multiple behaviour problems exhibited by a profoundly retarded adolescent. *Journal of Behaviour Therapy and Experimental Psychiatry*; **17**: 203–13.

Vukelich R., Hake D. F. (1971). Reduction of dangerously aggressive behaviour in a severely retarded resident through a combination of positive reinforcement procedures. *Journal of Applied Behaviour Analysis*; **4**: 215–25.

Wacker D. P., Steege M. W., Northup J. *et al.* (1990). A component analysis of functional communication training across three topographies of severe behaviour problems. *Journal of Applied Behaviour Analysis*; **23**: 417–29.

Whitman T. L. (1990). Self-regulation and mental retardation. *American Journal of Mental Retardation*; **94**: 347–62.

Wolfensberger W. (1980). The definition of normalisation: update, problems, disagreements and misunderstandings. In: *Normalization, Social Integration and Community Services* (Flyn R. J., Nitsch K. E., eds). Baltimore, MD: University Park Press.

Wolfensberger W. (1983). Social role valorisation: a proposed new term for the principle of normalisation. *Mental Retardation*; **21**: 234–9.

12 *The clinical measurement of aggression*

PER BECH

AGGRESSION: NON-CLINICAL VERSUS CLINICAL

The statement 'He is an aggressive person' would apply equally well to a man at work who is dynamic and creative and to the same man at home beating his wife. Thus, aggression has both a positive (creativity) and a negative (hostility) loading. Few have investigated the correlation between these positive and negative aspects of aggression, but it is outside the scope of this chapter to discuss further these aspects.

It is the negative aspect of aggression (hostility or socially dysfunctional behaviour) that is the topic of this chapter. From a clinical point of view the relationship between personality structure and clinical symptoms is relevant.

THE SPECTRUM OF CLINICAL AGGRESSION: PERSONALITY DIAGNOSES VERSUS CLINICAL SYNDROMES

A spectrum relationship between personality structure and clinical syndromes was proposed by Kretschmer (1921) between schizothymia and schizophrenia; by Bleuler (1922) between dysthymia and depression as well as between cyclothymia and mania; by Jung (1923) between extraversion and introversion; and by Schneider (1958) between dysphoria and the aggressive psychopathia. Among these 'classics of psychopathology' the work of Schneider on aggression has been discarded in the psychiatric systems of diagnoses like *DSM-III* (Bech, 1987).

MEASUREMENTS OF PSYCHOPATHOLOGY

Since the works of the 'classics of psychopathology' 60 years ago, methods for measuring clinical data have been developed. Among

Table 12.1 Aggressive rating scales

Self-rating scales	*Observer scales, nurses*	*Observer scales, psychiatrists*
Hostility subscale of MMPI (Cook and Medley, 1954) Hostility inventory (Buss and Durkee, 1957) Hostility and direction of hostility questionnaire (Caine *et al.*, 1967) State–trait anger inventory (Spielberger *et al.*, 1986)	Behavioural rating scale (Shatin and Freed, 1955) Irritability subscale, NOSIE (Honigfeld and Klett, 1965) Overt aggression scale (Yudofsky *et al.*, 1986) Staff observation aggression scale (Palmstierna and Wistedt, 1987)	Hostility factor (Wittenborn, 1951) Brief psychiatric rating scale (Overall and Gorham, 1962) Hostility subscale, AMDP (Pietzcker *et al.*, 1983) Social dysfunction and aggression scale, SDAS-11 (Wistedt *et al.*, 1990)

MMPI = Minnesota multiphasic personality inventory; NOSIE = nurses' observation scale for inpatient evaluation; AMDP = assessment and documentation of psychopathology.

these methods, rating scales have been most frequently used. According to their type of administration rating scales in psychopathology can be arranged into self-rating scales (self-report by the patients themselves), nursing staff observer scales (observational reports from the ward staff), and psychiatrist observer scales (observational interviews by the treating psychiatrist). All these types of rating scales have been developed for clinical measurements of aggression. Table 12.1 shows a historical overview.

SELF-RATING SCALES FOR AGGRESSION

The first self-rating scale measuring aggression was a subscale of the Minnesota multiphasic personality inventory (MMPI) and therefore a personality scale (Cook and Medley, 1954). As a dimension of outward aggression, the hostility inventory (Buss and Durkee, 1957) has obtained most use internationally in clinical research (e.g. Coccaro *et al.*, 1989). However, the use of self-rating scales in aggressive schizophrenic or manic patients is limited (Bech, 1981).

As a personality scale to be used in non-psychotic patients the hostility and direction of hostility questionnaire constructed by Caine *et al.* (1967) is of interest, because factor analysis pointed at two factors in this population – a factor for outward and another factor for inward aggression. Philip (1968) confirmed these results.

Table 12.2   Observer scales for aggression

Nurse's scale (NOSIE-30 subscale of irritability)	Psychiatrist's scale (AMDP subscale of hostility)
1. Is impatient	1. Aggressiveness
2. Gets angry or annoyed	2. Dysphoric
3. Becomes easily upset	3. Uncooperativeness
4. Refuses to do ordinary things	4. Irritability
5. Is irritable and grouching	5. Suspiciousness
6. Quick to fly off handle	6. Lack of feeling of illness
	7. Lack of insight

In Table 12.1 is also included the state – trait anger inventory developed by Spielberger *et al.* (1986). This scale measures outward aggression using a spectrum between trait aggression (personality disposition) and state aggression (aggressive symptoms) parallel to the 'classics of psychopathology', e.g. between schizothymia and schizophrenia.

STAFF OBSERVATION SCALES

Observations made by skilled observers as contrasted to self-reports by the patients themselves are, in the field of aggressive behaviour, most naturalistically performed by the nursing staff who are tallying behaviour as it occurs.

Among the first nurses' observation rating scales was the behavioural rating scale for mental patients constructed by Shatin and Freed (1955). From this scale (Table 12.1) the nurses' observation scale for inpatient evaluation (NOSIE, Honigfeld and Klett, 1965) was developed. A factor analysis of NOSIE (Guy, 1976) pointed at seven factors of which one was an outward aggression factor (Table 12.2). This scale measures the day-to-day level of aggression in the psychiatric ward, i.e. generalized aggression (outward).

The first staff observation scale to measure episodes of aggression (i.e. peak aggression or aggressive attacks) was developed by Yudofsky *et al.* (1986). According to this scale the nursing staff observe aggressive incidents of the patient being rated and then make an assessment of four items:

1.   Verbal aggression against others or self.
2.   Physical aggression against objects.
3.   Physical aggression against self.
4.   Physical aggression against other people.

The duration of the incident is indicated, as is the intervention. The overt aggression scale (OAS) by Yudofsky *et al.* (Table 12.1) measures, thus, both outward and inward aggression along the same dimension of severity of aggressive peak episodes or incidents.

The staff observation aggression scale (SOAS; Palmstierna and Wistedt, 1987) measures factors provoking aggressive episodes or incidents rather than the psychopathological behaviour of aggression.

The psychometric properties of the various staff observation scales, the NOSIE factor of generalized aggression and the OAS and SOAS for aggressive incidents are still insufficiently understood.

OBSERVER RATING SCALES BY PSYCHIATRISTS

In a comprehensive review by Frank (1975) on the psychometric evidence for the disorders included in *DSM-II* (American Psychiatric Association, 1968) it was, among other things, shown that a factor of general psychotic symptoms with aggressive behaviour was important. This factor seemed independent of diagnostic categories like schizophrenia or mood disorders. The rating scales referred to in this respect by Frank (1975) were observer rating scales completed by a psychiatrist after an interview with the patient and by reference to various ward observations, e.g. the scales developed by Wittenborn (1951) or Lorr (1953). Factor analysis of this scale (Table 12.1) pointed at a factor characterized by such items as 'unawareness of feelings of others', 'oppositional behaviour', 'deceptive behaviour', and 'assaultive behaviour'.

The brief psychiatric rating scale (BPRS, Overall and Gorham, 1962) has a general factor, that emerged in a factor analysis of Lorr's scale, which includes symptoms of improvement during neuroleptic treatment. The BPRS contains both psychotic items and items of aggressive behaviour.

By use of the assessment and documentation of psychopathology (AMDP) in a large sample of psychiatric inpatients, Pietzcker *et al.* (1983) showed that a factor of aggression was clearly present. This AMDP subscale includes both psychotic and aggressive symptoms (Table 12.2).

In this context it is of interest to refer to axis 5 (social functioning) in *DSM-III-R* (American Psychiatric Association, 1987), which is a global rating scale reflecting the current need for treatment. This global assessment of functioning scale (GAF, *DSM-III-R*) contains both symptoms of illness and social self-care. Table 12.3 shows the modified GAF for psychopathology as ascribed by Bech (1993). As can be seen, the GAF goes from 100 – no symptoms – to 1 – persistent danger of severely hurting self or others. The transitivity of the GAF scores (i.e. a lower score, such as 41–50 – marked symptoms includes

Table 12.3   Global assessment of functioning (GAF) reflecting
the current need for treatment (DSM-III-R)

Score	Symptomatology (psychiatric)
91–100	No or uncertain symptoms
61–90	Some mild symptoms
51–60	Moderate symptoms
41–50	Marked symptoms
31–40	Some impairment in reality testing
21–30	Psychotic symptoms (delusions, hallucinations)
11–20	Some danger of hurting self or others
1–10	Persistent danger of severely hurting self or others

Modified from Bech (1993).

also higher scores e.g. 51–60 – moderate symptoms) has the consequence that aggressive behaviour (outward as well as inward) is
considered as a psychotic behaviour.

The first observer scale for psychiatrists specifically developed to
measure aggression like the OAS, i.e. independently of psychotic
symptoms, was the social dysfunction and aggression scale (SDAS,
Wistedt *et al.*, 1990). This version contained 11 items (SDAS-11), of
which 9 items (SDAS-9) measure outward aggression and 2 items
(SDAS-2) measure inward aggression.

The SDAS-9 is shown in Table 12.4. In the study by Wistedt *et al.*
(1990) it was shown that the SDAS-9 was a promising scale for
measuring outward aggression. No correlation was found between
SDAS-9 (outward) and SDAS-2 (inward) aggression. The SDAS-9
was originally designed to measure generalized aggression like the
BPRS, AMDP factor and the Wittenborn factor (Table 12.1).

THE VALIDITY AND RELIABILITY OF A NEW OBSERVER AGGRESSION SCALE: SDAS-21

The social dysfunction and aggression scale (SDAS) has been further
developed in a multicentre study by the European Rating Aggression
Group (ERAG, 1992). The SDAS-11 was enlarged to contain 21 items
(SDAS-21), to cover more items relevant for measuring inward
aggression. The other objective in the ERAG study with SDAS-21
was to measure generalized aggression versus incidental (peak) aggression analogous to the use of the Hamilton anxiety scale when
assessing generalized anxiety versus panic anxiety (Bech *et al.*, 1986).

Table 12.4   Outward aggression (Mokken's
coefficients of homogeneity): Social dysfunction and
aggression scale (SDAS-9)*

0.84	Irritability
0.53	Negativism
0.19	Dysphoric mood
0.51	Socially disturbing behaviour
0.50	Non-directed verbal aggressiveness
0.51	Directed verbal aggressiveness
0.53	Physical violence towards things
0.65	Physical violence towards staff
0.63	Physical violence towards non-staff

*Generalized aggression ($n = 206$).

Construct validity of SDAS-21

Factor analysis of the SDAS in the ERAG study including 654
patients for generalized aggression and 206 patients for peak episodes
of aggression pointed at a two-factor solution (both for generalized
and peak aggression).

The first factor was the SDAS-9 (outward) aggression, including
the items shown in Table 12.4. Other tests for construct validity
(Cronbach's coefficient alpha, Loevinger's and Mokken's coefficient
of homogeneity, and Rasch's latent structure analysis; see Bech 1993)
confirmed that the SDAS-9 is a valid scale for measuring severity of
outward aggression, although both the Mokken and Rasch analyses
focused on item 3 (dysphoric mood) as problematic. Table 12.4 shows
the Mokken coefficients. A coefficient less than 0.30 means not
acceptable. The rank order shown in Table 12.4 equals the latent
structure of hierarchy found by the Rasch analysis, indicating that the
items of irritability and negativism are most inclusive, while the items
of physical violence are most exclusive. The same structure was found
for peak episodes.

The second factor that emerged in the ERAG study is shown in
Table 12.5. This factor included the SDAS-11 items of inward
aggression (self-mutilation and suicidal impulses) and might be considered as a subscale (SDAS-7) for inward aggression. The other tests
for construct validity seemed to confirm that SDAS-7 is a scale for
inward aggression, although the item of self-mutilation was the most
problematic of the items from a psychometric point of view. Thus, the
Mokken coefficient of homogeneity was just acceptable (0.31, see
Table 12.5). The Rasch analysis clearly rejected this item, as no item-
characteristic curve emerged for this item in contrast to the other
items. The rank order shown in Table 12.5 equals the latent structure

Table 12.5   Inward aggression (Mokken's coefficients of homogeneity): Social dysfunction and aggression scale (SDAS-7)*

0.63	Anxiety, psychic
0.47	Anxiety, somatic
0.34	Social withdrawal
0.54	Depressed mood
0.49	Self-dislike
0.58	Suicidal impulses
0.31	Self-mutilation

*Generalized aggression ($n = 206$).

of homogeneity found by the Rasch analysis, indicating that the items of anxiety are most inclusive and the previous SDAS items of inward aggression (suicidal impulses and self-mutilation) are most exclusive. Apart from self-mutilation the SDAS-7 items seem to measure a dimension of melancholia (e.g. the melancholia scale; Bech, 1981; Maier *et al.*, 1988).

Concurrent validity of SDAS-9 and SDAS-7

The ERAG (1992) study showed that SDAS-9 had a much higher correlation to the global assessment scale of aggression (0.75) than to the GAF scale (0.47) in terms of Spearman coefficients. The peak aggression measured by OAS (3 items for outward aggression) correlated 0.44 with SDAS-9 peak scores. The OAS (1 item for inward aggression) correlated 0.28 with SDAS-7 peak scores. As the OAS seems insufficient from a psychometric point of view (ERAG, 1992) it can be recommended to use the SDAS as an observer scale where the nursing staff and the treating psychiatrist collaborate as observers and raters.

Discriminant validity of SDAS-9 and SDAS-7

The ability to discriminate across psychiatric diagnoses – organic psychoses ($n = 38$); schizophrenia ($n = 298$); manic-depressive psychosis ($n = 122$); reactive psychoses ($n = 57$), and personality disorder ($n = 129$) – showed that SDAS-9 had highest scores ($P \leqslant 0.05$) in schizophrenia while SDAS-7 had highest scores ($P \leqslant 0.05$) in manic-depressive psychosis (ERAG, 1992).

The validity of the SDAS-7 in this respect loaded for the scale to measure melancholia rather than inward aggression (Freud, 1959, equalled melancholia and inward aggression).

The application of SDAS-7 in borderline disorder remains to be

Table 12.6   Schizoid borderline scale (Anhedonia)

1. Excessive social anxiety
2. Affective instability (marked shifts from dysphoria
   to euphoria)
3. Inappropriate anger
4. Lack of empathy
5. Expansive sense of self-importance
6. Feelings of emptiness or boredom
7. Self-mutilating behaviour

After Bech (1991).

evaluated. It might well be (as suggested by Bech 1993) that self-mutilation is an indicator of anhedonia in schizoid borderline disorder. Table 12.6 shows the schizoid borderline scale (anhedonia). Only further studies can elucidate the nature of self-mutilating behaviour as an indicator of anhedonia rather than of inward aggression.

Reliability of SDAS-9 and SDAS-7

There exist only few studies in the literature in which the interobserver reliability of aggression scales has been evaluated because such studies are difficult to perform (e.g. Palmstierna and Wistedt, 1987). The SDAS-9 (generalized) was found acceptable in the first study (Wistedt *et al.*, 1990). In the ERAG (1993) study the centre in Mainz performed an evaluation on 14 patients for generalized aggression and 10 of these patients also had peak aggression. The results showed that acceptable intraclass coefficients emerged, and were highest for SDAS-9.

CONCLUSIONS

In this review on clinical measurement of aggression it has been stated that clinical aggression refers to hostility or social dysfunction behaviour and not to the non-clinical aspects, including dynamic or creative behaviour. As measurement of clinical phenomena only rating scales have been considered in this review.

Self-rating scales for aggression have focused on the personality spectrum of aggression while observer scales have focused on the spectrum of aggressive syndromes.

The studies with self-rating scales have focused both on a dimension of inward aggression and on a dimension of outward aggression. A state – trait dichotomy of outward aggression has been suggested parallel to the state – trait anxiety.

The studies of nursing staff scales have differentiated between generalized aggression (NOSIE) and peaks or incidents of aggression (OAS).

A new observer scale to be administered by psychiatrists, the SDAS, has been evaluated in a large multicentre study performed by the ERAG. The results with this scale have focused on a 9-item subscale (SDAS-9) with adequate validity and reliability for measuring outward aggression, both generalized and peak aggression. The ERAG study pointed also at an inward aggression scale (SDAS-7). The construct validity of this scale, was, however, problematic as the most important item (self-mutilation) had insufficient properties psychometrically. In the evaluation of discriminant validity the SDAS-7 seemed associated with depression. Only further studies can clarify to what extent self-mutilating behaviour is an indicator of inward aggression.

The main conclusion is that the distinction between generalized aggression and incidents or attacks of aggression is important. Within observer scales the time has come to integrate nurse's and psychiatrist's reports and observations. Further studies are needed to assess the relationship between inward aggression, melancholia and anhedonia.

REFERENCES

American Psychiatric Association (1968). *Diagnostic and Statistical Manual of Mental Disorders* 2nd ed (DSM-II). Washington, DC: American Psychiatric Association.

American Psychiatric Association (1987). *Diagnostic and Statistical Manual of Mental Disorders* 3rd revised ed (DSM-III-R). Washington, DC: American Psychiatric Association.

Bech P. (1981). Rating scales for affective disorders: their validity and consistency. *Acta Psychiatrica Scandinavica*; 64 (suppl. 295): 1–101.

Bech P. (1987). *DSM-III and ICD-9: Developments and Levels of Communicative Validity. Psychometric and International Perspective*. Kalamazoo: Upjohn.

Bech P. (1993) *Rating Scales for Psychopathology, Health Status and Quality of Life. A Compendium on Documentation in Accordance with the DSM-III-R and WHO System*. Berlin: Springer

Bech P. Kastrup M., Rafaelsen O.J. (1986). Mini-compendium of rating scales for states of anxiety, depression, mania, schizophrenia with corresponding DSM-III syndromes. *Acta Psychiatrica Scandinavica*; **76** (suppl. 326): 1–37.

Bleuler E. (1922). Die Probleme der Schizoidie und der Syntonie. *Zeitschrift für die Gesamte Neurologie und Psychiatrie* **78**: 122–9.

Buss A.H. Durkee A. (1957). An inventory for assessing different kinds of hostility. *Journal of Consulting Psychiatry* **21**: 343–9.

Caine T.M. Foulds G.A., Hope K. (1967). *Manual of the Hostility and Direction of Hostility Questionnaire*. London: University of London Press.

Coccaro E.F. Siever L.J. Klar H.M. (1989). Serotonergic studies in affective and personality disorder patients: correlates with suicidal and impulsive aggressive behaviour. *Archives of General Psychiatrys* **46**: 587–99.

Cook W.N. Medley D.M. (1954). Proposed hostility and pharisaic-virtue scales for the MMPI. *Journal of Applied Psychology*, **38**: 414–18.

European Rating Aggression Group (ERAG) (1992). Social dysfunction and aggression scale (SDAS-21) in generalized aggression and in aggressive attacks. A validity and reliability study. *International Journal of Methods in Psychiatric Research*; **2**: 15–29

Frank G. (1975). *Psychiatric Diagnosis: A review of Research*. Oxford: Pergamon Press.

Freud S. (1959). *Mourning and Melancholia* (first published 1917). *Collected Papers*, vol. 4, pp. 152–70. New York: Basic Books.

Guy W. (1976). Early clinical drug evaluation (ECDEU) assessment manual for psychopharmacology. Publication no. 76–338. Rockville: National Institute of Mental Health.

Honigfeld G. Klett C.J. (1965). The nurses' observation scale for inpatient evaluation. A new ward behaviour rating scale. *Journal of Clinical Psychology*; **21**: 65–71.

Jung CG. (1923). *Psychological Types*. London: Routledge & Kegan Paul.

Kretschmer E. (1921). *Körperbau und Charakter*. Berlin: Springer.

Lorr M. (1953). Multidimensional scale for rating psychotic patients. *Veterans Administration Technical Bulletin* **10**: 507–17.

Maier W. Philipp M. Heuser I. Schlegel S. Buller R., Wentzel H. (1988). Improving depression severity assessment. Reliability, internal validity and sensitivity to change of three observer scales. *Journal of Psychiatric Research*; **22**: 3–12.

Overall J.E., Gorham D.R. (1962). The brief psychiatric rating scale. *Psychological Reports*; **10**: 799–812.

Palmstierna T., Wistedt B. (1987). Staff observation aggression scale (SOAS). *Acta Psychiatrica Scandinavica*; **76**: 657–63.

Philip AE. (1968). The constancy of structure of a hostility questionnaire. *British Journal of Social and Clinical Psychology*; **7**: 16–17.

Pietzcker A., Gebhardt R., Strauss A., Stöckel M., Langer C. Freudenthal K. (1983). The syndrome scales in the AMDP system. In: *The AMDP System in Pharmacopsychiatry* (Bobon D., Bauman U., Angst J., Helmchen H., Hippius H., eds), pp. 88–99. Basel: Karger.

Schneider K. (1958). *Psychopathic personalities* (1st edn 1923). London: Cassell.

Shatin L., Freed E.X. (1955). A behavioural rating scale for mental patients. *Journal of Mental Science*; **101**: 644–53.

Spielberger C.D. Johnson E.H., Jacobs G.A. Krasner S.S., Oesterle S.E., Worden T.J. (1986). *The State – Trait Anger Inventory*. Palo Alto: Consulting Psychologists Press.

Wistedt B., Rasmussen A., Pedersen L., *et al.* (1990). The development of an observer scale measuring social dysfunction and aggression (SDAS). *Pharmacopsychiatry*; **23**: 249–52.

Wittenborn J.R. (1951). Symptoms patterns in a group of mental hospital patients. *Journal of Consulting Psychology*; **15**: 290–302.

Yudofsky S.C. Silver J.M., Jackson W., Endicott J., Williams D. (1986). The overt aggression scale for the objective rating of verbal and physical aggression. *American Journal of Psychiatry*; **143**: 35–9.

Part 4 *Historical interlude*

13 *Richard Dadd: Violence and creativity in Victorian Bedlam*

PATRICIA ALLDERIDGE

On the morning of Monday 28 August 1843, the young painter Richard Dadd called at his father's house and place of business, no. 15 Suffolk Street, Pall Mall East, which was just round the corner from the recently built National Gallery. He wanted his father to come out for a day in the country, to the village of Cobham in Kent, a favourite childhood haunt in the days when the Dadd family had lived in the nearby town of Chatham. Cobham Hall contained a well known collection of paintings on which he had, so to speak, cut his artistic teeth, and Cobham Park had been one of his early sketching grounds.

His father was reluctant, suggesting that they should go instead to the new pleasure gardens at Rosherville in Gravesend, but Dadd was adamant. He said that he wished to 'unburden his mind' to his father, after which he would be 'quite well and perfectly himself again', but he would do it nowhere else but in the country. Dadd's mind had been a source of high anxiety to all his family and friends for the last three months, and he was currently under the eye, if not actually under the care, of Dr Sutherland, physician to St Luke's Hospital and a specialist in the treatment of insanity. His father was convinced, however, that he would eventually be cured by rest and quiet – as, indeed, they had originally been advised: also that Richard was less disturbed in his company than with others, and that he could always 'manage' him. Dadd's wish to unburden his mind in the peace of this familiar countryside seemed to confirm his hopes, and he was persuaded.

They took the 1 o'clock steamboat to Gravesend, and hired a chaise for the remaining five miles or so to Cobham, arriving at the Ship Inn at about 6 o'clock in the evening. There was no accommodation available here, but the waiter went out and found them beds for the night in two cottages in the village. After tea they went for a walk together, returning sometime before 8 to a light supper. Dadd then asked his father to come out for another walk, but his father protested that he was tired. Dadd went out alone, but on his return, was able once more to persuade his reluctant father to fall in with his wishes.

They walked the short distance to the outskirts of the village and on towards Cobham Hall, turning off the lane by a stile and setting out across the park. By now it must have been at least a quarter past 9, probably later, the moon was only three days from new, and it would certainly have been dark. The equivalent time now, allowing for summertime, would be at least a quarter past 10, and at the end of August it is by then very dark indeed in Cobham Park.

About thirty yards into the park from the lane, on the far side of a gloomy ravine then called Paddock Hole but which later came to be known as Dadd's Hole, Richard Dadd suddenly turned on his father, and with a brand new razor which he had bought the previous week in Covent Garden, tried to cut his throat. There was a violent struggle, during which the father was dragged some way towards Paddock Hole by his coat collar, and received a deep gash in his neck. Dadd then produced a rigger's knife with a four-inch spring blade, which he had bought at the same time as the razor, and stabbed his father in the chest between the second and third ribs and through the upper lobe of the left lung. Partially withdrawing the blade, he gave it a turn and thrust it in again, penetrating the lung in a different place. He left the body where it fell on top of the razor (where it was found the following morning), threw the knife a few yards away, climbed back over the stile, leaving the imprint of his hand in blood on the rail, and set off down the road for Rochester.

Calling at the Crown Inn he washed his hands, taking the towel away so that the bloodstains would not be seen, and from here posted to Dover, arriving in the early hours of Tuesday morning and explaining his dishevelled appearance by saying that he had had an accident and fallen off a coach. He had plenty of money with him and immediately hired an open boat to take him to Calais, where his passport was found to be in order, having been acquired in his own name during the previous week. He bought a new suit of clothes in Calais, leaving behind his own which were later found to be saturated with blood.

By the night of 30 August he had crossed Paris and was travelling on a *diligence* (the French version of a stage coach) near Fontaine-bleau, on his way, as he later mentioned, to kill the Emperor of Austria, when he was overtaken by a sudden impulse. There was one other passenger in the coach, and Dadd's impulse was to kill him. This gentleman seems to have possessed a singular reserve of *sang froid*, for according to his own account, Dadd had spent about fifteen minutes or so messing around with his companion's cravat and lowering his collar, before being asked to desist: whereupon he produced another razor from his pocket and set about trying to cut the Frenchman's throat. The man, though injured, managed to overpower him, and Dadd was arrested at the next staging post, where he handed over all his money so that his victim could be cared for.

Taken before the local magistrate, he quietly announced that he was Richard Dadd and had just arrived from England where he had murdered his father. Subsequently elaborating on these rather stark facts he explained that he was the son and envoy of God, sent to exterminate all those possessed of the devil, and that in killing the man who was said to be his father he had destroyed an enemy of God. His greatest wish was to be returned to London so that he could explain his actions, which he believed to be good. What was not mentioned at the time, but later emerged to be the case, was that the God in whose name this murderous mission had been undertaken was the Egyptian god Osiris.

This, except for the information about Osiris, was the narrative which gradually unfolded itself to the thrilled and horrified newspaper readers of 1843 and 1844. But what made Dadd remarkable, of course, was not just that he was a talented young man whose promising career was destroyed by mental disorder; nor even that the dénouement should have taken place in such violent, dramatic, and to all concerned, such devastating circumstances – both aspects of his story which must appear sadly familiar.

What made Dadd different in the first place, was that by all accounts he was regarded as the most talented and most promising young artist of his generation, who already at the age of 26 was beginning to have some considerable success and was clearly marked out for future triumphs; so that his early demise, as it was seen at the time, was accompanied by much genuine sorrow and disappointment in the contemporary art world. What makes him more interesting to us, is the fact that he spent the remaining 42 years of his life confined within the walls of the two state criminal lunatic asylums at Bethlem Hospital and then at Broadmoor, cut off from his former associates and from all contact with his own professional milieu, without motivation or stimulus beyond the memories of his own youthful aspirations, without need of reward, but equally without hope of recognition, pursuing with total dedication the career which had supposedly come to an abrupt end in Cobham Park in 1843. And the work which he produced is remarkable not for its curiosity value, but for its extraordinary artistic qualities: in particular for its meticulous draughtsmanship, its cool and delicate colouring, its haunting dream-like atmosphere, and occasionally, though not so often as many people think, for its richly exotic fantasy. As an artist, Dadd is quite simply unique, whether or not there may be anything remarkable about his case from a clinical standpoint.

Richard Dadd's early life had been a great deal more favourable than that of many aspiring young artists. He was born and brought up in Chatham, on the River Medway, where his father Robert was a chemist and druggist and his grandfather had been timbermaster in the Royal Naval Dockyard for many years. Robert Dadd was well known in the town, where he was popular and respected – 'amiable and talented' is how he was recalled in one local paper after his death, and this seems a fair description. Though a chemist by trade, he was known in the locality as an able lecturer on geology, and he was also instrumental in helping to found educational establishments in the area. In politics he was active in the reform movement. It is clear that Dadd grew up in a cultivated and liberal environment.

He was born on 1 August 1817, the third son and fourth child in a family of four sons and three daughters. His mother Mary Ann Martin, who came from another well established local family, died when he was not quite 7. Two years later Robert Dadd married again, but his second wife died at the age of 28 after only four years of marriage, having borne him two more sons. The oldest daughter, who was nearly 16, now took charge of the household, acting as a mother to the younger children. In a letter written nearly seventy years later, she recalls how her stepmother 'Gave The two Babes to me on Her Death Bed, begging Me to be Mother to Them'.

The subsequent history of Richard Dadd's siblings is not without interest. The oldest son Robert was apprenticed to his father, and practised as a chemist before joining a business firm of some kind. He appears to have achieved a remarkably stable and happy family life of his own, against a background of events which would not have been out of place in a Greek tragedy. Until his death at the age of 63 he was the focal point for his brothers and sisters, maintaining contact by letter with those who were farthest flung. Two of his sons became professional artists, as did at least two of his grandchildren. Mary Ann, the oldest daughter, lived to be 89, dying unmarried in America. She had emigrated in her sixties, following a man to whom she may have been housekeeper, or there may have been a closer relationship. She was deeply attached to all her family, and kept in contact even with younger members whom she had never met. The second son, Stephen, became his father's partner in the London business which I will be mentioning shortly. He died before he was 45, leaving a widow and three children in Manchester. There is one reference to a Dadd brother which indicates, by a process of elimination, that Stephen became insane and was looked after by a private attendant.

The second daughter, Sarah Rebecca, two years younger than Richard Dadd, died aged 78, also unmarried. She seems to have led a rather roving life, probably acting as a governess, companion, nurse, etc., but also joining Stephen's widow in some business enterprise in Manchester. Maria Elizabeth, the youngest daughter, married the Scottish painter John Phillip, one of Dadd's closest friends, and had two children. She began to show signs of mental disorder at the age of 23, but did not become permanently insane until about nine years later. After threatening violence to her husband she was confined in a private asylum for some years, where she tried to attack members of the staff. She was transferred to the Royal Lunatic Asylum at Aberdeen when she was 42, remaining there until her death thirty years later. At the time of her move to Aberdeen she was in a very deluded state, believing that she was being punished and tortured at night by various people, sometimes by electricity but more often by spiritual influence, and also that she and her children were persecuted by the Inquisition.

Richard Dadd's youngest full brother George William became a carpenter in the Chatham Dockyard. He began to show signs of insanity at the age of 20, the principal recorded manifestation being that he refused to go to bed, believing the bed to be on fire. He was admitted to a private asylum immediately after the murder, having arrived home naked one night. He was then transferred to Bethlem Hospital, where he died of consumption after twenty five years in the incurable department. He was violent for some time after admission, but later became 'dull, slow and indolent', though when urged he would 'work like a horse', excelling particularly at carrying coal, and would occasionally converse with considerable acuteness.

The two half brothers both emigrated to America and settled in Milwaukee. Arthur John was trained as a decorative artist and was also a talented watercolourist, but was never very successful in providing for his large family, a situation which was not improved by drink. He died at the age of 49. John Alfred, the youngest, had been apprenticed to his brother Robert, and established a pharmacy business in Milwaukee which passed to his only son. He became eminent in his field, and was elected the first president of the Wisconsin Pharmaceutical Association, dying at the age of 67.

In compiling the family tree so far, I have not encountered any other case of mental disorder outside Richard Dadd's own generation, except for one probable shellshock victim of the First World War. Artistic ability is another matter entirely, and professional artists are liberally scattered throughout the family.

To return to Richard Dadd himself: he began drawing seriously when he was about 13, and his talent was soon recognized and encouraged. It is not certain that he had any formal drawing lessons at all as a child, but it is obvious that he learnt some of the techniques of miniature painting while still quite young, particularly the use of hatching and stippling for painting shadows. This is a technique which eventually he was to refine and develop to the point at which it became uniquely his own, painting whole pictures which are stippled throughout with the tip of the brush in minute and exquisite detail. In subject matter, these early days by the Medway must have inspired the deep love of shipping subjects which was still in evidence even after thirty years of incarceration, and the surrounding countryside of Kent gave him an equally strong feeling for landscape.

The family moved to London in 1834, when he was 17, his father having taken over a carving, gilding and ormolu manufacturing business. Dadd entered the Royal Academy Schools at the age of 20, where he won a number of medals and soon began exhibiting his work. His first pictures were mainly the scenes from history and literature which were more or less *de rigueur* at the time, and are now known chiefly from their titles: amongst others, a *Don Quixote* (who did not paint a *Don Quixote* in those days, I wonder?) which gave him his first sale; *Elgiva the Queen of Edwy in Banishment*; and the still more lugubrious sounding *King Alfred the Great in Disguise of a Peasant, Reflecting on the Misfortunes of his Country*, which was nevertheless praised as a promising work. Among other Shakespearean subjects was a scene from *Hamlet*, which has survived. He also exhibited seascapes, landscapes, portraits and other subjects, including one entitled *Mackerel*.

The perfect vehicle for his talents emerged however in 1841, when he exhibited his first two fairy paintings, both subjects from *A Midsummer Night's Dream* and both surviving today. These and other fairy pictures which followed were highly praised for their originality and above all for their poetical imagination, and poetry is indeed the outstanding quality of these luminous and highly theatrical little microcosms of mystery and magic. It is sometimes claimed that Dadd's early works were conventional Victorian productions of no particular merit; but this is said either by people who have not actually seen the early fairy paintings at all, or by those who subscribe so wholeheartedly to the Romantic myth of his latent talent being in some vague way 'liberated' by insanity, that they do not wish to see. As it happens, the Victorians did not yet exist at the time when Dadd's style was being formed (even Queen Victoria herself can hardly be accused of being one a mere three years into her reign): but in any case, far from his being a mere follower of contemporary fashion, it was his fairy paintings which, if anything, served as prototypes for some of the more vapid products which later graced the drawing-room walls of the genuine Victorians.

Following the success of these imaginative works he began to receive commissions, the most important of which was for a large number of decorative panels for Lord Foley's new house in Grosvenor Square, for which he chose his own subjects. Both have their own prophetic significance: one series was from *Jerusalem Delivered* by the sixteenth century poet Torquato Tasso, who spent seven years of his life in the Asylum of St Anne at Ferrara; the other was from Byron's long narrative poem *Manfred*, a demon-haunted Gothic fantasy if ever there was one. Dadd could not have known that Byron had described it in a letter as 'a sort of mad Drama...a Bedlam tragedy'; but he could not have missed the words of Manfred himself at the height of his torments:

My solitude is solitude no more,
But peopled with the Furies. I have gnash'd
My teeth in darkness till returning morn,
Then cursed myself till sunset; I have pray'd
For madness as a blessing. . .

During this period Dadd had moved out from his father's house and was sharing rooms with a friend, though still on excellent terms with his family. As everyone recalled him, he was an amiable, intelligent, good humoured and generous young man, a lively and sociable companion, but also a serious and dedicated artist. 'A person more invariably gentle, kind, considerate, and affectionate, did not exist', we are told, 'emphatically one who could not deliberately injure a fly'. There was comment on his bright smile, 'his full rich voice, as full of music as a joy-bell, and his sportive humour, exciting innocent mirth'. It was remarked that his studio was more orderly than was usual among artists; also that he had been the most regular and attentive student who had ever studied in the Academy Schools. And again: 'All who knew him speak of the exceeding gentleness and sweetness of his nature, which, though sensitive, was anything but irritable; he was satisfied with small praise for himself, but ready and lavish of his praise of others'. His friend of their student days, the painter W.P. Frith, wrote many years later: 'I can truly say, from a thorough knowledge of Dadd's character, that a nobler being, and one more free from the common failings of humanity, never breathed'.

He was a general favourite within the family, but particularly with his father, whose pride and hopes centred on his third son. The most telling evidence for this comes from his brother Stephen, writing only four days after the murder to break the news to a close family friend. Referring to 'my poor unfortunate brother', he laments:

My poor Father in his affection for him allowed his prudence to be over-ruled and accompanied him alone, and thus has fallen a victim to his affection. My God to think he should fall by the hands of his Son Richard who loved him so dearly and whom he so dearly loved, tis more than I can bear. . .

This, then, was Richard Dadd in 1842, his 25th year. At the Royal Academy exhibition that year he showed a painting based on Ariel's song from *The Tempest*, 'Come unto These Yellow Sands', which again received considerable attention and almost rapturous reviews: '[It] approaches more nearly to the essence of the poet than any other illustrations we have seen', wrote one reviewer: 'the picture is fraught with that part of painting which cannot be taught – in short, the artist must be some kind of cousin to the muse Thalia'. Certainly there is nothing of the nursery mafia about Dadd's fairies: they are true elementals, born in this case of the sea and rocks as previously they had belonged to the natural world of the countryside; though with hindsight there is, perhaps, something a little odd, beyond the mere strangeness of moonlight magic, about this picture, and perhaps something a little over intense in the almost frenzied self-absorption of the dancing figures which are its main subject.

In July of 1842 Dadd left England on a new and immensely promising commission. He was to travel and make drawings for the best part of a year with Sir Thomas Phillips, a lawyer from South Wales who, as Mayor of Newport, had attracted public attention for quelling the Chartist riots. Phillips, then aged 40, was one of those self-possessed and capable people who seem always to be at home wherever they fetch up, and thus in many ways the ideal travelling companion; and from all that is known of his character there is no reason to suspect any clash of personality between him and Dadd. He was, however, an exceptionally hard-working tourist with an insatiable desire for knowledge.

They travelled first through Switzerland, Italy and Greece, then Asia Minor, Lebanon, Syria and Palestine, arriving in Egypt in time to be sailing up the Nile on Christmas Day. While this was undoubtedly a wonderful opportunity for any young artist, there were frustrations for Dadd on top of the general hardships of travelling in what were often very primitive conditions, and in considerable heat. The pace was relentless, and there was very little time for drawing at all. One of his sketch books from this journey is in the Victoria and Albert Museum, and contains a medley of minute, sharply observed and immaculately drawn, but rarely completed, figures, heads, boats, trees, camels, snatches of landscape, and fragments of architecture, all crammed into the tiny pages this way up and that. The whole book is a testimony to his urgent determination to capture something from this kaleidoscope of new experiences, before they should slip by into mere memory.

His few surviving letters are for the most part full of excitement and enthusiasm, with the merest hint (again only visible with hindsight) that he may have begun to experience passing episodes of anxiety and even of altered perception quite early in the journey. It was not until after they had left Egypt in February, however, that there was any outward sign of trouble. On the boat to Malta he suffered six days of what he himself described as nervous depression, for which he could not account; but already, as it emerged later, he had begun to feel irrational hostility towards Sir Thomas Phillips, and to think himself pursued by devils.

In Rome in April he felt an impulse to attack the Pope in a public place, but decided against it because the Pope was too well protected. According to Phillips he now became excited and gave way to 'violence of expression' whenever religion, politics, or the condition of the people was under discussion, contrasting the effects of Christianity unfavourably with those of paganism; and he believed that attempts were being made to injure his health, and that he was being watched. Eventually his behaviour towards Phillips became so disagreeable that Phillips decided to part from him, but he seemed to recover, and expressed sorrow. However, on the journey home through Italy things got worse again until Phillips no longer felt safe in his company; but at Paris it was Dadd himself who parted abruptly from Phillips, and returned to London alone and in great haste.

It was ten months since he had left home apparently perfectly well, embarked on the great adventure which would carry him to the heights of success. Nothing, I think, had been communicated to those at home to prepare them for the condition in which he returned, deluded, possibly hallucinating, and quite clearly deranged, though it is plain from the chronology of events that the behaviour of his younger brother George William must already have been causing concern before Dadd's appearance on the scene. Despite this his father, at least, clutched at the straw offered by Phillips on his own return, that Dadd had suffered a mild attack of sunstroke one day in Egypt, which had obviously been more serious than they thought. I would guess myself that what was taken for an attack of sunstroke may have been the first episode in his breakdown which was noticeable to those around him.

Medical advisers at first told the family that with complete rest and quiet he should eventually recover, and under this treatment his symptoms did appear to subside. He continued to work during the three months following his return, producing one major painting which he sent for exhibition. Now known as *Caravan Halted by the Sea Shore*, it shows a scene at a spring near Fortuna in Syria, and is striking for its restrained composition, subtle low-key colouring, and general air of calm and tranquility. Many who saw him during this period could not believe that there was anything wrong, though others recorded strange episodes such as his sudden flight from the company of friends, unaccustomed reserve and suspicion in his conduct, and occasional hints that he was haunted by evil spirits and was seeking out the devil. A mere six weeks before the murder Phillips breakfasted with him to discuss the drawings which Dadd was now making for him, having had so little time while travelling, and thought him perfectly recovered, but a short time before the crisis he had relapsed. His behaviour had become so bizarre that his landlady was afraid of him. He had cut out a birthmark from his forehead, believing it had been implanted by the devil. He had begun to live entirely on eggs and ale, and when his rooms were searched after the murder large quantities of eggs were found in bowls and littering the floor: there were said also to be portraits of his friends with their throats cut.

Only two days before the murder Robert Dadd had been told by Dr Sutherland that his son was dangerous, and must be put under restraint. Given a little more time, he would probably have accepted the necessity for this; but no one, even then, seems to have imagined that the father himself could come to harm.

After Dadd's arrest in France he spent ten months in an asylum at Clermont, where he appears temporarily to have lost all contact with reality. The governor reported that 'his mind is an utter and irreclaimable blank' and that he did nothing but stand in the courtyard gazing at the sun, 'which he calls his father'. Given the language difficulties, however, this could mean only that he was muttering incomprehensibly about his father. Certainly he had no interest in painting at this time, ignoring the pencils, paint and canvas which had been sent over by his family. In July 1844 he was extradited, and while in Maidstone Gaol he alternated between fits of frenzied violence, when he would hurl himself against the bars of his cell, and periods when he was mild and amenable and could be taken out for exercise in the prison yard. He was formally committed for trial, but on being certified insane he was sent to the State Criminal Lunatic Asylum attached to Bethlem Hospital, on the authority of the Home Secretary and under the Insane Prisoners Act of 1840.

Dadd remained in Bethlem for the next twenty years, and was transferred to Broadmoor when it opened for male patients in 1864, dying there on 8 January 1886. The Criminal Lunatic Department at Bethlem was no more than a prison block at the back of the hospital proper, with a bleak airing ground devoid of vegetation behind it. A small bare cell into which he was locked at night and a hundred-foot-long bare gallery lit by one barred window at each end were to be his home for thirteen years, until a more comfortable ward in the main hospital was converted for some of the 'better class' of criminal patients in 1857. The London sky above the high walls of the airing ground was, throughout his time at Bethlem, his only remaining contact with the world of nature which had once provided his inspiration; though the move to Broadmoor, with its terraces and magnificent views, did eventually restore to him at least the sight of one broad sweep of English countryside.

The astonishing thing is not just that Dadd continued to paint during this lifelong incarceration, but that he continued to paint the world which he had irrevocably lost, his sharply observed little landscapes, seascapes and river scenes becoming ever more ethereal as they were distilled through the visionary processes of his memory. Sometimes they appear only in the background of his pictures, as with the many examples occurring in the series of dramatic 'Sketches to Illustrate the Passions' which he painted in Bethlem in the 1850s: sometimes they are the main subject, often of tiny watercolours which are executed in his microscopic stippling technique to produce images of breathtaking delicacy. It is these fragile little vignettes, above all, which can still haunt the imagination as their subjects must once have haunted Dadd's.

His best known pictures are inevitably the two virtuoso fairy paintings on which he worked for many years in Bethlem, *The Fairy Feller's Master-stroke* and *Contradiction. Oberon and Titania.* In these, his undoubted masterpieces, the prodigality of Dadd's inventiveness seems inexhaustible, as his skill in controlling the complexities of the intricately woven designs seems little short of miraculous. Most of his works are not fantasies, however, but dreamlike reminiscences of the real world which he had left behind, or of the sort of pictures which he had painted while he was living in it, products of that essentially poetic vision which the critics of his early work had so astutely identified, and which only intensified as time wore on. Apart from some of the figure compositions of the early 1850s, in which there is considerable tension and occasional violence, they leave an overall impression which is gentle, contemplative and sometimes rather wistful. It is worth remembering this, when considering Dadd's actual condition during the time that he was working on them.

He began painting again within months of his admission to Bethlem, but remained fairly severely disturbed for many years, and retained his delusions to the end. No detailed notes were written for the first ten years, when it was recorded:

> For some years after his admission he was considered a violent and dangerous patient, for he would jump up and strike a violent blow without any aggravation, and then beg pardon for the deed. This arose from some vague idea that filled his mind and still does so to a certain extent that certain spirits have the power of possessing a mans body and compelling him to adopt a particular course whether he will or no.

Dadd himself spelled this out more specifically in a history of his own case which he wrote for the apothecary of Bethlem, of which this infuriating man published only a very brief extract:

> On my return from travel, I was roused to a consideration of subjects which I had previously never dreamed of, or thought about, connected with self; and I had such ideas that, had I spoken of them openly, I must, if answered in the world's fashion, have been told I was unreasonable. I concealed, of course, these secret admonitions. I knew not whence they came, although I could not question their propriety, nor could I separate myself from what appeared my fate. My religious opinions varied and do vary from the vulgar; I was inclined to fall in with the views of the ancients, and to regard the substitution of modern ideas thereon as not for the better. These and the like, coupled with the idea of a descent from the Egyptian god Osiris, induced me to put a period to the

existence of him whom I had always regarded as a parent, but whom the secret admonishings I had, counselled me was the author of the ruin of my race. I inveigled him, by false pretences, into Cobham Park, and slew him with a knife, with which I stabbed him, after having vainly endeavoured to cut his throat. Now the author of this act is unknown to me, although, as being the cat's-paw, I am held responsible. I do not extenuate my act; but as men are reasonable, or *capable of reason*, I think I have said enough to prove that I have no other concern than with an act of volition, blindly, it is true, but, as I thought, rightly accorded.

And he was still telling pretty much the same story towards the end of his life in Broadmoor, with Osiris still the Supreme Being. The Bethlem notes also record that he gloried in not being influenced by the same motives as other people, paid no attention to decency in his acts or words if he did not feel like it, and would gorge himself with food until he vomited, before returning to the meal. It is interesting that his brother George William is recorded as having acquired in Bethlem the name 'Tiger' from the voracious manner in which he ate. In spite of all this Dadd could be a very sensible and agreeable companion, if kept off the subject of the murder, 'and shew in conversation a mind once well educated and thoroughly informed in all the particulars of his profession'. Again, this was still true more than twenty years later in Broadmoor, where he was still reading classical poetry, playing the violin, and conversing with considerable interest about what was going on in the art world – and still willing, if pressed, to recapitulate with 'sickening exactitude' the details of his crime. Here, in 1877, he was interviewed by a journalist who later published an account of the meeting in *The World*, and who has admirably summed up the extraordinary career of this extraordinary artist:

> it is to his beloved brush that he clings, and wields continuously, with that enthusiasm and unwearying ardour the true painter alone can know. Many works will live after him, the product of these thirty odd years of absolute seclusion – melancholy monuments of a genius so early shipwrecked, but which never went actually to ruin.

The copyright for this chapter is held by Patricia Allderidge.

Part 5 *The consequences of violence*

14 Children who witness parental killing

DORA BLACK, TONY KAPLAN and JEAN HARRIS HENDRIKS

Our project on children who witness parental killing began because of a long-standing interest of one of us (DB) in bereaved children (Black, 1978; Black and Urbanowicz, 1985, 1987) which led to increasing numbers of referrals of children bereaved as a result of one parent killing the other. A complementary interest in the forensic psychiatry of childhood and adolescence enabled us to identify a number of key issues which have widened our remit and have led to our current project.

Children bereaved by the death of one parent, overwhelmingly the mother, at the hands of the father, lose both parents (father is usually arrested and on remand at the time of referral, or may be in a psychiatric hospital, or dead by his own hand). The children lose both parents, their school, their friends and almost everything they possess. Bereavement is only part of this story and the mourning process may remain uninitiated in children who are dislocated and traumatized.

It is not possible to determine the incidence or prevalence of this event from official data. The prison service, the probation service and the Department of Health do not keep records of children of convicted killers; death records of individuals contain no information about their children; many do not become involved with departments of social services, nor do they have legal representation and what records do exist are not coded in such a way as to enable retrospective identification.

We calculate a figure of 40–50 families affected per year in England and Wales (Home Office statistics 1984), given that of 500–600 cases of homicide, 20% are likely to be of a man killing his wife or cohabitee, of whom 40% will be in their child-bearing years. Thus, we have available a selected clinic sample.

The project began 7 years ago and a literature search preparatory to our first publication (Black and Kaplan, 1988) revealed only a small number of reports (Schetky, 1978; Pruett, 1979; Malmquist, 1986), each reporting on only a small number of cases. Our first report was based on 28 children from our own and other colleagues' clinical experience.

Table 14.1   Psychological problems of children of uxoricides

Problem category at referral	*(n = 50)* % *of referrals*
Post-traumatic stress disorder	26
Bereavement problems	48
Emotional problems	70
Conduct problems	44
Learning difficulties	48
Difficulty in relating to peers	38
Difficulties in relating to adults	38
Psychosexual difficulties	14

N.B.: Most children had more than one problem.
(From Black *et al.*, 1992).

Table 14.2   Post-traumatic stress disorder in children of uxoricides

		Post-traumatic stress disorder (n = 30)
Child witness (assessed by clinical interview; *n* = 80)		
Saw or heard killing	27	24
Did not witness killing	36	2
Not known	17	4

In asking for help, referrers in general did not make use of the conceptual framework of post-traumatic stress disorder (Table 14.1). These 50 cases, some directly known to us, were identified as showing a variety of problems of behaviour, emotion, socialization and learning.

The analysis of 80 cases given in Table 14.2 reflects an underestimate of children who may have seen or heard the killing. It includes, for example, 3 preverbal children found in the house with the body of their dead mother, 5 children said by those caring for them to have been asleep or out of earshot at the time of the killing and a family of 3 children referred for foster placement because of difficulties during adolescence. Twelve years earlier, all 3 had been in the house at the

Table 14.3 Post-traumatic stress disorder in childhood

---

1. Existence of a recognized stressor which would evoke significant symptoms of stress in almost anyone

2. Re-experiencing of the trauma indicated by at least one of the following:
   a. recurrent and intrusive recollections of the event
   b. recurring dreams of the event
   c. suddenly acting or feeling as if the traumatic event were occurring because of an environmental or an ideational stimulus

3. Numbing of responsiveness to or reduced involvement with the external world, beginning some time after the trauma, as shown by at least one of the following:
   a. markedly diminished interest in one or more significant activities
   b. feelings of detachment or estrangement from others
   c. constricted affect

4. At least two of the following symptoms which were not present before the trauma:
   a. hyperalertness or exaggerated startle response
   b. sleep disturbance
   c. guilt about surviving when others have not, or about behaviour required for survival
   d. memory impairment or trouble concentrating
   e. avoidance of activities arousing recall of traumatic event
   f. intensification of symptoms by exposure to events that symbolize or resemble the traumatic event
   g. *DSM-III-R* symptoms should have been present for at least a month

---

time when their mother killed their father and there were no records contemporaneous with that event recorded from the point of view of the children. They themselves claimed to have no memories of this period.

The diagnosis of post-traumatic stress disorder made by ourselves is possible only when we are able to examine the children shortly after the killing. We have achieved this in 30 of the 80 cases detailed in Table 14.2.

Our diagnoses have become more confident as, the work becoming known, we have received referrals within 3–28 days of the killing. The diagnosis is made according to *DSM-III-R* criteria (Brett *et al.*, 1988; Saigh, 1989). Symptoms must have been present for at least a month (Table 14.3).

In collating data we are influenced by the work of Pynoos and Eth (1984, 1986, 1990), basing our interviews on a semistructured interview designed by Pynoos for work with traumatized children. Terr (1991) provides a valuable overview of the diagnostic classification and natural history of trauma in childhood.

Case study 1

Two boys, 9 and 11, were referred to DB for advice on where they should live and whether they should see their father in prison. The affidavit of their social worker stated only that they had been outside playing when father stabbed mother, yet the transcripts of criminal evidence recorded that the younger boy had witnessed his father cut the telephone line to the house and then kill mother. Clinically, he demonstrated post-traumatic stress disorder, whereas his brother did not.

Case study 2

D, aged 5, was referred, together with her siblings, after father had battered their mother to death. It was claimed that D had been asleep at the time of the killing.

Ten years later D, aged 16 was assessed in the same clinical department with a severe disorder of eating. Her history was that father had served a sentence for manslaughter, resumed care of D and her siblings and had remarried. D herself had described being struck many times by her father as she became adolescent and, at a point when father and stepmother were having a physical fight, D had a flashback to a similar scene preceding her mother's death which, she had repeatedly been told, she did not see and did not remember.

Our data indicate that most children who witness or hear a killing develop symptoms of post-traumatic stress disorder, and few children who do not witness the killing develop the syndrome. There is confirmation of this from work with adults in mass disasters (Bravo *et al.* 1990; Ursano and Fullerton, 1990; Holen, 1991), as well as with children who witness violence to a parent (Pynoos and Nader, 1988). We have hypothesized that an immediate intervention may prevent the onset or mitigate the severity or duration of the symptoms (Mitchell, 1983; Pynoos and Eth, 1986). Of the 3 child witnesses who did not develop post-traumatic stress disorder, 2 were debriefed effectively within 1 week of the unlawful killing. A third, aged 16, was determined that she must be a witness in the forthcoming murder trial of her father. Perhaps because of this, she functioned extremely well during the pretrial period. When father pleaded guilty to manslaughter and evidence was not called, clear anger and some depression were expressed but classical post-traumatic stress disorder did not occur.

We lack a control group for work such as this and to achieve one would be problematical. Our problems, as with those researching rape (Mezey, 1990; see also Chapter 16) are:

1. problems of sample recruitment and selection;
2. conflict between collection of data for research purposes and delivery of clinical services; and
3. related moral and ethical issues.

An additional problem common to other researchers into disaster during childhood (Yule and Williams, 1990; Terr, 1991), is the extreme reluctance of both professionals and caretakers to talk with – still less to ask – children about what they have seen and heard. There is a wide gap between children's description of their suffering and that attributed to them by the adults most directly concerned.

Case study 3

J, aged 6, was supposed to be asleep in bed at the time when his father killed his mother with an axe. J's drawing shows father with the axe, mother dead, an ambulance and mother's uncle taking J and his sister to his uncle's house. (He draws himself with no legs and no face, though other figures are drawn complete as appropriate to the child's age.) The composition then includes a picture of the father in prison, although the boy had been told that his father was in hospital.

PLACEMENT ISSUES

It is commonplace that the conflict surrounding the killing is enacted and re-enacted in the maternal and paternal families. We have attempted mediation, but with limited success (Table 14.4). The commonest short-term placement, which tends to become long-lasting, is with the family of the victim, commonly the maternal aunt and her husband or the maternal grandparents. Other emergency placements are in foster homes or, usually for sibling groups, in children's homes. A minority are placed with members of the family of the perpetrator. This group includes 2 children whose mother killed their father. Of the children placed long-term with relatives of their father, 8 were the product of cousin marriages. However, the placement and contact with the father in prison were planned and maintained by father's family whose authority was superior to that of mother's kin.

A proportion of those children in foster care long-term are the subject of legal procedures to free them for adoption and 3 of 6 children in children's homes await long-term placement as a sibling group.

Of 4 children remaining with the perpetrator of the crime, 1 is a 5-year-old returned to the care of his mother who killed his father, 1 an

Table 14.4   The immediate and long-term placement
of children of uxoricides

	Immediate	Long-term
Killer's family	11	10
Victim's family	37	33
Foster home	20	16
Children's home	12	10
Adoption		7
With killer		4

adolescent who split with his mother's family and moved in to live with his father after the latter's discharge from psychiatric hospital, and 2 are adolescents who have lived with their father for 10 years after the latter completed a sentence resulting from the manslaughter of his wife.

These data, however, are cross-sectional. Longitudinal studies are of the essence. It is difficult to identify a suitable comparison group; many children and their caretakers are unreceptive to follow-up and resources are limited. Our clinical impression is that there are major difficulties for children irrespective of the placement. The kin of the perpetrator (usually father's kin) tend, in our view, to preserve the child for the killer coming out of prison, wishing to sustain that relationship and often intending that the killer will resume care of the child. There is a tendency to denigrate the victim and also an insistence on regular visits to the father, whether or not the children wish for this.

By contrast, the family of the victim, besides being plunged in grief, have difficulty in speaking to the child about what has happened, and are extremely reluctant for contact with father or his family.

There are problems for 'parents by default' (Brinich, 1989) where the dynamics of the relationship differ from those where parenthood is undertaken voluntarily. These caretakers, themselves grieving and sometimes traumatized, both overprotect and subtly reject the foster child. A further problem is that grandparents, often infirm and with limited accommodation, as well as bereaved, suddenly find themselves moving back a generation whereas maternal aunts and uncles have financial problems and young children of their own. One foster placement broke down after 2 children, aged 8 and 6, were placed with their maternal aunt who had 4 of her own children under the age of 7 years.

Our interest in civil forensic work leads to the preparation of written and oral expert opinions. In order of frequency, we are asked whether the child should visit the perpetrator, where the child should live, and to give an opinion on or to help resolve disputes within the wider family group about contact and issues of compensation and inheritance.

PRINCIPLES FOR PRACTICE

Immediate care

1. The children require a safe place, preferably with friends or a family well-known to them, but emergency state provision may be necessary. Caretakers will need immediate advice and support.
2. The children require urgent decisions about legal guardianship and should be given independent representation and advocacy. Preferably, the state should act as parent to the children while plans are made for them.
3. Primary health care services should be alerted about the children and early consultation sought with child mental health services with particular reference to the assessment of post-traumatic stress disorder, and the need for crisis intervention, bereavement counselling or psychiatric treatment. Expert advice should be sought regarding the planning of contact with key relatives.

PLANNING FOR THE FUTURE

Emergency placements should not become permanent by default and planning must take place irrespective of the outcome of criminal proceedings concerning the father. The advantages and disadvantages of placement with kin must be weighed against those of legal security in alternative families. Wherever they live, children have a right to information about their past and careful consideration about continuing contact with key relatives. The guiding principle must be that the rights of the child are paramount. Therapeutic help must be offered as needed by child mental health services convenient to the child in its new family setting.

DISCUSSION

Much disaster research is undertaken by clinicians with limited financial resources who respond to trouble pragmatically, as it arises. Control groups are lacking and their achievement is problematical if not unrealistic. We are studying, from the point of view of psychiatry, complex dysfunction at the interface between traumatic stress and bereavement; another interface is between disaster research and life events studies (Goodyer, 1990). Children who witness the death of a parent have a very high incidence of post-traumatic stress disorder, and require effective emergency intervention followed by more systematic assessment. There are resource implications both for this work and for the increasing demand, by the courts, for relevant expert opinion.

Comparative studies could include those of children who witness marital violence which does not end in death and children who witness other adult violence in community settings. Inevitably, aetiological factors in relation to post-traumatic stress disorder will be multifactorial; it is requisite that these be teased out and classified. The issue of resilience in relation to traumatic stress requires detailed study.

We have identified, and tentatively begun to map, an important field of knowledge from the perspective of child victims and survivors of violent crime. Our map links with and overlaps with related fields of study into disaster research, the psychology of murder, criminology, the psychopathology of bereavement, attachment theory and child development and life events studies. We need to set up a focused longer-term study with limited, realistic aims and objectives.

REFERENCES

American Psychiatric Association (1987). *Diagnostic and Statistical Manual of Mental Disorders (DSM-III-R)*. Washington D. C. APA.

Black D. (1978). Annotation: the bereaved child. *Journal of Child Psychology and Psychiatry*; **19**: 287–92.

Black D., Kaplan T. (1988). Father kills mother. Issues and problems encountered by a child psychiatric team. *British Journal of Psychiatry*; **153**: 624–30.

Black D., Kaplan T., Harris Hendricks J. (1992). Father kills mother: effects on the children. In: *International Handbook of Traumatic Stress Syndromes* (Wilson J., Raphael B., eds), New York: Plenum Press

Black D., Urbanowicz M. A. (1985). Bereaved children – family intervention. In: *Recent Research in Developmental Psychopathology* Stevenson J. E., ed., pp. 179–87. Oxford: Pergamon.

Black D., Urbanowicz M. A. (1987). Family intervention with bereaved children. *Journal of Child Psychology and Psychiatry*; **28**: 467–76.

Bravo M., Rubiostipec M., Canino G. J., Woodbury M. A., Ribera J. C. (1990). The psychological sequelae of disaster stress prospectively and retrospectively evaluated. *American Journal of Community Psychology*; **18**: 661–80.

Brett E. A., Spitzer R. L., Williams J. B. W. (1988). DSM-III-R criteria for posttraumatic stress disorder. *American Journal of Psychiatry*; **145**: 1232–6.

Brinich P. M. (1989). Love and anger in relatives who 'adopt' orphaned children: parents by default. *Bereavement Care*; **8**: 14–16.

Goodyer I.M. (1990). Recent life events and psychiatric disorder in school age children. *Journal of Child Psychology and Psychiatry*; **31**: 839–48.

Holen A. (1991). A longitudinal study of the occurrence and persistence of post-traumatic health problems in disaster survivors. *Stress Medicine*; **7**: 11–17.

Home Office (1984) *Criminal Statistics*. London: HMSO.

Malmquist C. (1986). Children who witness parental murder: post-traumatic aspects. *Journal of the American Academy of Child and Adolescent Psychiatry*; **25**: 320–5.

Mezey G. (1990). Victims and survivors. *Current Opinion in Psychiatry*; **3**: 739–44.

Mitchell J.T. (1983). When disaster strikes: critical incident stress debriefing. *Journal of Emergency Medical Services*; **8**: 36–9.

Pruett K. (1979). Home treatment of two infants who witnessed their mother's murder. *Journal of the American Academy Child and Adolescent Psychiatry*; **18**: 647–57.

Pynoos R.S., Eth S. (1984). The child as witness to homicide. *Journal of Social Issues*; **40**: 87–108.

Pynoos R.S., Eth S. (1986). Witness to violence: the child interview. *Journal of the American Academy of Child Psychiatry*; **25**: 306–19.

Pynoos R.S., Nader K. (1988). Children who witness the sexual assaults of their mothers. *Journal of the American Academy of Child and Adolescent Psychiatry*; **27**: 567–72.

Pynoos R.S., Nader K. (1990). Children's exposure to violence and traumatic death. *Psychiatric Annals*; **20**: 334–44.

Saigh P.A. (1989). The validity of the DSM-III post traumatic stress disorder classification as applied to children. *Journal of Abnormal Psychology*; **2**: 189–92.

Schetky D.H. (1978). Pre-schoolers' response to murder of their mothers by their fathers: a study of four cases. *Bulletin of the American Academy of Psychiatry and the Law*; **6**: 45–7.

Terr L.C. (1991). Childhood traumas – an outline and overview. *American Journal of Psychiatry*; **148**: 10–20.

Ursano R.J., Fullerton C.S. (1990). Cognitive and behavioral responses to trauma. *Journal of Applied Social Psychology*; **20**: 1766–75.

Yule W., Williams R. (1990). Post-traumatic stress reactions in children. *Journal of Traumatic Stress*; **3**: 279–95.

15 Psychological research in disasters: some snags and methodological issues

RACHEL ROSSER, GARY M. JACKSON, MAN CHEUNG CHUNG
and JAMES THOMPSON

INTRODUCTION

We know a great deal descriptively about the psychological consequences of disasters. Their phenomenology and natural history
suggest that they form a cluster of syndromes overlapping with long-
recognized and validated psychiatric disorders. Much of the information we have about the natural history of post-trauma syndromes is
retrospective. Indeed it is likely to continue to be so; the degree of
psychological distress, interpersonal, social and occupational disruption which accompany these syndromes has demanded a focus on
attempts at treatment and it will be very difficult in the future to get
ethical consent to study prospectively, without intervention and hence
to document, their natural histories. It would now be unthinkable not
to offer treatment to direct survivors of disasters and a strong case for
service provision to those much more remotely involved has been
established.

Twenty years ago treatment was erratic; people made their way
as best they could to whoever they could for help and the outcome
was not systematically documented. The situation has transformed
rapidly – the USA, the Netherlands, Scandinavia and Australia have
taken a lead and the UK is trailing somewhat behind. Treatment
interventions are very costly to those who receive them as they may
involve repeated, long and stressful visits to clinics. They are also very
costly to the community which has many competing demands on its
limited resources. An essential issue thus arises: are the treatments
being used for post-trauma syndromes effective or indeed, as Florence
Nightingale (1863) would have said, do we in fact do harm?

Even in the relatively straightforward experiment of a drug trial,
where double-blind control methodology is well-formulated, our
knowledge is constrained; trials continue to be flawed in their techniques of sampling, control and measurement. Issues such as defining

Table 15.1   Assessment of research studies

---

1. Hypotheses must be clearly stated so as to be testable
2. Alternative explanations for the results must be ruled out, necessitating adequate controls on the experiment
3. Measures must be reliable, valid and standardized in normal populations
4. Researcher bias must be avoided or corrected
5. The sample must be representative of a defined population
6. The method must be specified sufficiently to permit replication
7. The statistical techniques must be appropriate to the data

---

From Rosser and Kinston (1978).

the treatment factors, retrospective data collection and length of follow-up continue to confound findings. The fundamental conditions for sound outcome research designs are given in Table 15.1. Drug trials in disaster survivors have generally failed to meet the highest methodological standards and their findings need to be interpreted with this in mind (McFarlane, 1989; Davidson *et al.*, 1990; Kosten *et al.*, 1990). When it comes to evaluating psychological treatments, these issues become much more complex. Many people still take the view that psychological treatments cannot be evaluated systematically and all efforts ranging from traditional literature reviews to meta-analyses have failed to lay to rest the question of whether any therapies, particularly those with a dynamic approach, are effective. Evaluating psychotherapy in disaster survivors is even further complicated by sampling factors, time factors and control factors.

At the end of the 1970s the US National Institute for Mental Health (NIMH) review of psychotherapy experimental design defined a hierarchy which began with a single case account and ended with a factorial design. The factorial design (Fig. 15.1) accommodates factors whereby the patients are classified: for example in disaster research, by stressor-dependent threat and loss, pre-existing personality and coping styles, and treatment factors. An initial approach could be to include no specific treatment factor (control) comparing this with specific types of psychotherapy, if one could hold constant a number of non-specific factors such as support and social intervention. Preliminary measurements are required as well as measurements during and at the end of therapy and at 1-year follow-up, using instruments which are well-tested and give internationally comparable results. This baseline operation is in itself far from simple but the moment one moves on and starts to compare doses of psychotherapy, numerous other problems arise, largely due to sampling.

The NIMH factorial design has in part been achieved in a few psychotherapy studies, including the NIMH depression study which,

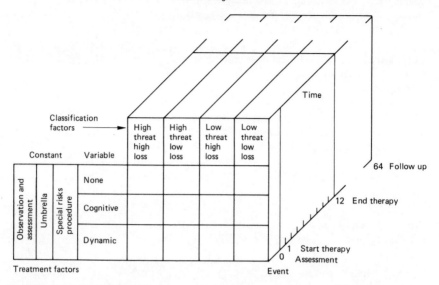

Fig. 15.1   *Factorial study design for scientific research in psychotherapy.*

in 1991 after 15 years produced its first paper on the subject (Sotsky *et al.*, 1991), and our own group used it for a sample of 64 (Rosser *et al.*, 1983). Even these studies are not without flaws. This design has not so far been achieved in disaster research and there is little prospect of this being attempted in the immediate future. Brom *et al.* (1989) conducted a waiting list controlled trial on a heterogeneous sample consisting mostly of bereaved subjects. Despite the heterogeneity of the sample, their efforts to set a standard for dynamic therapy studies on trauma survivors have not yet been superseded. Unfortunately, the small traumatized subgroup in their sample was not analysed separately.

In the late 1980s, however, the ideal trial design became more sophisticated and it is now expected that we use not only ordinal clinical rating scales but also measure quality of life on cardinal scales of utility. This opens up a wide range of statistical manipulations. In this chapter we report an attempt at a study employing such cardinal measurement techniques. As far as we are aware, no previously reported study of disaster survivors has used this approach.

THE STUDY

Results on 39 subjects entered into a psychotherapy trial are presented in Table 15.2. Twenty-eight of the subjects survived major disasters (for example, the King's Cross underground station fire and the

Table 15.2   Results of subjects entered into psychotherapy trial

Survivors ($n = 32$)
$+$
traumatically   } of major or small scale and personal disasters
bereaved
relatives ($n = 7$)

136   subjects met entry criteria and were offered a place in therapy trial
 70   (51%) accepted the offer
 39   (56%) completed therapy and therapy assessment
(31   did not start therapy or dropped out)

Source of referral
Self-referral
Postal outreach programme
Social services
Legal services
Voluntary organizations
Medical and health professional

Marchioness river boat sinking); a further 4 survived life-threatening personal disasters (for example, road traffic accidents or assault) and 7 were traumatically bereaved by a major disaster. These 39 are subjects on whom a complete data set is currently available; a further 31 subjects were offered therapy, but did not engage or were lost to 8-week follow-up. Subjects entered the trial by various routes–referral from other professionals, self-referral or as a result of an outreach programme. Subjects were clinically screened, then they completed psychological questionnaires at the start of therapy, at the end of 8 weeks of therapy and on completion of psychotherapy (Fig. 15.2). One-year follow-up of all subjects, including those who did not engage or prematurely left therapy, is under way.

The psychotherapy was conducted by experienced therapists (psychiatrists and psychiatric social workers) varying in their orientation and subjects received a mean number of 9.7 (with a range of 1–54) weekly 1-hour sessions. The mean number of weeks between the index event and trial entry was 50.

The design employed approximates the third level in the NIMH design hierarchy. This represented the highest degree of rigour we found possible; beginning within a few days of the King's Cross fire we were under pressure to offer a service to those directly and indirectly affected and we were working with a dispersed multidisciplinary team employed by three different agencies, in co-operation with voluntary agencies. For these reasons, a simple waiting list design which could be quickly operationalized was chosen.

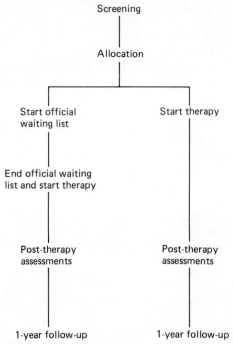

Fig. 15.2   *Flow chart of first psychotherapy trial design.*

Initial screening of trial subjects was done using standard instruments: the general health questionnaire (GHQ) 28-item version and the impact of events scale (IES) designed by Horowitz and frequently used in disaster research (Goldberg and Hilltes, 1979; Horowitz *et al.*, 1979). Subjects admitted to the trial were assigned to the immediate treatment or the waiting list condition. There was no difference between these two groups in terms of mean initial GHQ and IES scores. The instruments used for subsequent assessments included the screening instruments supplemented by the symptom checklist-90 (SCL-90; Derogatis, 1977) and the index of health-related quality of life (IHQL; Rosser *et al.*, 1992).

RESULTS AND DISCUSSION

The interpretation of psychotherapy trial results is difficult even with the simplest design. A complex data set, such as that generated in this study, can be analysed at various levels of detail and different levels can sometimes deliver different findings. In presenting our data, we begin with coarse, total instrument scores. We then pursue a finer analysis, concentrating on some of the scales and subscales which make up the instruments. Hence we illustrate a stepwise approach to

Table 15.3 Results of the whole sample (combined group)

	GHQ	IES	SCL-90	IHQL
Start therapy	14.93	38.30	1.40	0.28
End therapy	9.30	30.30	1.04	0.23
	($P<0.000$)	($P<0.011$)	($P<0.001$)	($P<0.032$)

GHQ = General health questionnaire; IES = impact of events scale; SCL-90 = symptom checklist-90; IHQL = index of health-related quality of life.

data interpretation. This type of analysis is facilitated by the inclusion of a cardinal instrument.

The first stage in descriptive statistics is shown in Table 15.3. For the combined groups ($n = 33$) the score changes on the GHQ, IES and SCL-90 during active psychotherapy (in other words, excluding the waiting list period for those in that condition) represent a significant improvement ($P<0.01$) with the biggest change measured on the GHQ. The IHQL score did not change significantly during the active psychotherapy stage. At this initial level of analysis then, the results, at least in terms of symptom reduction, are encouraging.

The next step was to determine the differential therapeutic effect of the two treatment conditions (Table 15.4). It emerges that there is a marked difference. Over the course of their therapy, subjects in the immediate treatment condition improved significantly ($P<0.018$) as measured by the GHQ, IES and SCL-90, but not as measured by the IHQL. For the waiting list control group however, over the complete therapy 'package' (i.e. beginning of waiting list to end of active psychotherapy) statistically significant improvements were measured only on the IES and IHQL ($P<0.02$). This package can be split into the two phases of the waiting list condition. During the waiting list itself, no improvements approaching statistical significance at the $P<0.05$ level were recorded by any of the instruments. Also, during the active therapy phase no significant changes at the $P<0.05$ level were recorded on any of the instruments. Thus only when the two phases are summed do two of the instruments suggest significant improvement. The IHQL reflects statistically significant changes in quality of life only in the waiting list control group.

A potential source of bias here is the difference in the two sample sizes, with the immediate therapy group being twice the size of the waiting list control group (although the two groups did not differ significantly on other characteristics). This inequality might be expected to bias results in favour of the larger group.

The sharp contrast between the change measures in the two conditions invites speculation. As the two groups had a similar mean number of therapy sessions – although delayed in the one condition –

Table 15.4

	GHQ	IES	SCL-90	IHQL
Immediate				
Session 1	15.54	40.72	1.43	0.29
End therapy	9.04*****	30.50**	0.98****	0.24
Waiting list				
Start waiting list	16.53	43.58	1.43	0.33
Session 1	13.76	35.33	1.31	0.26
End therapy	9.81	31.60***	1.14	0.21*

$*P < 0.023$; $**P < 0.018$; $***P < 0.016$; $****P < 0.004$; $*****P < 0.002$.
GHQ = General health questionnaire; IES = impact of events scale; SCL-90 = symptom checklist-90; IHQL = index of health-related quality of life.

could these results suggest that being on a waiting list reduces the potential gains to be made in subsequent active psychotherapy and perhaps limits the overall improvement?

To confirm this differential finding, subjects from the two treatment conditions were paired by sex and age; no significant outcome differences between the two treatment conditions were found. Pairing by initial symptom and distress scores once more revealed no significant differences between the two treatment conditions. Although the pairing process limited the number of subjects included in this analysis to a maximum of 13 pairs, thus increasing the risk of type 2 error, the inability of the initial differential analysis findings to stand up to the pairwise analysis must cast doubt on their validity or raise methodological questions. The heterogeneity of the sample is one problem but there are others. Figure 15.3 shows that there is a large number of people who do not show up to start therapy, particularly if they had been on the waiting list, while others left therapy after one session. Although the mode is 8 sessions, there is a tail of people who have twice as much or even more (trial protocol encouraged therapists to offer 8 sessions only, but time-limited renegotiation was allowed). These factors are bound to have introduced artifacts influencing our analyses. We will attempt to resolve some of these questions with our 1-year results; this will include following up as many non-engagers as possible.

Whereas the combined group and initial differential analyses suggest recommending immediate therapy, this is based on the findings of the three instruments which are fundamentally symptom-focused – the GHQ, IES and SCL-90. The IHQL, however – the most complex of the instruments – measured no statistically significant improvement in those in the immediate therapy condition, but did measure significant improvement ($P < 0.02$) over the combined wait-

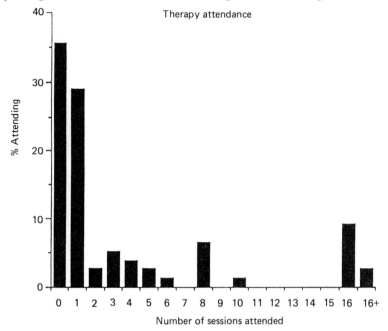

Fig. 15.3 *Bar chart indicating therapy attendance by trial subjects.*

ing list plus active psychotherapy phases in the waiting list condition sample. If one were thus to prioritize quality of life, the recommendation may be different, favouring a waiting list plus active therapy intervention package. The discrepancy between the IHQL and the cluster of other instruments invites investigation which is facilitated by the multiconstruct and subscale nature of the IHQL.

The IHQL measures quality of life in terms of three constructs – disability, discomfort and distress (Fig. 15.4). It also contains a utility scale. It delivers a single measure of the global impairment of quality of life of a patient or population as prejudged and prevalued by

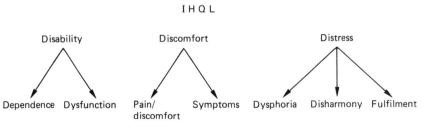

Fig. 15.4 *Outline of structure of the index of health-related quality of life research instrument.*

standard population samples. The constructs of disability, discomfort and distress split down into dependence, dysfunction, pain and discomfort symptoms, dysphoria, disharmony and fulfilment. There are five tiers giving 10/52 combinations of the different items on the instrument, each with a utility score.

A focus on the disability construct reveals that, when establishing the number of sessions of therapy as an independent variable, subjects who had more than 8 sessions of therapy improved significantly in disability. Focus on the dysfunction subscales of the disability construct shows that during the waiting list period itself subjects improve significantly, and then further gains are made during the active therapy phase, so that there is an overall statistically significant ($P < 0.05$) reduction in dysfunction. With regard to dependence, there is also a statistically significant improvement over the waiting list plus active therapy.

The distress construct subscale of dysphoria shows a somewhat similar pattern. Subjects in the immediate therapy condition who had more than 8 sessions improved significantly more than those who had shorter therapies ($P < 0.039$), although there was a mean significant improvement during therapy independently of therapy duration. Also, during the waiting list itself, subjects improved with regard to dysphoria ($P < 0.05$). So with indepth analysis we get the impression that different forms of interventions may have different fairly specific effects.

The interpretation of these findings is not, however, clear. What seems to emerge is that, apart from gains made during psychotherapy, there is some value in a period when a subject anticipates entry into active therapy, which may be supplemented during subsequent active therapy. There may also be a time factor involved, as suggested by the differential gains made by those in therapy of longer duration. This could suggest a duration – response curve and that a waiting list, like most other placebos, is not inactive. Still, no clear recommendation arises from this. Certainly we have no evidence that time-unlimited therapy is optimal (our practice is to renegotiate if there is clear indication for more than 8 sessions) but there does seem to be evidence that where renegotiation seems appropriate, either as a request from the patient or on other clinical grounds, it may prove beneficial.

The complexity of the interpretation of this small segment of one of our data sets underlines the conditionality of any recommendation based on initial analyses. Depending on what one sees as the major aim of therapy – for example maximum symptom reduction or improvement of quality of life, which seem not necessarily to be the same – one might make different recommendations. It may prove impossible to ascertain the potential influence of the missing data on subjects who dropped out.

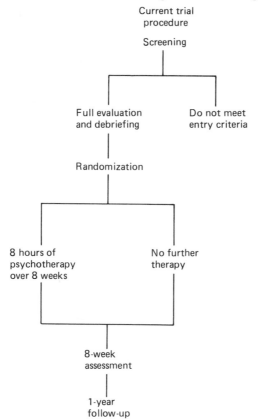

Fig. 15.5   *Flow chart of current psychotherapy trial design.*

THE NEXT STEP

To use funded time and available cases maximally, we started our second trial before we had analysed the first completely. To reduce the likelihood of losing patients in need as a result of their being placed on a waiting list after assessment, we extended our initial face-to-face contact with the patient to incorporate an active therapeutic element (Fig. 15.5).

Initial postal screening determined trial eligibility and entered subjects were interviewed in depth for several hours. Established instruments and assessment techniques were used, including amongst others a psychiatric mental state assessment, a comprehensive standardized psychiatric disorder classification interview (CIDI; Robins *et al.*, 1988) and a standardized post-traumatic stress disorder diagnostic scale (Robins *et al.*, 1988). These assessments were followed on the same day by a debriefing session, lasting between $2\frac{1}{2}$ and $3\frac{1}{2}$ hours. Psychological debriefing is a technique well-used but underevaluated

(Dyregov, 1989). In this trial, one-to-one sessions were undertaken, involving an exhaustive review of the event, in which all details of objective and subjective experience and associated emotions were worked through, followed by a process of rebuilding before the patient left the hospital. At the end of this full day patients were strictly randomized into one of two conditions: either monitoring or a further 8 sessions of therapy, renegotiable, with reassessment at the end of either 8 weeks of monitoring or 8 weeks of therapy. One-year follow-up is planned.

DISCUSSION: THE ROAD AHEAD

One of the most difficult aspects of psychotherapy research is sampling. A random population, for example, people caught in an underground fire, is ideal and allows researchers to randomize into different treatment conditions, providing the subjects don't meet up again. However, if subjects in your sample are connected in some way (as were many people on the Marchioness river boat), enormous design difficulties arise. Confusion is caused by differential expectations in patients receiving different treatments and they may find this unacceptable. The setting up of survivor organizations occurs soon after disasters nowadays, which further increases the likelihood of contamination within samples. Furthermore, potential patient numbers can be enormous; after the King's Cross fire we had contact with 1200 people, but 12 000 people contacted the police in the 2 days following the fire (Turner *et al.*, 1992). This raises difficulties in assessing the representativeness of your sample. Should patients have been subjected to multiple disasters, this heterogeneity creates statistical noise which can be ill-afforded and alternatively, carefully choosing subjects solely exposed to one simple disaster raises questions about the generalizability of findings.

In conclusion, we seem to be moving to a point where the state of the art in post-trauma syndrome research is to make assessment, in so far as possible, of natural history and certainly of outcome with drug treatment, psychological interventions and combined interventions. These studies have to be undertaken by international teams using common instrumentation, serially or in parallel in different groups, and with different designs.

REFERENCES

Brom D. Kleber R.J., Defares P.B. (1989). Brief psychotherapy for posttraumatic stress disorders. *Journal of Consulting and Clinical Psychology*; **57**: 607–12.

Davidson J.R.T., Kudler H., Smith R.D. (1990). Assessment and pharmacotherapy of posttraumatic stress disorder. In: *Biological Assessment and Treatment of Posttraumatic Stress Disorder* (Giller E.L., ed.), pp. 205–221. Washington, DC: American Psychiatric Press.

Derogatis L.R. (1977). *SCL-90: administration, scoring and procedures manual I.* Baltimore: Clinical Psychometrics Research.

Dyregrov A. (1989). Caring for helpers in disaster situations: psychological debriefing. *Disaster Management*; **2**: 25–30.

Goldberg D.P. Hillies V.G. (1979). A scaled version of the general health questionnaire. *Psychological Medicine*; **9**: 139–45.

Horowitz M., Wilner N., Alvarez W. (1979). Impact of events scale: a measure of subjective stress. *Psychosomatic Medicine*; **41**: 209–18.

Kosten T.R., Frank J.B., Dan E., Giller E.I. (1990). Treating post-traumatic stress disorder with phenelzine or imipramine. In: *Biological Assessment and Treatment of Posttraumatic Stress Disorder* (Giller E.L., ed.), pp. 175–202. Washington, DC: American Psychiatric Press.

McFarlane A.C. (1989). The treatment of posttraumatic stress disorder. *British Journal of Medical Psychology*; **62**: 81–90.

Nightingale F. (1863). *Notes on Hospitals* 2nd edn. London: JW Parker.

Robins L., Wing J., Wittchen H.U. *et al.* (1988). The composite international diagnostic interview. *Archives of General Psychiatry*; **45**: 1069–78.

Rosser R.M., Kinston W.J. (1978). Psychotherapy research. In: *Essentials of Postgraduate Psychiatry* (Hill P., Murray R., Thorley A., eds), pp. 725–42. London: Academic Press.

Rosser R.M., Denford J., Guz A. *et al.* (1983). Breathlessness and chronic morbidity in chronic bronchitis and emphysema. A study of psychotherapeutic management. *Psychological Medicine*; **13**: 93–110.

Rosser R., Allison R., Butler C., Cottee M., Rabin R., Selai C., (1992). The index of health related quality of life (IHQL): a new tool for audit and cost per QALY analysis. In: *Quality of Life Assessment: Key Issues in the 1990s* (Walker S.R., Rosser R., eds). In press.

Sotsky M.S., Glass D.R., Shea T. *et al.* (1991). Patient predictors of response to psychotherapy and pharmacotherapy: findings in the NIMH treatment of depression collaborative research program. *American Journal of Psychiatry*; **148**: 997–1008.

Turner S.W., Thompson J.A., Rosser R.M. (1992). The Kings' Cross Fire: early psychological reactions and implications for organizing a 'phase two' response. In: *The Handbook of Traumatic Stress.* (Wilson J., Raphael B., eds). In press.

16   *The effects of rape and sexual assault*

GILLIAN C. MEZEY

Rape is a criminal assault committed against a person that generally involves threats, often involves physical violence and occasionally results in the death of the victim. Rape is, however, legally defined not in terms of violence or brutality but in terms of a single aspect of the assault – genital penetration. This sets the act of rape apart from other personal disasters or life-threatening violent assaults. It is conceptualized as a sexual act and therefore, unlike any other form of criminal assault, implicates the victim in an unwitting partnership and collusion with the perpetrator, questions her complicity, stigmatizes the victim of rape more than any other form of assault and attracts a societal response combining prurient interest, moral outrage and condemnation often directed more towards the woman than the perpetrator. Examination of the woman's morals, personal habits, lifestyle and sexuality is justified as being a matter of public interest in a way that would be condemned if applied to victims of community disasters or non-sexual criminal assaults.

The act of rape perverts what is normally an intimate act of love between consenting adults into an act in which the victim is terrorized, humiliated and objectified by the assailant. The fact that rape is an act committed by men against women has led to a politicization of rape and a possessiveness about the issues by feminist groups which initially focused attention on the problem but the continuation of which may paradoxically act against the interests of rape victims, through their reluctance to collaborate with or share their knowledge and experience with the criminal justice system and professional carers.

PREVALENCE OF SEXUAL ASSAULT

Accurate estimates of the prevalence of rape are virtually impossible because of the underreporting of the offence, which has led sociologists such as Betsy Stanko to refer to sexual violence towards women as representing the 'hidden face of crime' (Stanko, 1988). Underreporting of rape ranges from 8% (Koss, 1985) to 84% (Kilpatrick and Best, 1990). The British Crime Survey and the Scottish Crime Survey noted the reluctance of women to disclose experiences of sexual assault to interviewers (Hough and Mayhew, 1983, 1985; Chambers and Tombs, 1984). Hough and Mayhew found only one case of attempted rape amongst 11 000 women surveyed – an improbably low figure: the impersonality and official tone of these large-scale surveys may inhibit women from reporting. A smaller-scale survey in Leeds found 4 cases of serious sexual assault in only 129 subjects (Hanmer and Saunders, 1984) and locally based surveys have consistently reported higher rates of sexual assault on women than the 'official' British Crime Survey (Kinsey, 1984; Jones *et al.*, 1986).

There are over 3000 reported rapes a year in England and Wales (Criminal Statistics: England and Wales, 1990) – at least three times this number are not reported. In the USA the lifetime prevalence of rape lies between 15 and 25% of women (Koss *et al.*, 1987; Russell, 1984; Kilpatrick *et al.*, 1987), although many more are affected by less serious forms of sexual victimization including indecent assault, sexual harassment and intimidation on the streets and in the work place and obscene telephone calls. However one may wish to argue the reliability of various figures published on prevalence, one is left with two conclusions: firstly, that the problem is a serious and significant one in terms of numbers of women affected and secondly, that there has been a noticeable lack of rigorous epidemiological investigation in the UK.

METHODOLOGICAL PROBLEMS ASSOCIATED WITH RAPE RESEARCH

Disaster research including the investigation of rape reactions has tended to lack the methodological rigour of life event research (MacFarlane, 1985). Research difficulties which are inherent to rape victim research fall into the following categories: sample selection, conflict between the 'researcher' versus 'service delivery' role, moral/ ethical issues and political considerations (Holmes and Williams, 1979).

Sample selection

Researches vary in their definition of what constitutes a sexual assault; certain studies include only victims of rape and exclude victims of forced fellatio and anal penetration. Other studies include victims of all kinds of sexual assault including exhibitionism and indecent assault. Certain studies include child as well as adult victims. Many studies lack any control or comparison groups, have very small numbers, or rely on retrospective recall. The source of the research sample may, in itself, bias results: the majority of American studies select women from hospital- or community-based rape crisis centres or from mental health clinics. Although the women described may not be representative of the population as a whole, it is impossible to predict in what way the experience of women who report and who choose to participate may differ from those who refuse. Long-term follow-up is difficult because survivors of this kind of experience tend to move away or simply wish to forget the experience and the dilemma is to what extent these women should be pursued for research purposes.

As stated previously, underreporting of rape occurs on a massive scale: of those women who report the rape, only a proportion will agree to be 'studied'. Even the better studies suffer from low rates of participation ranging from 62.9% (Murphy *et al.*, 1988) down to only 9% (Resick *et al.*, 1981) of subjects approached and report high attrition rates during follow-up. The majority of sexual assault victims do not report the experience to the police, to physicians or even to family members or confidants.

A number of studies of psychiatric patients have found that the prevalence of sexual assault increases dramatically when women are asked direct questions about the subject rather than relying on spontaneous disclosure by the patient. The use of an appropriate screening instrument gives more than a threefold increase in the identification of sexual assault victims (Saunders *et al.*, 1989).

It is rare, however, for psychiatrists to ask women and even rarer to ask men about their past experiences of sexual abuse and assault, although psychiatry implicity recognizes the role of life events and past adversity in the genesis of psychiatric disorder. Although social factors are often implicated in the finding of excess psychiatric disorder in females over males, the role of past sexual assault and abuse is often glossed over or euphemistically referred to as 'relationship problems'. There is a common assumption that the mere questioning of a woman about past sexual abuse will result in some catastrophic psychological reaction. Professionals may understimate the significance or extent of the problem either because of a failure to confront the issue, or because women who have been sexually assaulted are simply not presenting for psychiatric treatment. Failure to disclose sexually abusive experiences may be related to other factors such as guilt, fear of blame, stigmatization, perceiving that no help is available or the presence of the avoidance symptoms of post-traumatic stress disorder, which may include avoiding treatment which would necessitate the woman recalling and relating her experiences.

The dual role conflict

A second obstacle to good empirical research with rape and disaster victims is that research is often regarded as being incompatible with working with highly distressed individuals – the dual role conflict. This refers to the potential conflict between the 'researcher' and the 'service delivery' role, which is particularly acute when dealing with individuals who are traumatized and extremely vulnerable. Psychiatrists who wish to research these individuals are often accused of churning up feelings without offering any help, and they find themselves criticized for medicalizing a problem which is more to do with a society that endorses negative and objectifying images of women while at the same time encouraging male violence and aggression. Research is often criticized in so far as it reinforces the notion of rape victims as sick and in need of help, as being helpless, out of control and irrational.

A disaster such as rape is a life event which appears to induce a state of panic not only in the victim but in the would-be researcher. Because of the nature of a crime such as rape the researcher has to seek the subjects, rather than relying on the subjects seeking psychiatric help. Any investigation concerns subjects in considerable distress, where the onus is on the observer to offer help and support rather than adopt an objective and dispassionate approach, possibly even adding to the woman's distress.

Moral and ethical issues

There are moral/ethical problems in investigating this area, such as the difficulty of pursuing subjects who become reluctant to continue with the research who do not wish to discuss their experiences further and for whom persistent questioning may seem to make matters worse rather than better. There is also the problem of attempting to document the natural history of recovery from rape or a natural disaster and therefore being precluded from offering treatment or support at an early stage.

Political considerations

A major obstacle to conducting rape research in the UK is a political one: rape had been 'owned' for many years by feminists before criminologists and psychiatrists began to focus their attention on the fact that behind the statistics were a growing population of women whose problems were undefined and whose needs were not being adequately addressed. In the metropolitan area relations between the police and the London Rape Crisis Centre have reached such a low point that there is virtually no dialogue between them. The Rape Crisis Centre does not, on principle, advise women to report to the police. Psychiatrists who are identified with the police in terms of being authoritarian, establishment and overwhelmingly male are similarly vilified by Rape Crisis workers who regard research as essentially dehumanizing and undermining in terms of the woman's confidence and sense of control. More specifically, they baulk at the idea of a researcher coming in and implying mental abnormality in a woman either prior to or resulting from the rape. Symbolic of this approach is the way that the word 'victim' has been outlawed in favour of the word 'survivor', dismissing the idea that women may continue to have profound adjustment problems even when the acute threat has dispersed. The fact that a number of raped women do develop mental illness afterwards has been disregarded or seen as irrelevant.

Another reason for the near complete absence of good victim research in the UK as compared to the USA comes down to funding. In 1976 a National Center for the Prevention and Control of Rape was established within the National Institute of Mental Health in Washington. This provided and continues to provide substantial funding for rape-related research along with two other bodies, the National Institute of Drug Abuse and the National Institute of Justice. Federal funding of rape crisis centres in the USA was established through block grants in 1981 and the Victims of Crime Act in 1984 ensured substantial resourcing of rape victim work and research. By contrast, in the UK rape-related research has never been seen as a priority, either by the state or by mental health professionals. The Government, having stated their intent to combat crime (Home Office 1990, Waddington 1990), depend wholly on untrained volunteer bodies to provide treatment and services for rape victims – services which are certainly cheaper than professionals but which have no real interest, motivation or the training to carry out research and whose efficacy in terms of preventing long-term morbidity remains unproven. It may be no coincidence that in the UK we have simply not had the terminology to describe individual responses, by the absence of Post-Traumatic Stress Disorder within our classification system. The absence of a label has meant the absence of a disorder.

A fundamental problem is how to measure pathology in rape victims. Clearly some kind of reliable and replicable measure is to be desired but, arguably, existing instruments of meaurement used in research lack the sensitivity or specificity to document the real impact of rape on the individual. Empirical studies and simple statements of fact – such as whether the subject is depressed or not; whether she is anxious or not; whether she is phobic or not – fail to convey the more subtle but often profound and wide-ranging effects: the woman's sense of vulnerability, persisting threat, betrayal, self-blame, rage, loss and isolation which may persist for years after the attack. They fail to document subtle changes in the woman's behaviour and lifestyle that arise directly as a result of the rape: a woman stopped wearing high heels and skirts and started wearing flat shoes and trousers when she went out so that if she were attacked, she would be able to make an escape; another woman, having returned to her parents' home to live, was infantilized and protected (by her parents) against possible reminders of the rape to the extent that the television and radio were switched off whenever the word 'rape' was mentioned; articles in the newspaper were cut out by her parents to protect her from possible distress. The experience of rape had transformed her from being an autonomous, independent and confident young woman into an dependent, insecure and overprotected child.

There is a basic conflict in victim research between the necessity of conveying the individuality of the woman's experience through qualitative studies and descriptive accounts and the need for empirical research using validated instruments of measurement, but which in essence reduce the woman's experience from the extraordinary to the ordinary. Even if we do detect morbidity in rape victims, there is often uncertainty about what may constitute the traumagenic aspect of the experience. The rape occurs at a moment in time on a woman who has certain attitudes, expectations and preconceptions of rape, and the likely causes and consequences of the act. Certain reactions triggered by the rape are modified and influenced by these expectations and also by the response of the woman's social network, the police and the criminal justice system. It is likely that some of the 'pathology' that develops is due less to the injury of the single traumatic assault than from a chain of events triggered off within the woman's immediate environment, in response to her new status as 'rape victim'.

Perhaps not surprisingly, virtually every piece of research on the subject of rape-related psychiatric disorder has been done by women. This may be because rape is a subject that concerns women and to which women are drawn, or it may be that men are simply disallowed from the possibility of getting involved – access to rape victims is generally filtered through rape survivor groups which are often wary and suspicious of men. It has also traditionally been an area dominated by psychologists, sociologists and nurses, which may reflect a view that rape-related post-traumatic stress disorder is a 'normal' reaction to an abnormal event, as opposed to a simple adjustment reaction which is viewed as an abnormal reaction to a normal event, therefore coming more naturally into the remit of psychiatry.

EFFECTS OF RAPE AND SEXUAL ASSAULT

The term 'rape trauma syndrome' was originally described in the early 1970s by Ann Burgess, a nurse, and Linda Holmstrom, a sociologist (Burgess and Holmstrom, 1974). Their original work was highly influential in terms of focusing attention on the fact that rape was a violent and often life-threatening event which could precipitate considerable psychological problems in the survivor: this spawned dozens of papers and books. However their original study was purely descriptive with undefined sampling techniques, no validated instruments of measurement, no control groups and therefore questionable validity. Since then, cumulative evidence points to the fact that the experience of rape leads to psychiatric morbidity in a significant minority of women. Controlled follow-up studies report raised levels of generalized and phobic anxiety, depression, post-traumatic stress disorder, somatic complaints and increased drug use over non-victims, as do a number of community victimization studies of sexual assault survivors (Kilpatrick *et al.*, 1985; Bagley and Ramsey, 1986; Frank and Anderson, 1987; Burnam *et al.*, 1988; Mullen *et al.*, 1988).

Post-traumatic stress disorder

Following rape, the majority of women experience high levels of distress that would define them as cases in the first few weeks of recovery. Steketoe and Foa (1977) found that more than 90% could be diagnosed as having post-traumatic stress disorder (American Psychiatric Association, 1987) immediately after the rape. However on this and all studies levels of distress show an initial rapid decline so that within 4–6 weeks the majority of women are no longer significantly different from a control group of non-victims. This means that the rate of spontaneous recovery following rape is similar to that which has been described in outpatient populations of women with reactive depression.

DSM-III-R defines criterion A of post-traumatic stress disorder as 'a psychologically distressing event that is outside the range of normal human experience that would be markedly distressing to almost anyone, usually an experience that induces fear terror and helplessness' (American Psychiatric Association, 1987). Rape represents a markedly distressing event, which is often life-threatening and in certain cases gives rise to symptoms characteristic of post-traumatic stress disorder. Re-experiencing and avoidance phenomena were reported in one controlled study in over 80% of women 3 years after the rape and numbing of responsiveness, reduced involvement in people and former interests including sexual activity has been noted by a number of researchers (Kilpatrick *et al.*, 1979b; Atkeson *et al.*, 1982; Becker and Skinner, 1983).

The impact of conceptualizing the response to rape as post-traumatic stress disorder rather than rape trauma syndrome is threefold. First, post-traumatic stress disorder is a more respectable diagnosis than rape trauma syndrome, simply through its inclusion in the *DSM-III*. Second, it reframes the impact of rape as a generic stress response, and allows the recognition of features common to other victim symdromes, e.g. post-Vietnam syndrome (Shatan, 1973) and battered woman syndrome (Walker, 1984). Third, categorizing the response to rape as post-traumatic stress disorder gives the clinician and researcher the advantage of a broader knowledge base. It is also a more popular diagnosis with psychiatrists who are increasingly being required to act as expert witnesses in court. However, by changing the terminology away from rape trauma syndrome which had popular appeal but no empirical support and by substituting post-traumatic stress disorder, the area of rape was moved out of the hands of volunteer agencies and adopted by professionals.

Symptoms of post-traumatic stress disorder appear to persist for years after the original assault. In a national survey of adult women, 16.5% were still diagnosed as having post-traumatic stress disorder over an average of 17 years following the rape (Kilpatrick *et al.*, 1987). Amongst victims of crime in general, three elements make a significant individual contribution to the development of crime-related post-traumatic stress disorder. These are perception of life threat, actual injury and being the victim of a completed rape as opposed to an attempted rape. If all three features were present a woman was 8.5 times more likely to develop post-traumatic stress disorder than a woman with none of those features (Kilpatrick *et al.*, 1989). Rape victims are more likely to develop post-traumatic stress disorder than victims of other forms of crime and this holds true even if elements of violence and dangerousness are controlled for, which suggests that there are other elements present in a rape attack which are particularly pathogenic.

Generalized and phobic anxiety

Rape-related phobias appear to be generated initially through classical and then by operant conditioning. The phobias relate to three main areas: rape-associated fears such as fear of the dark, fear of strange men, fear of the sexual act; secondly, fear of the consequences of the rape, and thirdly, fear related to the woman's sense of her own vulnerability. The pattern of fear appears to change over time so that vulnerability fears increase as rape-associated fears decrease (Kilpatrick *et al.*, 1979a). Kilpatrick and colleagues at the Charleston Victims of Crime Centre carried out a 3-year follow-up study involving 45 recently raped women and 35 controls matched for age, race and social class (Kilpatrick *et al.*, 1985). Subjects were interviewed at 6–10 days, 1, 3 and 6 months, 1, 2 and 3 years post-rape using a number of instruments. They found that initially victims had significantly raised levels of generalized and phobic anxiety compared with non-victims. Anxiety levels dropped rapidly in virtually all subjects regardless of therapeutic intervention. Levels of distress at the 21-day assessment were more highly predictive of continuing distress at 3 months than other variables examined. About 25% of women appear to recover by the 21-day assessment and do not require further therapeutic intervention. Levels of distress did not continue to diminish significantly from the 3-month to the 3-year assessment post-rape.

Depression

Atkeson and colleagues in Georgia investigated the prevalence of depression in a 1-year follow-up of 115 rape victims compared with the non-victimized control group. (Atkeson *et al.*, 1982). Although depression, as measured by the Beck and Hamilton inventories, was initially significantly raised in rape victims, in virtually all cases this depression rapidly improved within 4–6 weeks. At 1 year just over a quarter (26%) still scored above normal range on the Beck depression inventory but were no longer significantly different from controls. Women with prior psychosocial problems had an increased risk of becoming depressed. A 4–6-week controlled follow-up study of 60 recent rape victims also found they were significantly more likely to meet a diagnosis for depressive illness (38 versus 16%), generalized anxiety (82 versus 16%) and drug abuse (28 versus 3%) after the rape (Frank and Anderson, 1987). In their national survey of over 2000 women the Charleston group found that compared with non-victims, victims of completed rape were 8.7 times more likely to have made a suicide attempt (19.2 versus 2.2%) and twice as likely to be diagnosed as having a major depressive illness (54.4 versus 21.9%; Kilpatrick *et al.*, 1985).

Social adjustment and self-esteem

Further epidemiological studies have indicated substantial impairment in work and self-esteem. Impaired work performance has been demonstrated up to 8 months post-rape (Resick *et al.*, 1981), impaired relationships up to 1 year post-rape and decreased self-esteem at 18 months post-rape (Murphy *et al.*, 1988).

Physical health

In a study of over 2000 women, based on one work site, 57% of them reported having been the victim of a physical assault, a burglary or a rape since the age of 14. Of these, a third had been raped. On measures of general health, total symptoms and mental health, crime victims as a group were significantly less healthy than non-victims: burglary victims, for example, had increased rates of medical consultation up to 1 year after the offence, while rape victims showed increased rates of medical consultation at up to 2-years follow-up. Victimization was a more powerful predictor of medical consultation than other life stressors studied (Koss, 1988).

The frequency of physical and psychological complaints and absenteeism in victims of sexual assault has considerable economic impact in terms of personal as well as institutional costs. Clearly there are different rates of recovery between individuals which depend on a number of factors. Recovery is affected by the woman's age, socioeconomic status, past personality, the nature of the assault and her social support system (Hilberman, 1976). Impaired recovery has also been related to being a recidivist victim (Miller *et al.*, 1978; Ellis *et al.*, 1981; Santiago *et al.*, 1985), previous psychosocial problems Frank *et al.*, 1980; Atkeson *et al.*, 1982; Streit-Forest and Goulet, 1987 and a delay in reporting a rape (Duffy-Stewart *et al.*, 1987) although results are contradictory.

Ellis and colleagues found that rape by a stranger, which tends to be more violent, creates more depression and anxiety in the victim (Ellis *et al.*, 1981), but other studies have found a poorer outcome associated with acquaintance rape together with an increased tendency for the victim to blame herself for the rape and have long-term problems in psychosocial and psychosexual adjustment (Frank *et al.*, 1980; Duffy-Stewart *et al.*, 1987). The precise nature of the assault itself does not influence recovery to a great extent (McCahill *et al.*, 1979; Frank *et al.*, 1980) – a finding that echoes findings from other disaster research (MacFarlane, 1989), except for the association of completed rape and the victim's perception of life threat with more severe pathology (Kilpatrick *et al.*, 1989). A curious finding that has been replicated in a number of studies has been that levels of distress fall more rapidly simply through frequent face-to-face contacts with the researcher. In the absence of any formal treatment, simply the process of being seen and given the opportunity to ventilate problems can be therapeutic. Spontaneous recovery effected by simple researcher contact has even been noted to occur in non-victimized control groups. This observation raises the question of whether there is any specific component of therapy that benefits the woman or whether improvement is related to something as general and non-specific as the expression of care and concern.

CONCLUSIONS

Victims of rape and other forms of violent crime fit uneasily in the area between disaster work and life event research. There has been a lack of epidemiological work and good empirical research, which is partly due to methodological difficulties specific to this area and partly because of the anomalous position it occupies. Many of the results to date have been confusing and contradictory; however there is convincing evidence that rape survivors demonstrate an increased risk of long-term, generalized fear and phobic anxieties, drug abuse, post-traumatic stress disorder and long-term difficulties with social adjustment and lowered self-esteem following rape.

It is likely that conventional psychiatric instruments of measurement underestimate the extent to which women adapt their lives and alter their expectations, attitudes and cognitions to make sense of their experience. Most of the instruments currently used have not been developed for the separation of distress from psychiatric disorder, their accepted specificity and sensitivity having been defined in a clinical population. Further research into the effects of crime will contribute towards greater understanding of the relationship, adversity and psychiatric illness.

Although the role of adversity in creating psychiatric disorder has been recognized, the significance and extent of sexual assault have consistently been underestimated and underresearched due the emotive nature of the subject matter, the elusiveness of the subjects and the failure of clinicians to question women directly about experiences of sexual assault in the view that crimes such as rape are more properly dealt with by the criminal justice system. We should be able to look at why some women recover following rape and some do not, and to identify vulnerable individuals in order that services can be targeted appropriately.

Finally, there are real concerns about the validity of the current definition of criterion A in the diagnosis of post-traumatic stress disorder in terms of whether it is reasonable on practical or phenomenological grounds to separate out diagnoses such as adjustment disorder and post-traumatic stress disorder primarily on the basis of the quantity of stressor. Post-traumatic stress disorder has only just been incorporated into the *ICD-10*: its definition of criterion A as 'exposure to an exceptionally threatening mental or physical stressor' is not only ambiguous but also confusing in its failure to clarify the meaning of the word 'exceptionally'. How is the cut-off point for criterion A determined? Is there a continuum of experience between, for example, divorce and moving house, burglary, road traffic accidents, rape, and natural disasters such as floods, crashes and fires? Does the victim of a deliberate human malevolent act experience more severe or persistent or simply qualitatively different reactions from victims who have experienced an act of God? Finally, by defining a disorder on the basis of some pre-existing precipitant, is there a risk of putting the cart before the horse? A collective diagnosis such as post-traumatic stress disorder may only serve to deny the individuality of each person's response to trauma.

REFERENCES

American Psychiatric Association (1987). *Diagnostic and Statistical Manual of Mental Disorders* (*DSM-III-R*). Washington, DC: American Psychiatric Association.

Atkeson B.M., Calhoun K.S., Resick P.A., Ellis E.M. (1982). Victims of rape: repeated assessment of depressure systems. *Journal of Consulting and Clinical Psychology*; **50**: 96–102.

Bagley C., Ramsay R. (1986). Sexual abuse in childhood: psychological outcomes and implications for social work practice. *Journal of Social Work and Human Sexuality*; **4**: 33–47.

Becker J.V., Skinner L.J. (1983). Assessment and treatment of rape related sexual dysfunctions. *Clinical Psychologist*; **36**: 102–5.

Burgess A.W., Holmstrom C.C. (1974). Rape trauma syndrome. *American Journal of Psychiatry*; **131**: 981–6.

Burnam M.A., Stein J., Golding J.M. *et al.* (1988) Sexual assault and mental disorders in a community population. *Journal of Consulting and Clinical Psychology*; **56**: 843–50.

Chambers G., Tombs J. (1984). *The British Crime Survey, Scotland*. London: HMSO.

Duffy-Stewart B., Hughes C., Frank E., Anderson B., Kendall K., West D. (1987). The aftermath of rape. Profiles of immediate and delayed treatment seekers. *Journal of Nervous and Mental Disorders*; **175**: 90–4.

Ellis E.M., Atkeson B.M., Calhoon K.S. (1981). An assessment of long term reaction to rape. *Journal of Abnormal Psychology*; **90**: 263–6.

Frank E., Anderson B.P. (1987). Psychiatric disorders in rape victims: past history and current symptomatology. *Comprehensive Psychiatry*; **28**: 77–82.

Frank E., Turner S.M., Steward B.D. (1980). Initial response to rape: the impact of factors within the rape situation. *Journal of Behavioral Assessment*; **22**: 39–53.

Hanmer J., Saunders S. (1984). *Well Founded Fear*. London: Hutchinson.

Hilberman E. (1976). *The Rape Victim*. New York: Basic Books.

Holmes K.A., Williams J.E. (1979). Problems and pitfalls of rape victim research: an analysis of selected methodological, ethical and pragmatic concerns. *Victimology: An International Journal*; **4**: 17–28.

Home Office (1990). *Victim's Charter*. London: Home Office.

Hough J.M., Mayhew P. (1983). *The British Crime Survey: First Report* Home Office research study no. 76. London: HMSO.

Hough J.M., Mayhew P. (1985). *Taking account of crime: key findings from the second crime survey*. Home Office research study no. 85. London: HMSO.

International Classification of Diseases (10th Revision), (*ICD-10*). (1992). World Health Organisation.

Jones T., MacLean B., Young J. (1986). London: HMSO. *The Islington Crime Survey: Crime, Victimisation and Policing in Inner City London*. Aldershot: Gower.

Kilpatrick D.G. Best (1990). Sexual assault victims: data from a random probability sample. Presented at the 36th Meeting of the South Eastern Psychological Association, Atlanta, Georgia.

Kilpatrick D.G., Veronen L.S., Resick P.A. (1979a). Assessment of the aftermath of rape: changing patterns of fear. *Journal of Behavioural Assessment*; **1**: 133–48.

Kilpatrick D.G., Veronen L.J., Resick P.A. (1979b). The aftermath of rape: recent empirical findings. *American Journal of Orthopsychiatry*; **49**: 658–69.

Kilpatrick D.G., Veronen L.J., Resick P.A. (1982). Psychological sequelae to rape. In: *Behavioural Medicine: Assessment and Treatment Strategies* (Doleys D.M., Meredith R.L., Ciminero A.R., eds). New York: Plenum Press.

Kilpatrick D.G., Veronen L.J., Best C.L. (1985). Factors predicting psychological distress among rape victims. In: *Trauma and its Wake* (Figley C.R., ed.) New York: Brunner/Maazel.

Kilpatrick D.G., Best C.L., Veronen L.J., Amick A.E., Villeponteaux L.A., Ruff G.A. (1985). Mental health correlates of criminal victimisation: a random community survey. *Journal of Consulting and Clinical Psychology*; **53**: 866–73.

Kilpatrick D.G., Saunders B.E., Veronen L.J., Best C.L., Von J.M. (1987). Criminal victimisation: lifetime prevalence reporting to the police and psychological impact. *Crime and Delinquency*; **33**: 479–89.

Kilpatrick D.G., Saunders B.E., Amick-McMullan A., Best C.L., Veronen L.J., Resnick H. (1989). Victime and crime factors associated with the development of crime related post traumatic stress disorder. *Behaviour Therapy*; **20**: 199–214.

Kinsey R. (1984). *The Merseyside Crime Survey, First Report*. Liverpool: Merseyside Metropolitan Council.

Koss M.P. (1985). The hidden rape victim: personality, attitudinal and situational characteristics. *Psychology of Women Quarterly*; **9** 193–212.

Koss M.P. (1988). Criminal victimisation among women: impact on health status and medical service usage. Paper presented at the American Psychological Association, Atlanta, GA. (Unpublished conference paper.)

Koss M.P. Gidycz C.A. Wisniewski N. (1987). The scope of rape: incidence and prevalence of sexual aggression and victimisation in a national sample of students in higher education. *Journal of Consulting and Clinical Psychology*; **55**: 162–70.

McCahill T.W., Meyer L.C. Fishman A.M. (1979). *The Aftermath of Rape*. Lexington, MA: D.C. Heath.

MacFarlane A.C. (1985). The effects of stressful life events and disasters: research and theoretical issues. *Australian and New Zealand Journal of Psychiatry*; **19**: 409–21.

MacFarlane A. (1989). The aetiology of post traumatic morbidity: predisposing, precipitating and perpetuating factors. *British Journal of Psychiatry*; **154**; 221–8.

Miller J. Moellar D., Kaufman A., Divasto P., Patnak D., Christy J. (1978). Recidivism among sex assault victims. *American Journal of Psychiatry*; **135**: 1122–4.

Mullen P.E., Romans-Clarkson S.E. Walton V.A. Herbisan G.P. (1988). Impact of sexual and physical abuse on women's mental health. *Lancet*; **1**: 841–5.

Murphy S.M. Amick McMullan A., Kilpatrick D.G. *et al*. (1988). Rape victims' self esteem: a longitudinal analysis. *Journal of Interpersonal Violence*; **3**: 355–70.

Resick P.A., Calhoon K.S., Atkenson B.H., Ellis E.M. (1981). Social adjustment in victims of sexual assault. *Journal of Consulting and Clinical Psychology*; **49**: 705–12.

Russell D.E.H. (1984). *Sexual exploitation: Rape, Child Sexual Abuse and Workplace Harrassment*. Newbury Park, CA: Sage.

Santiago J.M, McCall-Perez F., Gorcey M., Beigel A. (1985). Longterm psychological effects of rape in 35 rape victims. *American Journal of Psychiatry*; **142**: 1338–46.

Saunders B.E., Kilpatrick D.G., Resnick H.S. Tidwell R.P. (1989). Brief screening for lifetime history of criminal victimisation at mental health intake. *Journal of Interpersonal Violence*; **4** 267–77. 13.3–41.7

Shatan C.F. (1973). The Grief of Soldiers – Vietnam. Combat veterans' self help movement. *American Journal of Orthopsychiatry*; **43**: 640–53.

Stanko E. (1988). Hidden violence against women. In: *Victims of Crime. A New Deal* (Maguire M., Pointing J., eds). Milton Keynes: Open University Press.

Steketoe G., Foa E.B. (1977). Rape victims: post traumatic stress responses and their treatment. *Journal of Anxiety Disorders*; **1**: 69–86.

Streit-Forest U., Goulet M. (1987). Les effets du viol six mois après l'aggression et les facteurs associés au rétablissement. *Revue Canadienne de Psychiatrie*; **32**: 43–56.

Waddington D. (1990). Home Secretary's speech to victim support volunteers seminar. Preston. (Speech available through HMSO.)

Walker L. (1984). *The Battered Woman Syndrome*. New York: Springer.

Index